INSEAD

From Intuition to Institution

JEAN-LOUIS BARSOUX

INSEAD

First published 2000 by
MACMILLAN PRESS LTD
Houndmills, Basingstoke, Hampshire RG21 6XS
and London
Companies and representatives throughout the world

ISBN 0–333–80398–1

A catalogue record for this book is available from the British Library.

This book is printed on paper suitable for recycling and made from fully
managed and sustained forest sources.

10 9 8 7 6 5 4 3 2
09 08 07 06 05 04 03 02 01 00

Printed in Great Britain by Creative Print & Design (Wales) Ltd, Ebbw
Vale

Contents

List of Plates

INSEAD

From Intuition to Institution

"Man proceeds in a fog. But when he looks back to judge the people of the past, he sees no fog on their path ... their path looks perfectly clear to him, good visibility all the way." Milan Kundera, *Testaments Betrayed.*

ACKNOWLEDGEMENTS

Many people have lent their thought and time to the completion of this book. The originator of the project was Claude Rameau and, before I was even involved, he had conducted numerous interviews with key figures, while Micheline Dehelly had researched and summarised masses of background material. Their extensive preliminary work and the fact that they had long held pivotal positions within the school, gave them a unique understanding of its history. To their immense credit, in our regular discussions together, they made no attempts to impose their views nor to present information in a self-serving manner. As Uwe Kitzinger put it at the end of our interview: "I would say that Claude and Micheline could have written the history of Insead, but probably in far too much detail and with far too many embarrassing stories. So it's very good that you have them as sources, and that they have you as a filter."

Others also contributed 'beyond the call of duty'. On several occasions, Gareth Dyas, with his extra-sensory knowledge of the school, helped to identify dominant themes where no *leitmotiv* was immediately obvious. Claire Pike offered helpful suggestions on the text and took care of the publishing side, allowing the author to concentrate on the writing.

Special thanks are also due to Claude Janssen, Olivier Giscard d'Estaing, Roger Godino and Pierre Cailliau for delving repeatedly into their personal archives in order to enrich the text or to eliminate glaring errors.

Louis d'Arras, Isabel Borges and Christine Poupat had the unenviable task of reorganising the long-neglected archives which greatly facilitated the subsequent research. Similarly, Gerrit Kohler and Micheline Dehelly sorted through jumbles of unlabelled photographs in order to come up with a selection capable of illustrating the text.

In the course of over a hundred encounters, I was particularly struck by the candour and impartiality of interviewees; the lack of score-settling and the tributes to figures who might otherwise be undervalued by posterity. It was a fitting testimony to the enduring fascination exercised by the school on those who come to know it.

INTRODUCTION: ECRIRE, C'EST CHOISIR.

This book charts the metamorphosis of Insead from the first flutters in the mind of Georges Doriot to a fully fledged academic institution. Given the way the world has evolved, it is difficult, today, to imagine that the school could be anything but a resounding success. In truth, it was anything but a foregone conclusion. A key aim in relating this story was to convey some of the confusion and contradictions, setbacks and tensions encountered *en route*. The only way to do justice to this unfolding drama was to take a chronological approach.

Insead's history has some key inflexions, but a lot of incremental evolution. This made it difficult to find natural breaks in the narrative. Various options suggested themselves. The chapters could evolve in rhythm with the changes of leadership, the major strategic developments, or the progressive thresholds of external visibility. The last dimension was particularly pertinent given that the status of 'institution' is conferred by external perceptions rather than internal developments. The resulting structure is actually a compromise between all three dimensions: chapters begin or end with changes in academic leadership or strategic deviations; while the overarching structure reflects changes in visibility: from inception to obscurity (chapters 1 and 2), from obscurity to respectability (chapters 3 and 4), from respectability to prominence (chapters 5 and 6), and from prominence to impact (chapters 7, 8 and 9).

The book focuses heavily on the 'early years'. Indeed, two whole chapters are devoted to the period which precedes the launch. There are several reasons for this bias: first it is the least known period; second, given the parallels with any business start-up, it is probably the most exciting period; and third, the strategic choices made at that time conditioned and constrained much of what was to follow. To understand the present, one needs to understand the challenges and legacies of the past.

The bulk of the information came from three complementary sources. First there were lengthy interviews with faculty, staff, students and others associated with Insead's past or present. These were excellent for potted histories, thumbnail sketches of people and perceptions of critical incidents. But memory provides unreliable material for historical purposes. Management professors, in particular, are prone to post-hoc rationalisation. That, after all, is their business. So it was important to cross-check with contemporary written sources to see how much was known or foreseen at the time. Press clippings served as an important gauge of the school's growing visibility and its aspirations; and the mass of 'invisible literature' – the minutes and memos, the annual reports and brochures – provided the documentary evidence to corroborate impressions and recollections.

The third source of information, in many ways the most precious, was the personal correspondence of several key figures including Georges Doriot, Olivier Giscard d'Estaing and Claude Janssen. In contrast with the sanitised version of events contained in the official accounts, these documents gave real insight into the evolving preoccupations of the main players. The correspondence, much of it hand-written and confidential, provided snapshots of their beliefs and doubts, their triumphs and disappointments, as well as the extent of their personal affinities. Readers will note that the weight of written correspondence wanes as the narrative progresses. This reflects the steady shift from letters to telephones as the staple means of communication. Sadly, for corporate historians, telephone exchanges leave no trace.

Some consider that a historian's role is to assemble the facts rather than to intrude with opinions or to offer conclusions. But for a management researcher, facts do not speak for themselves; the interpretation is key. Who, what, where and when provide a platform for explorations about how and why. The result is a series of essays about, rather than a definitive guide to Insead.

Some of those who contributed their time and energy may not feel properly acknowledged. To mention all the members of staff, faculty, alumni, supporters and philanthropists from the business community who allowed the school to achieve its academic destiny would have been richly deserved, but would have impeded the investigation of the defining moments in the school's history. The author's choice was to focus on the organisational and strategic, rather than the social or anecdotal; on those who pushed the school forward, rather than those who made it an educational experience to remember.

In such an endeavour there is no recipe for success, but there is a recipe for failure and that is to try to please everyone. The reverse is equally hazardous. Clement Attlee, a former British Prime Minister, once commented that Winston Churchill's History of the English-Speaking Peoples should have been entitled "Things in history which interested me". Hopefully, this book steers a course between these two extremes.

PART I

From inception to obscurity

CHAPTER I

Getting to the drawing board

"A beginning is an artifice, and what recommends one over another is how much sense it makes of what follows." Ian McEwan, *Enduring Love.*

FESTIVE AND INSTRUCTIVE

In the space of four decades, Insead has developed from an entrepreneurial venture to an internationally regarded institution.[1] It is distinctive in having achieved this metamorphosis without university or government support and in a less-than-hospitable environment (to management education, to unrecognised diplomas or to fee-paying education). Moreover, the institute's spectacular growth has been achieved without major discontinuities which is a testament to the astute vision of the founders. It is an entertaining and enlightening story.

However, one of the consequences of its dramatic growth has been a lack of reflection on achievements, tributes to the builders or strong sense of corporate memory. Wander around the corridors and what you see are the images of the current faculty. There are no visible images of any of the school's former leaders. Only three people are physically represented at Insead. They are Georges Doriot, whose statue and photo greet visitors to the library, John Loudon whose portrait hangs in the lecture theatre that bears his name, and Henri-Claude de Bettignies whose bust adorns the Euro-Asia Centre.

The purpose of this book is, in part, to remedy these lacunae. But beyond tracing the unfolding history of the school, the book is also a reflection on institution building – and the particular challenges, dilemmas and risks

---

[1] Taking Pareek's definition of an 'institution' to mean "an organisation with a mission to serve, to project new values and become a change agent in the community." (Pareek, U., 1994, *Beyond Management: Essays on institution building and related topics.* New Dehli: Oxford & IBH).

which accompanied successive phases of growth. Insead has clearly 'done something right' to get to where it is today. The idea is to consider what that 'something' might be – and to restore a sense of the uncertainty and tension involved in achieving it.

WAITING FOR DORIOT

In 1920, Georges F. Doriot left France for the US to study the emerging science of business administration. He became the first Frenchman admitted to Harvard Business School (henceforth referred to as HBS). Thirty years later, he was still there, now as a tenured professor and the number of French students attending the business school had grown to a steady trickle of some four or five each year. Hardly a dramatic increase, but perhaps enough of one to suggest that something like Harvard was perhaps lacking in France, and more generally in Europe. Did this insight represent an opportunity? Only in the right hands.

Too often, opportunities are presented as independent entities. Business models developed by strategy and marketing researchers sometimes give the impression that opportunities exist 'ready made', simply waiting to be spotted and seized by the first enterprising passer-by. In reality, not everyone is equally equipped to perceive or capture an opportunity.

In the case of Insead, one could go further and argue that, if Doriot had not come along, nothing vaguely resembling Insead would ever have materialised – international institutions would certainly have been created and so would new business schools – but the two notions would not have been merged. So, although Insead took several years to come to fruition, there was never any danger of someone 'scooping' Doriot in creating the first international business school. Without Doriot, there was no opportunity.

Today, it seems almost inconceivable that an idea which reconciled management education and internationalism could fail, such is the demand for 'global managers'. Back in the early '50s, the demand was dormant to say the least. Moreover, it was a very complex venture to undertake – involving several parties, across national borders and integrating numerous unknowns. But Doriot's unique personal and professional history predisposed him to spot this opportunity, to consider it worthwhile and to make it happen.

BRINGING THE CASE METHOD TO FRANCE

In 1926 Georges Doriot, then 27 years of age, thought it was about time that business should be taught in Europe, the way it was being taught by Harvard in North America. In his view management education should be based on interactive teaching methods and exposure to real business situations in order to foster practical business skills and problem solving abilities. Remaining very attached to his native land, Doriot thought that France had much to gain both in terms of prosperity and reputation if it became known as a nation teaching business 'the right way'.

Though settled in the US, Doriot was in the habit of spending his summer breaks in France. So in August 1927, he made the most of his stay in Paris to meet up with the French Minister for Commerce and Aviation, Maurice Bokanowsky, and to tell him about his hopes. Evidently impressed by the young man, the Minister stopped off in Boston during his visit to the US, the following month. Dining at the Ritz, they spent the whole evening deep in discussion. They met up again for breakfast the next morning, then spent the day at HBS and, as Doriot later noted: "The decision to teach business with the case system, in France, was made that day."[2] The question, now, was how to go about it?

It first occurred to Doriot to try to introduce the Harvard case method into an existing school. However, with the HBS having no particular interest in what he was trying to achieve, Doriot had to wait until the following summer to pursue his idea in France. In July 1928 he met professors from the *Ecole des Sciences Politiques* who seemed keen to supplement their students' theoretical training with business courses. A few weeks later, Doriot had a return call in Boston from one of the French professors. His verdict, after visiting Harvard Business School was that "his school had nothing to learn from HBS", recalled Doriot. "He went right back to Paris, telling me that Descartes had figured it out several years back!" Doriot realised that it might be difficult to integrate a new teaching method and an unfamiliar discipline into an existing French educational structure.

Meanwhile, another contact made that summer started to look more promising. Through Maurice Bokanowsky, Doriot had met representatives of the Paris Chamber of Commerce in late July 1928. The four officials had responded enthusiastically to Doriot's ideas and promised to give them further thought. Among them was a young man in charge of education issues, Pierre Jolly, whom Doriot had known during the 1914–18 war and with whom he had kept in touch.

There followed numerous contacts between Doriot and the Paris Chamber of Commerce, both in Paris and Boston. Several alternatives were considered, including the creation of a French school in New York and the establishment of an all-French section at Harvard. Eventually, they decided instead to establish a school in Paris patterned closely on the Harvard principles and methods. This was a fairly natural development for the Paris Chamber of Commerce[3] which had a dynamic tradition of founding schools,

---

[2] Doriot, G. F. (1975) *The Creation of the CPA in Paris*, personal notes.
[3] The Paris Chamber of Commerce, unlike US Chambers which are strictly private organisations, was a semi-public organisation occupying a position of considerable prestige – advising central government and engaging in other activities, notably in the field of education and training.

counting among its successes both the *Ecole des Hautes Etudes Commerciales* (HEC) and the *Ecole Supérieure de Commerce de Paris* (ESCP).

Doriot spent the summer of 1929 working closely with Pierre Jolly, translating a number of Harvard cases for teaching purposes and helping to shape the concept of the new school. Initially, they envisaged some kind of postgraduate school which would prepare fresh graduates to make the transition into business, but then they switched to a school aimed at experienced managers and engineers. This may well have been the first middle management programme anywhere as HBS itself did not offer education to executives already in employment until 1943.

In early 1930, the school's curriculum was submitted for the approval of Harvard's executive council and Harvard's help was solicited to prepare case study material. Harvard's response, in April 1930, was to send Edna Allen, a research assistant, to France to organise the collection and writing of cases. Six months later she sailed back to New York, to be met by an eager Georges Doriot – and they were married the following month.

The *Centre de Perfectionnement aux Affaires* (CPA), as the new school became known, opened its doors in October 1930, based in Paris, with Pierre Jolly as its director and Dean Donham of Harvard giving the inaugural speech. The school itself was financed by the Paris Chamber of Commerce, the French government and student contributions. In 1931, each student paid 3,000 francs a year, equivalent to the monthly salary of a young engineering graduate. The education dispensed was very practically oriented, there was no permanent faculty and the instructors were all active in business. So as not to disrupt the employing organisations, courses were scheduled for evenings and weekends over 18 months, which later earned the CPA the unenviable label '*l'Ecole du divorce*'.

Understanding the historical development of the CPA is relevant for the story that follows. Several features are worth highlighting: the fact that the CPA represented a successful collaboration between Doriot and the Paris Chamber of Commerce; the role of Harvard as a source of educational material, inspiration and legitimacy; the fact that the CPA was a post-experience school, where teaching was based on the case method and group work; the early experience with fee-paying education which was virtually unknown in Europe at the time. These parallels are important: first, because they show how the CPA helped pave the way for the later creation of Insead; second, because they show that Insead was neither a blinding flash of vision nor a stroke of sheer luck, but rather a thoughtful development on a successful initiative. In many ways the CPA represented a kind of dry run for the ambitious undertaking that was to follow – and would also prove a tremendous source of technical support.

In July 1954, when Doriot was approached to participate in the 25th anniversary celebrations of the CPA, he told the Paris Chamber of

Commerce that anniversaries should not merely be times for reminiscence and self-satisfaction, but opportunities to think about the future. He suggested that the anniversary, to be held in October 1955, would be the ideal time for the Chamber of Commerce to announce its next step, which might be the creation of a graduate school at the European level. Somewhat taken aback by this proposed development, the representatives of the Paris Chamber of Commerce promised to go away and think about it.

A TEACHER WITH A DIFFERENCE

In the years between the creation of the CPA and its 25th anniversary, Doriot had not been idle. The intervening period had seen his reputation as a teacher grow to legendary proportions, his unforeseen promotion to the rank of General, and his involvement in pioneering a whole new industry, with the creation of the first public venture capital company. This period is worth dwelling on because it helps to explain why Doriot was uniquely placed to push the idea of a European business school and to elicit support from many quarters. One can better appreciate the creation if one understands the experience of the creator.

Doriot's course at Harvard started in 1926 and was misleadingly entitled 'Manufacturing'. In reality, it was a wide ranging sweep through topics as diverse as 'business and government', 'the development of a management team', 'analysing a company' or 'advertising, publicity and public relations'.[4]

Ironically, for the father of the case method in France, Doriot's class was not based on cases like other courses at Harvard. Rather it was a combination of lectures and workshops. In terms of teaching style, Doriot was said to favour a "studied technique of infuriating students into positive brilliance" and of being "purposefully rustic".[5] For the workshops, students were dispatched to companies in the Boston area to gain practical experience. Doriot was also a great believer in group work and an important part of the course was the preparation by student teams of 'topic reports'.

The course stressed hard work, learning, leadership, creativity and other common-sense virtues. Doriot introduced the course as "A possible method of conducting one's life in the world of business" but intimated that many of the principles might have implications beyond business.[6] The course was an enormous success and made a lasting impact on scores of business leaders who could recall Doriot's insights or aphorisms decades after leaving Harvard.[7]

[4] The "Manufacturing Class Notes" put together in 1993 by the Board of Trustees of the French Library in Boston, as a tribute to Doriot, give a good flavour of the spirit of Doriot's course.
[5] Cruickshank, J.L. (1987) *A Delicate Experiment: The Harvard Business School 1908–1945*, Boston: Harvard Business School Press, p. 171.
[6] Doriot, G.F. (1993) *Manufacturing Class Notes*, French Library in Boston, p. 11.
[7] During his forty years at Harvard, the 'Manufacturing' course was taken by over 7,000 students, including two generations of some families.

One former student remembered Doriot inviting the president of US Steel to their class in 1947. Doriot observed afterwards: "US Steel doesn't understand what business they are in. They are in the materials, not the steel business. They are completely ignorant of aluminium and plastics." This was over a decade before Theodore Levitt formulated his famous catch-phrase question "What business are we in?"[8] The student in question observed: "Doriot was the first person to think in those terms."[9]

In early 1942, Doriot's teaching activities were interrupted by the war. He served the US Army as director of military planning for the Quartermaster Corps and deputy director of research and development for the War Department general staff. These were opportunities to solve complex logistical problems, to find new, more efficient and faster systems of routing supplies across the North Atlantic. He also sought out the critical problems for the 'end user', nominating a select group of 'combat observers' who would go out into the field and report back on the troop's real needs so that efforts could be channelled towards solving them. Amongst other things, this process led to the famous 'K-ration' survival packs and to a redesign of the basic army boot to make it more water-proof or to provide better ankle support for parachutists.

Doriot emerged from the war with the Distinguished Service Medal and the rank of Brigadier General in the US Army – something of a first, for a one-time sergeant in the French armed forces. From this period until the end of his life he was affectionately known as 'The General'.

After the war, a third career grew out of the first two. Drawing on both his classroom teaching and his military experience, Doriot helped found the first publicly traded venture capital firm, American Research & Development (ARD). Dozens of start-ups were financed by ARD but probably the best known was the result of an encounter in 1957 with a young MIT engineer, Kenneth Olsen, who wanted to start a computer company. Doriot put up $70,000 of ARD's money in exchange for 70 per cent of the new venture's equity. The start up became Digital Equipment Corporation, one of the world's leading computer companies. ARD went on to spawn two sister companies in Europe and Canada, and was the precursor of what today has become an industry in itself. It was this contribution to the stimulation of innovation in the US economy which later earned Doriot a rare place in the *Fortune* 'Hall of Fame'.

So how did these experiences help to make Insead possible? First, Doriot's involvement with ARD gave him a closeness to business, and an enhanced understanding of the dynamics of entrepreneurialism – confirming the need to pick the right people for the right projects, to accompany them in their development and to show patience in nursing young companies towards

[8] Levitt, T. (1960) "Marketing Myopia," *Harvard Business Review*, July–August 1960, 45–56.
[9] *Forbes*, July 13, 1987.

maturity. It must also have reinforced his faith in his judgement, his taste for calculated risks and his determination to see projects through – qualities which would be sorely tested in the slower, more conservative European environment.

Then there is Doriot's inspirational influence on waves of former students, not just over time, but also across distance. This 'cult following' was critical in that it helps to explain how Doriot was able to push through a project in France while spending only limited time in the country. Three of his former students were charged with relaying his efforts. They were Olivier Giscard d'Estaing (HBS '51), Claude Janssen (HBS '55) and Jean Raindre (HBS '47).

Conventional wisdom counterposes reflection and action, often regarding them as mutually exclusive. In particular, there is a popular view that academics are never more than failed practitioners – as captured by Shaw's famous observation that "Those who can't, teach." Doriot showed a singular capacity to combine the two activities – to draw his experience into his teaching and to practise what he preached. Unlike most teachers, he had a record of acting on his ideas.

AN INTUITION UNFOLDS

By 1954, the CPA had become an established and respected management education centre, a leader in the field within Europe. With this successful collaboration behind him, Doriot saw the Paris Chamber of Commerce as a natural partner in his search to advance the idea of a European business school. Doriot had already tested out his idea informally on influential parties, including the French Minister for Education (in November 1953) and the head of the French Railways (in February 1954). Both had reacted positively in their letters. Both had also misspelled 'Harvard' referring to it as 'Haward Business School' – which gives an indication of the low visibility of the business school and more generally of business education in France at the time. European students attending HBS were still very much pioneers.

In late July 1954, representatives of the Chamber of Commerce met up with Doriot to follow up on his recent proposal. One of the representatives was Doriot's old friend, Pierre Jolly, now director general of the Paris Chamber of Commerce; the other was Gérard Ansieau, its vice-president. The discussions were rather different from those which had preceded the creation of the CPA, back in the late 1920s. Doriot had acquired considerable standing. He was no longer 'just' an energetic but inexperienced professor at Harvard. He was now a renowned figure – 'The General'. This time, when he talked about his idea, they listened and took notes.

Minutes of the meeting were written up by Jolly and Ansieau for the benefit of their colleagues at the Chamber of Commerce explaining what Doriot was proposing. A number of points are worth highlighting. First,

Harvard Business School having been approached by a number of European institutions for help, wanted to target its efforts. One of Harvard's leading professors being French-born, it was natural that France should receive special attention within continental Europe – just as it was natural to entrust the project to the Paris Chamber of Commerce which had a proven track record in the field. Second, the school would have a dual mission: to help train graduates for business and, 'from a moral point of view', to further European understanding within business. This 'dual mission' would help to set Insead apart from other management education establishments and, with hindsight, can be regarded as a key to the school's pulling power for students from the very first intake.

Doriot also had some fairly clear ideas on the shape of the European business school, which he shared with them. The course should be entirely residential; it should last one academic year (September to July); student recruitment should be pan-European; teaching should be based on the case method with a heavy preference for teaching by practitioners from different countries (to keep the courses on a practical footing); and the teaching should be bilingual (French and German) or possibly trilingual, but there was some expectation that there would be very limited British interest in a European school based in Paris. The bilingual or trilingual nature of the school would require access to simultaneous translation! Some of the principles proved premonitory, others were mainly relevant to the start-up phase, and one or two were off-target.

In terms of support, the technical help of Harvard would be guaranteed and Doriot speculated that the Ford Foundation might be willing to make a financial contribution once the school was running. The big sticking point for the Paris Chamber of Commerce was that it would be necessary to finance the set-up costs – purchase of educational premises, residential quarters and all the refurbishment requirements.

Seven months after these discussions, in March 1955, Doriot received a letter from Jacques Fougerolle, the president of the Paris Chamber of Commerce, announcing that after some deliberation they had agreed to support the idea. Fougerolle confirmed the willingness of the Chamber of Commerce to provide whatever technical assistance was necessary, notably the services of the CPA, but he would not promise any financial contribution. Doriot was asked to make a presentation of his project to an invited audience from the world of business and politics next time he visited France.

Thus, on 13 June 1955, Doriot made his first public presentation of the project at the CPA. In the fortnight that followed the presentation Doriot met two leading French business figures to tell them more about his project. They were Raoul de Vitry d'Avaucourt, President of Péchiney (with whom he had remained very close since a first meeting in 1939) and Hély d'Oissel,

President of Saint Gobain (succeeded two years later by Arnaud de Vogüé). As Doriot later recalled, these individuals, with their powerful business, social and political connections were key 'recruits' to the cause. "They gave their time, their support, their reputations. I made several speeches. They were always there."[10] Again, without Doriot's high-level connections and capacity to persuade busy people to give up their time and use their influence, the idea might simply never have gathered momentum.

On 13 July 1955, the Paris Chamber of Commerce held a big meeting to discuss Doriot's proposal in more detail – this time inviting important figures from outside France, notably Bertrand Fox, vice-dean of Harvard Business School and Thomas H. Carroll, the vice-president of the Ford Foundation (who also happened to be head of the Harvard Business School alumni association). Unfortunately, Doriot himself was unable to attend. An additional point of interest emerged at this stage concerning the site: Doriot's recommendation was that the school should be "established outside but near Paris" for the convenience of visiting instructors flying in from abroad.

The assembled parties strongly supported the idea of the school, considering that many of the implementation difficulties (to do with the cross-national nature of the project) were actually arguments in its favour and speculating that, once established, the school would "prove not only useful but indispensable".[11] This meeting was significant in that the idea was starting to make its way without Doriot's physical presence.

On reading the minutes of this meeting, Doriot made two hand-written notes in the margin which give important insights into his ambitions for the school. The first rectification concerned a passage asserting that the school would prepare students "for a career in any business organised on a European basis or concerned with trade between the different European countries". Doriot wrote: "Should not be limited to that." He foresaw that this was a school based *in* Europe but not exclusively *for* Europe.

Further along, the minutes stated that: "If 100 students were accepted, this would mean 10 to 15 from each country." Doriot wrote to Gérard Ansieau of the Paris Chamber of Commerce: "With reference to your limitation of 100 students, do you think that it might give the impression that the school would never grow larger than that? I think 100 is a good start, but certainly the school should become much larger later on."[12] There is no doubt that Doriot saw *big*.[13]

[10] Doriot, G.F. (1976) *The Creation of Insead*, personal notes.
[11] Mr. Spiette, General Secretary of the Brussels Chamber of Commerce, in the minutes of the Conference on the Establishment of a European Business School, held at the Paris Chamber of Commerce, 13/7/55.
[12] Doriot correspondence, 20/9/55.
[13] In Doriot's personal notes, from January 1957, he considers that the school "must be planned for 800 students at least (perhaps with affiliates elsewhere)".

THE ROCKY ROAD TO COMMITMENT

Perhaps the overriding impression from Doriot's written correspondence between late 1953 and mid 1957 is the long lead times between events. Each summer when Doriot came to France, he would stir things up, make presentations, bring new people on board, rekindle flagging enthusiasm. Similarly, when meeting French visitors in the US, Doriot would often ask them to return and urge the people at the Chamber of Commerce in Paris to move faster. But when Doriot was not there to inspire, coax or bully, progress seemed painfully slow. Jean Martin, the former head of education for the Paris Chamber of Commerce, recalled that "From 1954 through 1956, the project was inching forward and General Doriot was really starting to grow impatient."

Typically, once he was back in Boston, the news reaching him from France comprised a dispiriting mix of setbacks and indifference. For example, in November 1954, a letter from his friend Pierre Jolly, Director General of the Paris Chamber of Commerce, explained that if he had not written it was because "there were no new developments to speak of" and that the project was being side-tracked by the planned transfer of the *Ecole des Hautes Etudes Commerciales* (HEC) to a site in the Paris suburbs.[14]

In June 1956, Doriot received a letter from Ansieau, vice president of the Chamber of Commerce bemoaning "the little success solicited from abroad by our initiative ..." and telling Doriot of their plans to house the European school in the greenfield site being built for the HEC school.[15] Three months later, Ansieau wrote again telling Doriot that the summer break had prevented him from "assembling the French personalities who have shown interest in the school".[16] Compared with the sense of entrepreneurialism and 'can do' attitude that Doriot had grown used to in the US, the process must have been deeply frustrating – to the point that Doriot found himself writing to Pierre Dumont, the new president of the Paris Chamber of Commerce, in the summer of 1956, asking him: "Do you think there is any hope for it?"

In February 1957, Doriot received a letter from Claude Bouvard,[17] a company director and one of Doriot's many antennae in France, which seemed to confirm his worst fears. Bouvard noted that in his efforts to promote the idea, he had encountered "much kindness, lots of fine words, but little enthusiasm, little effectiveness, and little desire for change".[18] One could sense the exasperation in Doriot's response, dated 12 March 1957, where he noted that self-interest on the part of local management education establishments was preventing the project from advancing. "By hoping to

[14] Doriot's correspondence, letter from Pierre Jolly, Paris Chamber of Commerce, 26/11/54.
[15] Doriot's correspondence, letter from Gérard Ansieau, Paris Chamber of Commerce, 27/6/56.
[16] Doriot's correspondence, letter from Gérard Ansieau, Paris Chamber of Commerce, 20/9/56.
[17] Bouvard had attended the Harvard Advanced Management Program, on which Doriot taught.
[18] Doriot's correspondence, letter from Claude Bouvard, Compagnie Electro-Mécanique, 22/2/57.

protect little things, which are not bad in themselves, most people do not want to see the light and carry out a plan which will be infinitely better ... Therefore, nothing bigger or more interesting will be done." It is worth remembering that Doriot was doing this '*pour la gloire*'. He had no intention of returning to France; nor would he derive any commercial gain from the project.[19] It was driven by a simple urge, as expressed in his personal notes from early 1957: "My only desire is not to regret, and perhaps have them regret in ten years from now, that there really was a need for a distinguished European Graduate School of Business."

In reality, the initiative was inexorably moving forward, on one front or another. Each year, new people were attracted to the project. For instance, in mid 1955, Claude Janssen left Harvard with his freshly minted MBA to become another of Doriot's 'agents in France' – working behind the scenes, applying pressure where possible and reporting back on progress. And in the summer of 1956, whilst in Paris, Doriot renewed contact with a former student, Olivier Giscard d'Estaing. Alongside his business career, Giscard d'Estaing was teaching at the *Institut d'Etudes Politiques*. He, and another HBS alumnus, Jean Raindre had persuaded the school's authorities to offer a course in business as a fourth year elective. As a firm believer in management education and a committed proponent of a federal Europe, Giscard d'Estaing was an easy convert to Doriot's cause. Others, such as Georges Villiers, the influential head of the French employers' association,[20] were also coming round to the idea. Slowly, the project was gathering behind it a critical mass of active supporters. And once an idea becomes an inevitability, no one wants to be remembered for standing in its way.

Doriot had also taken the precaution to approach the Strasbourg Chamber of Commerce as a potential alternative to Paris. Its president, Jean Wenger-Valentin, had immediately shown a keen interest in the project. The Strasbourg option made a lot of sense given the established European credentials of the city (seat of the European Council) and its openness to Germany. Doriot's advances were genuine and Strasbourg was seriously considered, but there was also an element of gamesmanship involved. When the news was leaked, the idea did not go down particularly well with the Paris Chamber of Commerce. The whiff of competition seemed to have the desired effect in terms of speeding up the decision process.

Finally, in its annual general meeting of 5 July 1957, the Paris Chamber of Commerce agreed to take the plunge and establish a European business

---

[19] A Harvard colleague of Doriot's was invited to act as a consultant in the preparation phase of the new school and wondered whether he should charge a fee for this week's work. Doriot's exclamation mark in the margin suggests that he was surprised by the question, and responded: "I have always taken the point of view that the time I have given them, either when the CPA was formed or now, was part of my duty as a professor of the Harvard Business School." (4/4/58).

[20] *Conseil National du Patronat Français* since renamed *Mouvement des entreprises de France* (Medef).

school. It is easy to underestimate the courage behind this decision. Why should the Paris Chamber of Commerce commit to this novel international venture? Firstly, its geographical constituency was clearly the Paris region, not France and certainly not Europe. Secondly, the Paris Chamber of Commerce already supported several schools (including HEC, ESCP, CPA) which might conceivably lose out (if only in terms of funding) from the creation of the new school. Fortunately, the call of Europe was stronger. Four days after the annual general meeting, a public event was organised to make the news official. Immediately after the meeting, the creation of the school was announced in the newspapers and on the airwaves – with the first classes planned for the autumn of 1958.

The news was picked up by *Le Figaro* and *Le Monde*, numerous regional papers, the financial press and other trade papers (including the Montpellier-based *La Journée des Fruits et Légumes*!). It was several months before the foreign press picked up on the news, starting with the Dutch, Belgian, German and Swiss press (from December 1958 onwards), and then several months again before the English-speaking press took notice of it (from April 1959 onwards). The recurring commentary was that this was a timely initiative given the changing institutional context in Europe.

A TIME AND A PLACE

Ideas can be swept up or swept away by historical circumstance, so they cannot be considered apart from their context. This is particularly true of Insead, an initiative closely associated with the unification of Europe, and an initiative which embodied and projected new values.

The signing of the Treaty of Rome, in late March 1957, surely influenced the decision, barely three months later, to support the creation of a European business school.[21] The time was now ripe for such an initiative. The notion of European reconciliation and renaissance was part of the *zeitgeist*. One could argue that the context had finally caught up with the idea.

In many ways, France seemed a natural home for the European school. France, motivated by a desire to secure lasting peace in Europe and to 'be heard' in world affairs, had been at the forefront of the efforts to unify Europe. In 1950, it was Robert Schuman, the French Minister of Foreign Affairs, who had first proposed the creation of a kind of United States of Europe. Its earliest manifestation came just a year later when six western European states formed the European Coal and Steel Community (CECA – *Communauté Européene du Charbon et de l'Acier*).

---

[21] The Treaty of Rome was a vital and unexpected boost to the European construction which had been somewhat shaken by the failure to establish a common defence body. In early 1957, the reality of a unified Europe still rested on the uninspiring European Coal and Steel Community. The 248 articles of the Treaty of Rome agreement, promoting freer trade, were negotiated in a breathtaking six months.

The political drivers in favour of a European business school were reinforced by economic forces. The western economies, so badly shaken by the second world war, were starting to recover in the wake of the Marshall Plan. The growth of Europe as a major economic bloc looked set to create a demand for people trained in management with an understanding of countries and languages other than their own. Moreover, the growing presence of US multinationals in Europe led some to make a link between superior management know-how and the unprecedented productivity and prosperity of the US economy.

These were powerful influences on the decision to create a European business school and to do so in France – so powerful, in fact, that they have tended to obfuscate other contextual factors affecting the genesis of Insead. This makes the idea look more obvious than it really was. Two forces opposing the creation of the school are worth resurfacing.

First, there was the hospitality of France in the 1950s to 'foreign bodies', particularly in the domain of higher education. The French education system has a tradition of intellectual excellence and robust insularity as embodied by its unique network of *Grandes Ecoles*. The proposed school was not purely French and, back in the 1950s, management was certainly not regarded as a legitimate academic discipline. Indeed the school would be offering an unrecognised qualification. Nor was it obvious how French companies would accommodate the graduates into their career systems. So the local conditions were not entirely favourable.

A parallel can be drawn here, with a more recent attempt by an energetic and highly respected Insead professor to create an international business school near Munich. First mooted in 1988, the idea quickly attracted financial and moral pledges from Germany's largest corporations. As with Insead in the 1950s, the historical context was particularly propitious: intensifying global competition, post–1992 European integration and the opening of Eastern Europe all provided powerful arguments for creating such a school in the German-speaking region of Europe. In 1991, however, the project had to be abandoned, a victim of a hostile local environment, as explained in a 'post-mortem' report. On the one hand, there remained widespread scepticism, in Germany, regarding the value of producing mobile 'MBA-style' generalists in a business culture which valued corporate loyalty and functional specialism. On the other hand, the project threatened to interfere with and detract from local management education institutions which mobilised resistance against the project. A favourable European climate clearly has its limitations.

Returning to the case of Insead, a second situational factor menaced the creation of the school, namely the geographical distance between the originator of the idea and its intended home. Today, distance is often regarded as an irrelevance – both in terms of transport and communication.

Back in the mid-1950s, it was a non-trivial consideration. People, Doriot included,[22] were still crossing the Atlantic by ship, and getting hold of someone in France, with its archaic telephone exchange system, was something of a lottery. The sense of trust and enthusiasm generated by a face-to-face encounter could be said to have a kind of half-life, quickly decaying between encounters. Written correspondence was the only reliable 'technology' at Doriot's disposal to keep people 'hyped up' between summer visits. It therefore speaks volumes for Doriot's standing, persuasiveness and perseverance that the project made it onto the drawing board.

Later, reflecting on the time it took to create CPA and Insead, Doriot noted that, in both cases, several years elapsed between putting out the first feelers and attending the inaugural ceremonies. He thought that the process might have been accelerated had he not lived in Boston, but he also had a suspicion that this constraint had actually served the project. He even speculated that: "The fact that I was not in France may have been a help. It takes time for an idea to take root, and people must be given the opportunity to think and digest. They must not be rushed."[23] People needed to develop a sense of ownership and to realise what their contribution might be. Had Doriot been present, he would inevitably have taken a lead role, and others would not have got involved to the same extent or been capable of replacing him afterwards. A familiar refrain in entrepreneurial ventures is that everything takes longer than expected. In a perverse way, this may have actually helped the project succeed.

THE HINGE OF FATE

In order to give the new school momentum and visibility, two important positions – those of director-general and director of academic studies – needed to be filled quickly, especially given the scheduled October 1958 opening date.

Within three weeks of the official announcement of the project, a likely director general had been identified by the Paris Chamber of Commerce. His name was General Gustave Leroy. He had attended the CPA and was currently director of the prestigious French school, *l'Ecole Polytechnique*.[24] Doriot first met him, along with Jean Marcou, then treasurer of the Paris Chamber of Commerce (but soon to become its new president) in Paris on 6 August 1957. The arrival of Leroy, who seemed keen to appropriate the project, would allow Doriot to step back and adopt a more supervisory role.

Meanwhile, on 10 July 1957, Olivier Giscard d'Estaing had written to

[22] Doriot favoured the ship crossing to Europe. A French friend of his envied him, lamenting that he was forced to take the plane because he was a member of the airline's board. This was another age!

[23] Doriot, G.F. (1976) *The Creation of Insead*, personal notes.

[24] *L'Ecole Polytechnique* is always headed by an active general.

Pierre Dumont, President of the Paris Chamber of Commerce, to introduce himself and his two Harvard colleagues – Claude Janssen and Jean Raindre – and to offer their assistance.

Some time previously, Doriot had thought of Arnaud de Vitry (HBS 53) – whose father's relentless support had helped sway the Paris Chamber of Commerce in favour of the school – as a potential director of academic studies. On 20 August 1957, however, Doriot was forced to write to Pierre Dumont, President of the Paris Chamber of Commerce, informing him that Arnaud de Vitry did not accept the job.[25] Doriot proposed Olivier Giscard d'Estaing or Claude Janssen, with a preference for the former: "I have discussed them with General Leroy. I think a strong bid should be made for Olivier, who has very much of a European conception, and also he and his family seem to have a very sincere interest in public services." Another suitable candidate mentioned by Doriot was a Belgian former Harvard alumnus, Stefaan Cambien, who had started a business school in Lille (CEPI[26]) – and might be "ready to face something bigger". Having attended Harvard was a 'requirement'; French nationality was not.

On 27 August 1957, Doriot received a letter from Claude Janssen explaining that he had visited General Leroy in his 16th *arrondissement* apartment, together with Olivier Giscard d'Estaing. "We met a man who seems fully determined to carry this project through to a successful conclusion" and someone with "a dynamic personality".[27] Nevertheless, Janssen had a couple of misgivings about General Leroy's apparent plans for the school. Firstly, General Leroy seemed intent on integrating the school into the existing CPA set up, sharing cases, professors and premises. Janssen was also slightly concerned that in General Leroy's mind, the business dimension might be subordinate to the European dimension of the school. Janssen added that he, Giscard d'Estaing and Raindre had thought of another potential candidate for the director of studies position – Robert Posthumus Meyjes (HBS '56), then assistant to Dean Fox at HBS.

At around the same time, Doriot received a letter from General Leroy alluding to the meeting with Janssen and Giscard d'Estaing. After their lengthy and fruitful discussions, Leroy was able to "affirm that there are no glaring flaws in *my* project – only efforts to be made, as I suspected"[28] (italics added). Nevertheless, Leroy saw two potential impediments to ensuring the best quality education: first, there might be a shortage of qualified professors in some disciplines, notably marketing – he wondered whether Harvard

---

[25] Arnaud de Vitry would later help to found the European version of ARD – European Enterprise Development – headquartered in Paris. De Vitry was also on the board of Digital Equipment Corporation from the start.

[26] *Centre d'Etudes des Problèmes Industriels.*

[27] Doriot's correspondence, letter from Claude Janssen, 27/8/57.

[28] Doriot's correspondence, letter from General Leroy, Director of *l'Ecole Polytechnique*, 24/8/57.

would be prepared to help out on this matter. Secondly, he thought that "of the *40 students* expected to enrol" (italics added), 30 or so might find it difficult to finance their course fees plus their board and lodging. He wondered whether the Ford Foundation, which Doriot had mentioned in their previous meeting, might be willing to provide a grant of, say, $100,000 a year for the first three years, to launch the school under the best possible conditions.

Doriot's response was swift. He confirmed that the school might consider loaning one or two professors for the weaker subject areas. But there was also a note of irritation in his letter: "I want to tell you very definitely that the European School should not ask for anything in this country until it is done officially and only after a definite outline of the effort to be made by Europeans for that school has been worked out. As you know the Harvard Business School is interested in the idea, but neither the Harvard Business School nor the Ford Foundation nor anybody else should be asked to do anything until there is evidence of the effort to be made by Europeans ... In other words, let's see what your effort is, how much of a contribution you are making, and then we will help."[29] Doriot voiced another concern too. A couple of people who had heard about the school assumed it was some kind of postgraduate political sciences institute, as opposed to a business school. He concluded: "I think it is very important to make clear that the school will definitely be a business school for Europeans and not a school for Europeans to come and discuss the problems of Europe."

By September 1957, Leroy had still not been officially named. He was awaiting clearance from the Government, and ministerial decisions were heavily delayed in a context of massive social and political instability. But in a letter to Doriot, dated 10 September, he explained that he had already started working on the courses and articles of association. His next task would be to organise a round of visits to inform foreign chambers of commerce, and he expected to complete those visits early in the new year. As Pierre Dumont, President of the Paris Chamber of Commerce, wrote to Doriot in early October 1957: "General Leroy has only recently stepped down from running *l'Ecole Polytechnique*. I expect his detachment to our organisation to be completed in the current month."[30] Dumont added that while Doriot's former students were taking a lively interest in the project, none of them seemed prepared to abandon their careers, even temporarily, to devote themselves full-time to the school.

On 23 October 1957, André Morice, the French Defence Minister, wrote to the Paris Chamber of Commerce turning down General Leroy's request for secondment to the new European school. The decision was linked to the

[29] Doriot's correspondence, letter to General Leroy, Director of *l'Ecole Polytechnique*, 3/9/57
[30] Doriot's correspondence, letter from Pierre Dumont, 2/10/57.

upheaval in Algeria. General Leroy would be heading out to Africa in the coming months to take up an important military position in the Sahara.

Including the story of 'the director who never was' may appear like a quirky digression. However, it casts light on two important points. First, it shows again the impact that external events can have on the development of an institution, particularly in the preliminary phases when a project can be nudged in multiple directions. Second, it is important to restore some of the false starts, blind alleys and detours, long since forgotten, which demonstrate the uncertainty and delicacy of the whole venture. What might, or might not, have been if Leroy had been appointed? Had he stayed, the opening of the school would probably not have been postponed by one academic year, a delay which may actually have helped to build up demand and readiness; the school only had one chance to make an impressive debut. More significantly though, one can at least speculate that the new school might have become a rather French institution, drawing stronger inspiration from the CPA and *l'Ecole Polytechnique*. The Harvard alumni, who were to play a determining role in shaping the school, might well have been marginalised in the process – which would probably have inhibited the international scope of the project.

THE LEADERSHIP ISSUE

With less than a year to go to the scheduled start, efforts had been focused on finding a director of studies for the school.[31] Now the school found itself back at square one, with neither leadership position filled. Doriot was very disappointed. Writing to Claude Bouvard in France, he confided: "I am very much disturbed to learn that the European school does not have a director any more." He appealed to Bouvard: "Can't you and your friends help them to find someone? There must be someone, young or old, who is willing to give up two or three years to build up something which can be very wonderful, not only for France but for western Europe." Doriot, who had grown used to American positivism, bemoaned the lack of drive or spirit of adventure on the old continent: "I simply do not understand why it is so hard to find someone who can take on that most constructive and promising job. I must say that in this country it would be easier and that one could convince a person to get leave of absence for that kind of thing. Why can't it be done in France? Somehow most everybody is in favor of something as long as somebody else does it."[32] Again one senses the exasperation and helplessness occasioned by the distances involved, both geographical and cultural.

On 25 October 1957, Doriot learned that while they would continue to do all they could to support the school, neither Olivier Giscard d'Estaing nor

---

[31] See Gérard Ansieau's letter to Georges Doriot, 2/10/57.
[32] Doriot's correspondence, letter to Claude Bouvard, 31/10/57.

Claude Janssen was keen on taking up the director of studies position, as both had flourishing careers in their respective companies.[33] Doriot responded immediately with a plea to his former students: "All of you must get together and with whatever help you can get from your friends or family or whatever it is, you must take the bull by the horns and help more aggressively ... I have been ringing doorbells for three years, and I cannot do much more. This is a problem for your generation!"[34]

Doriot was partly reassured by Janssen who told him that the imminent accession of Jean Marcou to the presidency of the Paris Chamber of Commerce augured well for the project. As Janssen related it: "Marcou repeatedly affirmed ... his determination to overcome the numerous difficulties still separating us from the opening class." Janssen observed, "He is a very resourceful man and I am convinced that he will not want his first year as President to be marked by such a failure."[35] The new president would be joined by Jean Martin, replacing Gérard Ansieau, with responsibility for the CPA and the European school.

Back in Boston, Doriot continued to scout round for names. He talked again with Arnaud de Vitry about taking up the directorship, rather than the director of studies post previously proposed, but de Vitry could not envisage returning to France. The difficulty of finding people to fill the top jobs again indicates the anticipated life expectancy of the budding institution – people were not exactly lining up to take on the challenge.

Doriot then sent the CVs of three people to the Paris Chamber of Commerce: these included Willem Posthumus Meyjes whose name had been suggested by his son working at HBS. As Doriot put it: "I do not know the gentleman but his son told me that if the new European School did not have a Director, he thought that his father might be considered."[36] Willem Posthumus Meyjes was the retiring Dutch ambassador to Greece, with business experience as a former banker. Doriot's view was that the head of school should not be French and that the Director of Studies or Assistant Director should be a HBS graduate.

By early February 1958, Marcou was able to announce to Doriot that they had several promising candidates for the directorship of the school. The openness and frequency of the correspondence between the two men suggested this relationship differed from the previous ones between Doriot and the Paris Chamber of Commerce. Marcou was strongly committed to and ambitious for the project.

On 10th February 1958, Olivier Giscard d'Estaing wrote to Doriot telling

---

[33] Janssen was with Banque Worms, a large financial institution, and Giscard d'Estaing was working with the steel manufacturer, *Aciéries de Pompey* (which had supplied the elements for the Eiffel Tower).

[34] Doriot's correspondence, letter to Claude Janssen, 31/10/57.

[35] Doriot's correspondence, letter from Claude Janssen, 14/11/57.

[36] Doriot's correspondence, letter to Gérard Ansieau, 3/12/57.

him that Jean Martin of the Paris Chamber of Commerce had officially offered him the job of director of studies "with conditions which appear acceptable". After further talks, Giscard d'Estaing would be called upon to make a decision, but he remained equivocal. It would mean interrupting his industrial career for four or five years and he feared there might be no way back once he had taken an academic post. He was fully conscious of the risk in taking up this job. He was also concerned that, if he took the job, there was no guarantee that he would be given the discretion and resources needed to "create the kind of school we have discussed".[37]

Within minutes of receiving the letter, Doriot drafted a reply telling Giscard d'Estaing: "I do hope you will take the job. Do not think of the future. You will do well in that job and I am confident in my soul that the future will take care of itself ... I am quite certain you will get help from a great many people, therefore, please take it. I will do everything I can."[38]

In March 1958, Doriot received unofficial confirmation that the two positions were pretty much settled – with Olivier Giscard d'Estaing reporting to Willem Posthumus Meyjes – but would only be officially announced in June at the meeting of the European Presidents of the Chambers of Commerce. By this stage, with the delays in appointments, it had become clear that the school would not be launched until September 1959.[39]

Doriot probably breathed a sigh of relief that was audible in France. He could see that his idea would do more than survive – not just with the two prospective appointments, but also with the energetic duo of Marcou and Martin, at the Paris Chamber of Commerce, who seemed to share his vision for the school. To a certain extent, Doriot's mission was now accomplished.

From this point on, Doriot slipped out of the picture and got back to his 'day job'. He would continue to work behind the scenes on behalf of the school, providing a sounding board for the successive leaders, giving advice, straightening out 'diplomatic' entanglements, publicising the European school, eliciting support and raising funds for it in the US. But the destiny of the school was now in the hands of others.

In his 438 page tome on institution building, Udai Pareek proposes that: "The most crucial test of institution building is the extent to which a leader is able to dispossess the institute which he has been able to establish."[40] Doriot had shown he could do it with the CPA and he proved it again with Insead. Having assembled the necessary ingredients, he left others to make it happen.

[37] Doriot's correspondence, letter from Olivier Giscard d'Estaing, 16/2/58.
[38] Doriot's correspondence, letter to Olivier Giscard d'Estaing, 25/2/58.
[39] Doriot's correspondence, letter from Pearson Hunt, 16/3/58
[40] Pareek, U. (1994) *Op cit.*

ON GIANT'S SHOULDERS

Because the real origins of Insead are little known, there is a widespread belief, even internally, that its running start and rapid development were essentially the product of good fortune. As one twenty-five year veteran of the school summarised it: "Insead's success is really just chance of circumstances: that the General had his idea in the first place, that he had been to Harvard, that he got together with these people who also thought it was a good idea, that they managed to get funding for the idea because Europe was 'hot' and so on."

This first chapter has attempted to put straight that misconception. Inevitably there was an element of chance involved, but tracing the origins and development of the intuition suggests an incremental progression, not a series of random opportunities or lucky breaks.

The emergence of Insead was the result of a complex alchemy between an exceptional individual (with a compelling idea), an enlightened patron and an historical context. This chapter has tried to show how these three ingredients intertwined over time, rather than simply converging from nowhere. The terrain was unconsciously prepared by the creation of the CPA, by the Paris Chamber of Commerce's growing willingness to experiment with business education, and by Doriot's undimmed allegiance to France and Europe.

In particular, Doriot's bizarre itinerary gave him a unique potential to follow through on the idea – with his repertoire of experiences, competencies and connections. But capability is one thing, and action is another. It took a peculiar mix of self-belief, altruism and determination to pick up the challenge. As Doriot himself once said: "A creative man merely has ideas; a resourceful man makes them practical."[41]

The short answer to the luck versus judgement question is 'Look at the paternity'.[42] Doriot was a remarkable man. Insead was not conceived by a standing committee: it was the brainchild of perhaps *the* outstanding professor at Harvard Business School; someone who profoundly influenced generations of business leaders, who pioneered the venture capital industry, and who ended up in the *Fortune* 'Hall of Fame'. In Doriot's obituaries, in 1987, Insead was just one item in a long list of achievements.

Doriot's selfless and tenacious efforts are worth highlighting for another reason. A long-standing criticism levelled at Insead, from certain French quarters, is that it scatters domestic talent all over the world instead of pumping it into French firms. For some, Insead is 'working for the enemy'.

---

[41] *Forbes*, July 13, 1987.

[42] In the staircase leading to the dean's office, there is a plaque paying tribute to the founders of Insead. Tucked away in the list of 'contributors' is the name of Georges F. Doriot. Such is the nature of success, with its multiple paternity claims.

This is a very narrow view. First, it ignores the flip side: many 'foreign' MBAs end up working in France; and exposing an international managerial elite to French culture increases France's networks and potential reach in the world. Secondly, it assumes that France will be better off if it remains self-contained. Increasing France's physical presence in the world is an important way of defending its culture, its language, its commercial and industrial interests – as well as enhancing the capacity of returning expatriates to tackle France's problems, shortcomings or blind spots from a wider perspective.

Doriot's relentless efforts helped to set up the CPA, Insead, the Paris-based European Enterprise Development (providing venture capital for European start-ups) and the French library in Boston (one of the leading centres of French culture in the US). These initiatives were precisely the work of an expatriate Frenchman who wanted his experience to benefit his country of origin.

CHAPTER 2

Believing something into being

"In innovation, as in any other endeavor, there is talent, there is ingenuity, and there is knowledge. But when all is said and done, what innovation requires is hard, focused, purposeful work." Peter Drucker, *Harvard Business Review*, May–June 1985, 72.

TAKING MEASURE OF THE CHALLENGE

In July 1958, Willem Posthumus Meyjes and Olivier Giscard d'Estaing were officially appointed to head up what was still being referred to as the European business school. They set to work in the offices of the Paris Chamber of Commerce. With only 14 months separating them from the scheduled start, and one full-time secretary to assist them, they faced an uphill battle. The school remained a virtual entity, without premises or even a firm location, without professors, without a fixed legal status, without a selection process for students or a course outline to propose to them, and with only a portion of its funding guaranteed. Where should they start?

The problem of deciding where to start was compounded by the varying and uncertain lead times on many of these issues – and the fact that some issues could not be tackled until others had been resolved. For example, attracting students is not an overnight job – they need to manifest interest, to be sent application forms, to fill them out. These application forms then need to be processed – and to evaluate them correctly requires people who are familiar with the nuances of educational qualifications from different countries. This could entail setting up decentralised screening panels or examination centres close to the main sources of candidates. It is a lengthy process. And it gets more complex.

To attract students in the first place presentations have to be made to create awareness of and demand for a new type of education. Brochures must also be distributed. But to produce brochures one needs to be fairly precise about what is being offered – the location ('somewhere in the Paris region' sounds rather suspect), the facilities, the content of the studies, and who is putting their name behind it. Thus potential supporters or patrons have to be contacted internationally – and that involves a lot of time on the road, explaining what the school is about, and convincing people face-to-face. Thus, there are multiple 'chains' of interdependent actions and decisions which need to be tackled in considered sequences. A team of critical path analysts would have a field day.

Given the inspiration behind the European business school, rapid answers to some of these issues might be gleaned from Harvard. Giscard d'Estaing was certainly familiar with the practices and policies at Harvard and was well placed to leverage his Harvard connections, starting of course with Doriot. The Harvard model offered plenty of tried and tested 'solutions' – the question was which ones might work for Europe and which ones were affordable? Emulating Harvard with a tiny fraction of the resources would require considerable ingenuity.

The beauty of hindsight is that it makes everything seem obvious and perfectly logical. The questions raised in the introduction are merely intended to give readers an appreciation of the challenge as it presented itself, going forward rather than looking back.

THE CREDIBILITY GAP

Olivier Giscard d'Estaing began by touring some of the existing management schools and training centres in Europe looking for inspiration. The most prominent of these were IPSOA, established in 1952 in Turin and financed by Fiat; the CEI created by Alcan Alumimium in 1946, which had become an independent foundation in 1956, establishing a formal relationship with the University of Geneva; and IMEDE in Lausanne, opened in 1957 as a foundation of Nestlé in co-operation with the University of Lausanne.[1]

What made the new school different from most existing business schools was that it was independent, not linked to a university or a sponsoring corporation. It had managed to secure seed money from the Paris Chamber of Commerce, but this was guaranteed only for five years. It covered only a portion of the running costs and would be maintained only on condition that complementary financing was secured from the corporate sector. Thus, like any private entrepreneurial venture, the European school started with a huge credibility problem – compounded by the fact that this was an international entrepreneurial venture.

[1] IPSOA (*Istituto Post-Universitario per gli Studi di Organizzazione Aziendale*), CEI (*Centre d'Etudes Industrielles*), IMEDE (*Institut pour l'étude des méthodes de direction de l'entreprise* – International Management Development Institute).

Deprived of the instant legitimacy of university association, the new school would be hard-pushed to impress various parties – including prospective students, would-be professors, potential employers, bankers or resource providers, as well as peer institutions with which it might collaborate. What guarantees of quality existed for a school which was not part of a national education system and which would deliver an unrecognised diploma?[2]

The first priority for the school was, therefore, to attract patrons with high visibility who might lend it a kind of surrogate reputation, a promise of stability and seriousness. The support of the Paris Chamber of Commerce and of certain high profile business people – like Raoul de Vitry (Péchiney), Arnaud de Vogüé (Saint Gobain), René Perrin (Compagnie Française de Raffinage) and Paul Desombre (Compagnie Electromécanique) – was a good start, but they were all French.

The commitment of a core of like-minded people, speaking the same language (both literally and figuratively) was perhaps a necessary condition to launch the project. Had Doriot tried to marshall international support from the outset, the project would almost certainly have floundered under misunderstandings and clashing agendas. But now, the 'winning combination' of Doriot, the Paris Chamber of Commerce, the CPA, the French Harvard alumni, plus the big-name French industrialists threatened to put off potential international supporters – and without international patrons, the school was unlikely to attract international students, professors, employers or funds. Not for the last time in the school's development, a solution which had served the school well in the first place posed difficulties for further progress.

Yet there were clearly problems with obtaining international high level endorsement. However much they might applaud the idea, why should potential supporters commit to something they couldn't even see, which was not to the glory of their own country and which might never amount to anything? In any case, what was the evidence that there would be sufficient demand (either in quantity or quality) for what was on offer? And even if the demand existed, why should people come to France to receive an education in management?

Without belabouring the point, France in the 1950s was hardly considered an exemplar in the practice of management. A French alumnus of Harvard, quoted in a 1957 pamphlet advertising the business school's new fellowships for French students, gave his impression of the prevailing state of French business: "I have long believed that the point of view held by many

---

[2] The fact that the school did not belong to any 'national system' meant that accreditation could not be sought in advance from French or other European authorities. And the fact that it was a one-year programme was understood to preclude access to the MBA label. The qualification received was the Post-Graduate Diploma (*Diplôme Post-Universitaire*).

French business administrators towards their businesses, their employees, their customers, their suppliers, the general public and the nation itself, is rather on the selfish side. And the sum of my belief is that the attitude of many French businessmen tends towards the weakening rather than the strengthening of that country." France was highly respected in many domains – for its architecture, its art, music and literature, its cuisine and wines, its fashion and perfumes but not especially for its approach to business.

It fell upon Posthumus Meyjes and to a lesser extent Giscard d'Estaing and Jean Marcou, to try to enlist support outside France. Posthumus Meyjes embarked on an exhausting series of tours abroad to seek sponsorships, fully aware of the time lags involved. Writing to Doriot, before making a trip to Luxembourg, Germany, the Netherlands, and Belgium, he observed: "I cannot hope to come back with a wad of signed cheques from the institutions and large corporations of those countries. It will be several months before we can hope to harvest the fruits of our work."[3]

Of course, as a former ambassador, Posthumus Meyjes was in his element – explaining, persuading, cajoling was his business. He had international experience, he was fluent in several languages, he was a committed European and his son had attended HBS. He was also living proof that what might appear like a French initiative had a genuine European vocation.

Over the months that followed, Posthumus Meyjes was instrumental in securing the support of the honorary presidents, Prince Bernhard of the Netherlands and Paul-Henri Spaak, general secretary of NATO, as well as numerous other high profile Europeans.[4] Taken together with the institutional patronage of the European Productivity Agency, the International Chamber of Commerce, and the European League of Economic Co-operation, it gave the school impressive credentials. In December 1958, there was also a key meeting in London with John Loudon, chairman of Shell, who would later play a significant role in the development of the school.[5] The eventual list of patrons read like a roll call of the European Establishment as noted by a prominent American journalist, shortly before the school opened: "The list of those who have given their support and assistance... includes the names of virtually everyone who has been prominent in the post-war integration of Europe."[6]

[3] Doriot's correspondence, letter from Willem Posthumus Meyjes, 15/9/58.
[4] On Christmas eve 1958, letters were sent out by the Paris Chamber of Commerce asking people to confirm their willingness to be part of the patronage committee. Amongst those who accepted were Walter Hallstein (president of the European Economic Community), Piero Malvestiti (president of CECA), M. Benvenutti (chairman of the Council of Europe), René Sergent (secretary general of OECE), and Etienne Hirsch (president of Euratom).
[5] Referred to in letter from Posthumus-Meyjes to Mr. A.D. Vas Nunes, Shell Oil Company, 9/4/62.
[6] Jan Hasbrouck, "A school of business", *New York Herald Tribune*, 15/9/59.

STANDING ON A SHOESTRING

Another immediate priority for the school was to find suitable premises. The Paris Chamber of Commerce was still offering its CPA premises which were vacant during the day, the CPA running only evening and weekend courses. The new European school was perceived as a way of making greater use of the existing facilities and spreading maintenance costs. For the new school this presented an expedient solution, but not the most appropriate for two reasons: first, using the CPA premises would mean abandoning the idea of a residential course; second, it was anticipated that the location of the CPA in central Paris would disrupt the possibilities of group work and socialisation among the students. The idea was not simply to create a space where knowledge could be dispensed but to set up conditions where learning and cultural exchange would carry on outside the classroom. That meant keeping the students in close proximity, giving them a sense of *esprit de corps* and minimising external distractions. From the outset there was already a strong, though mostly tacit, concept of the learning process going far beyond the immediate course content.[7]

In an effort to find a viable alternative to the CPA solution, Giscard d'Estaing, together with Claude Janssen and Georges Doriot, over in France for the summer, toured the Paris region in late July 1958. They were looking for "any worthwhile available building", a provisional site for perhaps two to five years, until purpose-built premises could be financed.

Of course, the international nature of the school imposed a key constraint on the choice of location, necessitating access to an airport. There were other considerations influencing the specific choice of premises. The students would have to be lodged on the spot and the available space should be adaptable to the nature of the work (discussions, group meetings, quiet workrooms, library). Doriot also had a strong belief in reflection and self examination, so the site should be isolated and calm, ideally 20 to 40 kilometres from Paris, with surrounding grounds. The obvious solution seemed to be some kind of stately home or small château which might be rented at a low cost in exchange for renovation investments. But given the likely refurbishment needs, as well as the need to announce the location in the promotion material, it was becoming urgent to find something.

In August 1958, with Doriot back in the US, Posthumus Meyjes made several further visits with Giscard d'Estaing and an architect friend of his, Bernard de La Tour d'Auvergne. In the course of these visits, La Tour d'Auvergne wondered if it might not be possible to find some kind of

---

[7] An early confidential document which refers explicitly to "off-the-course" learning notes: "It goes without saying that 'inculcating a European spirit' among the students will be a constant concern, and every possible occasion will be used to promote exchanges and understanding. But the implementation of this crucial mission is not programmable, so no further mention will be made of it in this report." (4/11/57, *Visions of the Evolution of the European School.*)

temporary solution in conjunction with the American Art School in Fontainebleau where he happened to be a professor. The American Art School occupied the Louis XV wing in the Fontainebleau palace for two months every summer. The facilities were vacant for the rest of the year and there were also residential premises close by, in the town.

Quite apart from the 'neat fit' with the American Art School, there were several arguments in favour of this solution. France's main international airport, Orly, was within easy distance. The beauty of the town and the forest were obvious attractions. As an established tourist centre, Fontainebleau had an international reputation and abundant hotel accommodation; but the town also had an international feel thanks to the presence of a NATO base. Moreover, the historical and environmental characteristics of the setting upheld Doriot's belief in creating time and space for personal as well as professional development. Perhaps the biggest attraction though, was the lure of the palace. If the new school could be housed in the palace, it would bestow instant prestige and presence on the nascent venture.

By 20 October 1958, Giscard d'Estaing was able to write to Doriot that talks with the American Art School, presided over by the ambassador François Valéry, were progressing well. The idea of settling in Fontainebleau was further reinforced by the enthusiasm of the local authorities, under the leadership of Mayor Paul Séramy.

However, there remained a significant obstacle. The new school fell under the jurisdiction of three ministers – education, foreign affairs and industry – but approval for the use of the palace lay with the minister for culture, the writer André Malraux. A formal request to use the palace was duly dispatched. Some weeks later, this request was turned down on the grounds that the palace was reserved for artistic activities.[8] Doriot's response was that business *was* an art, which allegedly convinced the architect in chief responsible for the palace, but did not change the decision. Malraux was reported to have been outraged at the idea of turning part of a national palace into a business school.

Legend has it that there later followed a kind of showdown in the course of which Malraux finally succumbed to the argument that the initiative would not demean but rather ennoble the palace – that it would attract the cream, the European elite who would go on to become the builders of the Europe of tomorrow, and it would be very good for France. Such stories are vital to developing a young school's sense of identity. The truth is less pithy but more revealing of the realities of institution building.

It took several months of discussions with high ranking civil servants, plus the personal intervention of one of Doriot's friends, Paul Bertrand,[9] to get Malraux to acquiesce. In early July 1959, the new school was finally

---

[8] Doriot's correspondence, letter from Olivier Giscard d'Estaing, 24/3/59.
[9] His contribution is formally mentioned in the minutes of a meeting of the 'Coordination and Control Committee' (20/7/59), 4.

authorised to use the palace to house its lecture room and four offices. But by that time there were less than two months left before the opening date, set for 12th September 1959 – and new heating and lighting systems still needing to be installed. Malraux agreed to one year, non renewable, though at "a very nominal rent".[10]

Of course, gaining access to the palace was a tremendous marketing coup, giving an immediate impression of an elite institution. But this solution was not without its drawbacks: first, because a replacement solution would quickly be needed; and second, because of the incongruity between the setting and the mission – the palace had stronger connotations with the history of France than the future of Europe. Overall though, the palace provided a cadre befitting the endeavour and helped to justify the choice of France for the location. It would prove a key factor in the endeavour to 'create a reputation out of thin air' without a single student having graduated or a single course having been taught. Limitations on resources tend to activate ingenuity and perseverance.

MAKING RULES AND BENDING RULES

Concurrently with the search for premises, a small group of volunteers was working on the operating policies and course outlines. A *Comité Technique* was formed consisting of the three former Harvard graduates (Olivier Giscard d'Estaing, Claude Janssen and Jean Raindre) and three senior officials of the Paris Chamber of Commerce (Paul Minguet, Pierre Petot and Marcel Tourrenc) all three of whom had attended the CPA. Considerably older than their Harvard counterparts, the Paris Chamber of Commerce representatives tended to proceed with a certain caution. The Harvard alumni, on the other hand, benefited from a clear understanding of what a real business school looked like, as well as an international experience which had tended to sharpen their self-belief and impulsiveness. These differences in experience and outlook did not facilitate early discussions.

In particular, there were debates regarding the best means to launch. It was proposed that the school should start with short course programmes and then create the one year postgraduate programme later. Probably, starting with short courses would have been much easier – shorter sessions, lower fixed costs, a chance to test the water for a few years, then expand. But the Harvard alumni were fundamentally opposed and, with the benefit of more examples to draw on today, the difficulty for a management training centre to make the transition to a business school has become evident.

Another proposition was that the school start out as a French school, focusing on Europe, and become a truly European school once it had

[10] *France Actuelle*, 1/12/59.

gathered momentum. Again the Harvard alumni eschewed this solution, although it would surely have proved simpler. As numerous business schools have discovered since, the scope for 'internationalising' an existing school is limited. These policy choices seem obvious today, but the school could have been a very different entity had it pursued more expedient alternatives.

As mentioned earlier, the Harvard model was a useful reference in these discussions – there was no point reinventing the wheel – but given the difference in scale, in available resources, in cultural context and mission, the model needed to be handled with care. In truth, the committee had to determine what to copy, what to discard, what to adapt, and what to invent from scratch.

Meeting regularly, often twice a week, in the Paris Chamber of Commerce's 8th *arrondissement* offices, the technical committee steadily worked through the various issues. A document summarising the team's intense work, including 19 day-long meetings in the space of ten weeks, showed that by September 1958 many practical issues had been resolved, at least in theory. The impact of the three Harvard alumni, whose average age was 30, is particularly striking given the prevailing view of youth in France in the late 1950s; May '68 was still a decade away. But here again, they basked in the reflected authority of Doriot. They were perceived as his disciples.

Several features of the new school had been lifted directly from Harvard, thanks largely to the official intervention of Doriot. In particular, he had secured unlimited access to Harvard cases, and later a donation of several hundred books, for the new school. The standard Harvard application form was adapted to suit the new school's needs. Similarly, the course outline was heavily inspired by the Harvard programme, although the new school would also offer a unique course dealing with the European context, ponderously titled 'The Institutional, Economic, and Social Aspects of European Affairs'. Adopting Harvard's teaching approach was a formality in that the case method had been accepted from the start. However, as Giscard d'Estaing recalls, they did get dragged into a half an hour discussion as to whether it should be labelled the '*méthode* des *cas*' or '*méthode* du *cas*'.

The idea of fee-paying higher education was also imported, but this represented a real novelty in the European context. Higher education in France, like other European countries at the time, was free, and the most prestigious of France's *grandes écoles*, *l'Ecole Polytechnique*, even paid its students. The technical committee had calculated individual fees of 7,000 francs (then equivalent to about $1,400) which would include tuition fees, plus board and lodging. This compared to Harvard's total fees of around $2,300. High tuition fees would entail establishing a system of grants and loans so as to provide reasonable access to all candidates, irrespective of personal means. It fell to Jean Marcou, with his high-level banking contacts, to try to persuade financial institutions to pioneer such a scheme. Marcou's chief argument was that it would not be a bad investment to offer loans and build up goodwill with people who would later scatter across the world and keep accounts with French banks. It was a tenuous argument, but eventually Marcou managed to convince three of the nationalised banks, Crédit Lyonnais Société Générale and the Comptoir National d'Escompte de Paris (later to become BNP), to help out by creating a loan fund. This would allow students to take out study loans repayable over five years at an interest rate of under four per cent.[11] There was also a grant system, though this was not based on external bequests. Whatever reductions in tuition fees were accorded would simply diminish the size of the incoming revenues.

INTERNATIONAL DEPARTURES

In certain other respects, the new school would diverge from the Harvard model. For example, there was no question of moving towards a two year course. The feeling was that the duration of studies in Europe, together with the military obligations for many European students, did not allow a longer course to be envisaged. An additional consideration was the belief that a two year course might breed arrogance in students or raise corporate expectations unduly, giving companies the impression that the school was delivering a 'finished product'. The school's mission was to facilitate the transition between higher education and the practice of management. As expressed in the technical committee's report: "The learning must correspond to the needs of businesses and avoid giving the students the impression that they are all-knowing."[12]

Another departure from the Harvard model was the decision to call itself an 'institute' not a 'school'. The rationale behind this was that the term 'school' tended to mislead people as to the level of education dispensed, at least in Europe. The title 'Institut Européen d'Administration des Affaires' was officially adopted on the grounds that the two terms 'institute' and 'administration' had similar meanings in English and French. Of course, the abundance of vowels posed problems for the acronym, a *must* for any self-respecting international institution. Initially, it gave rise to the abbreviation INSAD, but a few months later, prompted by Edouard de Percin, a member of the Paris Chamber of Commerce, this was changed to INSEAD, in order to emphasise the European aspect of the school.[13] Indeed, the school's European character was symbolically reinforced spelling out its full name on letter heads in three languages.

The school would also distinguish itself by calling its students

[11] *Meeting of the Coordination Committee*, 20/7/59.
[12] *Activity Report of the Technical Committee* (July–August 1958), 6.
[13] An internal memo, dated 24/10/58, sent out by Pierre Jolly of the Paris Chamber of Commerce, states that the school will be known as INSEAD not INSAD.

'participants', a term proposed by Posthumus Meyjes, in order to emphasise the interactive nature of the learning experience. Another Insead peculiarity was the adoption of the French term *'promotion'* to designate a graduating class. Newcomers quickly adopt the jargon and soon forget that a phrase like 'participants in the latest promotion' is not especially meaningful to the uninitiated. Around such details are cultures built.

The international character of the school forced the technical committee to create new solutions since the Harvard model was of little help on this score. For example, Harvard selected students on the basis of written tests, references and qualities contained in the application form. HBS was dealing with a relatively homogeneous population. Its admissions committee knew where a particular qualification stood in the pecking order, and could work out what a reference was worth. Candidates were mostly familiar with the code of self-presentation and language expected in application forms. Processing application forms was therefore relatively straightforward. This was not the case for the population targeted by Insead. The school would need to decentralise its admissions process in order to avoid selection errors based on misjudgement or misrepresentation. Candidates would have to be interviewed. That would mean setting up pre-selection panels close to the main sources of candidates, and finding local associates qualified to help out – benevolently.

Also, in terms of the selection policy, the team wanted to ensure a spread of nationalities. How could this be achieved? One way would have been to set quotas based on the financial contributions of each country to ensure some kind of equity between the international mix and the international 'demand'. Another approach might have been to establish quotas favouring the six Common Market countries, then the other western European countries, while reserving a set number of places for students from the rest of the world. The committee eschewed the idea of quotas, opting instead for a ceiling of one third on students of any one nationality. This was a courageous decision in that it would result in mismatches between corporate donations and recruitment patterns. On the other hand, it also guaranteed a high degree of admissions flexibility. In terms of intake quality, there is a big difference between accepting students in order to satisfy national quotas and turning down students to avoid cultural dominance. The policy made no attempt to ordain in which direction the school should evolve, which would later prove decisive in helping Insead to develop its international diversity.

This 'one third' ruling was quickly extended to all of the school's supervisory and representative bodies. Again, with hindsight, this may appear like a routine measure. But at the time, all of the financial backing was French. Why should the running of the school be opened up to representatives of nations which were not even risking funds in the project? The assumption was that the international funds would flow in once the international credentials of the school had been established, but this was a gamble. Another potential sticking point was that part of the mission of the Paris Chamber of Commerce was to defend French commercial interests. Enlightened thinking was therefore required to foresee that only by allowing 'foreigners' onto the supervisory board could the school become authentically European, and an asset to France's international standing. Even in today's 'global' firms are there rarely more than a token number of non-nationals included on their boards.

Another original concept was the idea of trilingual education. The technical committee spent much time discussing how this trilingual intent might be achieved in practice. The possibility of simultaneous translation cropped up, but this was deemed incompatible with the interactive teaching methods. Eventually the team settled on three week long intensive refresher courses with Berlitz in Paris for those whose French, English or German was rusty. As the team saw it at the time: "The trilingual objective is clearly difficult to achieve, but for that very reason, it will constitute the originality and international standing of the institute."[14] This suggests that the team members discerned quite clearly what niche the school could appropriate. The lack of reputation and resources might impair the school's ability to approach the educational standards of Harvard, but by offering a business education 'with a difference', the school could at least hope to compete in terms of quality of intake. Rather than creating an abridged replica of Harvard, this would be the business school where one could learn to become a European.

A final dilemma posed by the international and independent objectives of the school concerned its legal status. Several alternatives had been proposed in the July 1958 meeting confirming the official appointment of Posthumus Meyjes and Giscard d'Estaing. One possibility was that the school be set up as a limited company. Another possibility was that it become a non-profit association. The third option was that it be integrated as an international arm of the Paris Chamber of Commerce. All three alternatives had their drawbacks. The first two would limit the participation of other European countries; the third would inhibit the independence of the school. Several months later, a hybrid status was proposed: the school could perhaps be registered, under the French 1901 law, as a foreign non-profit association, thus preserving its international dimension and its freedom to collect donations. In March 1959, this proposition was submitted to the Ministry of the Interior for approval.

[14] *Activity Report of the Technical Committee* (July–August 1958), 10.

RECRUITMENT MATTERS

The first priority in terms of recruitment were the professors. They would determine the character and quality of the institute. Of course, there was something of a gap between the school's 'wish list' of requirements and the recruits it could realistically attract. A complex set of imperatives and constraints compressed the possibilities of choice.

For instance, the teaching style demanded instructors with experience of the case method – they were mainly to be found in America. Conversely, the international focus demanded a mix of nationalities and people with an understanding of the European context. Or again, the reputation of the school demanded a professional faculty of international standing. Yet the resources of the school allowed for only a part-time faculty, and poorly paid at that time. Such contradictions could not realistically be resolved in a single profile, which probably accounts for the unlikely mix of backgrounds that characterised the initial faculty body; though given that only Olivier Giscard d'Estaing and Gilbert Sauvage were full-time, 'body' is perhaps a big word for it.

A list of possible professors had been drawn up by Giscard d'Estaing and the technical committee at the same time as they had considered the programme contents. It was particularly important to secure able professors to look after each course, even if they were assisted by less experienced professors and visiting professors. At the start of 1959, the search commenced in earnest, on multiple fronts.

As is the case with most start-ups, the first people contacted were immediate acquaintances – notably former classmates, like Stefaan Cambien and Roger Godino, who were Harvard educated and had returned to Europe. Giscard d'Estaing and Jean Raindre also featured on the faculty list, though the latter withdrew once a suitable replacement, Gérard Llewellyn of the BNP, was found to take over the finance course. A few people were recommended by Doriot, such as André Bisson, a Canadian alumnus of HBS or Pierre Bartholin, director of finance at Péchiney. But that list was quickly exhausted. Where should they look next? Who could do the job? Who would be interested? Who could they afford?

In keeping with the practical orientation of the school, and its lack of funds, the team decided to target experienced consultants. Again, this represented a notable deviation from the Harvard model, but fitted the multiple requirements of the school. Some consultants, notably those who had taught at the CPA, were already familiar with the case method; and those who were not, had enough experience of different business situations to handle it. In practical terms, their flexible agendas made it possible to block out teaching periods in advance. More significantly perhaps, they could be attracted. Having independent sources of income, they might be willing to forego adequate remuneration for the prestige of professorial status. The likes of Paul Planus, Pierre Sadoc and Maurice Teper (all French), Stanley Hillyer (American), Kenneth Most (British) and Paul Silberer (Swiss) were thus recruited.

With the CPA as a primary source of professors, the recruits were predominantly French. Concerned that the school build an international faculty, Giscard d'Estaing made trips abroad to try to identify likely talent. Returning from Germany in March 1959, he wrote to Doriot: "I met two young Germans, Gerhard Dahlke and Hanns-Martin Schönfeld, trained in the US, who would accept assistant professor positions for the sales and finance courses. Several others promised to help out as visiting professors."[15] They were later joined by Ernst-Bernd Blümle and Gilbert Sauvage, all strongly drawn by the European dimension of the school. Sauvage, who had been working for the *Bureau International du Travail* in Geneva, became the first full-time instructor responsible for the 'European context' course, which was both distinctive and symbolic for the school. He was also a very energetic prospector and presenter for the school. Such recruits were perfectly in line with Doriot's earlier recommendation to Giscard d'Estaing that he focus on young professors with a pioneering spirit, rather than trying to invite big name professors, as IMEDE had done.[16]

Nevertheless, the school still hoped to entice one or two established US professors, for reasons of reputation, international coverage and general guidance on policy. Without the funds to attract them, the school approached the European Productivity Agency which might help finance such professors. So it was that Paul Converse (Illinois) and Wilford John Eiteman (Michigan), two Fullbright professors from the US, were detached to Insead on a full-time basis for one year.

Of course, the most precious recruit to the cause would be Doriot himself. The school, via Jean Marcou, president of the Paris Chamber of Commerce, officially invited Doriot to come and teach for a year, with the title of dean: "This will confer the best possible guarantee of the quality of the school's teaching, right from the start."[17]

Surprisingly perhaps, Doriot refused. He explained that it would not be possible to find someone to take over his course at such short notice. Understandably, there was pressure from the dean at Harvard who was not keen to lose one of his leading lights for a year. But one can also imagine that if Doriot had insisted, he would have been released. Since Doriot had a huge emotional investment in the well-being of the school one can speculate that there were unspoken reasons for not participating directly, which he could not communicate without eroding the confidence of those involved. Firstly,

[15] Doriot's correspondence, letter from Olivier Giscard d'Estaing, 24/3/59.
[16] IMEDE's entire faculty came from the US thanks to the financing of Nestlé. Insead could not afford to do this, but nor was it considered desirable given the European vocation of the school.
[17] Doriot's correspondence, letter from Jean Marcou, 22/5/59.

he may have been concerned that it might raise student expectations unrealistically, cruelly exposing the gap between the neophyte professors and the best that Harvard could offer. Secondly, from his vast experience with new ventures, he may have been concerned that his presence might give an unsustainable boost to the school. Withdrawing after a year, leaving Giscard d'Estaing to pick up the pieces, would do the school no favours. It needed to learn to stand up on its own, from the outset.[18]

Besides the professors, there were administrative staff and research assistants to recruit. The chief concern in such recruitments was the international dimension. The first significant recruit was Dusan Radivojevic, taken on as administrative secretary. A Yugoslav, fluent in French, German and English, having studied in several European countries, he was the first symbolic appointment, setting the standard in terms of international aspirations. Subsequent appointments followed similar lines, favouring expatriates, polyglots, people with a wide exposure to different cultures. Madeleine Kinebanian, a Dutch librarian speaking four languages, was given responsibility for the embryonic documentation centre.

The recruitment of research assistants was not to be neglected, especially given the lack of full-time professors. As Pearson Hunt, a HBS colleague of Doriot's had observed when visiting Paris back in the spring of 1958: "Because of the proposed international character of the program, a part-time faculty is considered essential ... I made some comments about the difficulties in such an arrangement, and advised at least a permanent core of assistants."[19] Once the school got under way, the research assistants would play a front line role: they would organise, coordinate, liaise with the students and provide a sense of continuity. In many ways they would be the glue holding everything together. In the meantime, the four full-time research assistants were charged with preparing the 500 cases the school hoped to assemble before opening, from Harvard, CPA, IMEDE and the EPA.

In addition to the official personnel, a number of people were 'loaned' to the school to help with the launch preparations. For example, Claude Janssen was authorised by his company to help part-time on the project from January 1959 onwards. Similarly, the European Productivity Agency assigned two US professors, Merwin Waterman and Richard Clewett, to act as consultants to the school for the 10 weeks preceding the launch. Meanwhile, HBS, under the impetus of Doriot, had offered the services of two experienced research assistants, Hugo Uyterhoeven and George von Peterffy (Doriot's own assistant).

Initially, Harvard's generous offer was refused for the simple reason that

---

[18] Two years later, when Olivier Giscard d'Estaing renewed his request (15/2/61), Doriot responded: "I do not want to do it because I do not think I would do well. I am not accustomed to European students, and you know, you have had very bad experiences with American teaching there." (21/2/61).
[19] Doriot's correspondence, letter from Pearson Hunt, 16/5/58.

"it does not seem possible for us to take in charge the travelling expenses for those two gentlemen for the time being".[20] This gives a measure of the school's financial precariousness. Eventually the European Productivity Agency came to the rescue offering to foot their travel bill.[21]

IN SEARCH OF DIVERSITY

Conscious that the school's reputation could be made (or broken) by the quality of its first wave of students, Giscard d'Estaing and his associates knew it was important to attract high calibre applicants. But how could they achieve this when the school had no track record or big name, permanent professors? First, they sent out posters to the big companies and top universities; for example, the US schools targeted in the poster campaign were Stanford, Yale, Princeton, Columbia, Chicago and Harvard.[22] It was never a case of blanket bombing.

By 19 September 1958, 700 copies of a preliminary brochure had been produced. It was far from complete: it lacked a detailed outline of the courses, list of patrons or professors, or specification of location, details that would follow in subsequent versions. A standard letter was also established for students requesting information.

While posters and brochures may raise awareness they are unlikely to elicit action. So the next step was to organise press conferences and speeches in the elite academic institutions throughout Europe, and then to go out on the road and convince people. What moved people to apply were the impassioned visions of committed Europeans such as Posthumus Meyjes and Giscard d'Estaing, later relayed by Roger Godino and Gilbert Sauvage. The clinching argument in their sales pitch was that Europe would be made by business people, and not politicians.

As Giscard d'Estaing recalled: "I toured the big German universities, the *grandes écoles* and Oxbridge. We went round spreading the word – preaching to convince accomplished people to come to Insead." The problem they found, remembering that unemployment was not a serious issue at the time, was that students did not tend to plan very far ahead: "So when we went to see them early in the academic year, telling them to come to Insead in ten months time, it did not always have an immediate impact."

Giscard d'Estaing wrote to Doriot after one particularly successful press conference on 13 October 1958, to let him know that it had generated several press articles, some radio coverage, as well as 15 new applicants. By this stage, a French pre-selection committee comprising two HBS alumni and two CPA alumni had been constituted, with Belgian, Dutch and

[20] Doriot's correspondence, letter from Willem Posthumus Meyjes, 17/3/59.
[21] Doriot's correspondence, letter from Willem Posthumus Meyjes, 6/5/59.
[22] Doriot's correspondence, letter from Olivier Giscard d'Estaing, 11/2/59.

German committees to be formed imminently.[23] The idea of decentralised pre-selection committees was enlightened in that it allowed applicants to be judged by their own nationally accepted standards, and enabled more subtle evaluations of a candidate's accomplishments.

Two members of each pre-selection committee would conduct separate interviews with each candidate, then the assembled candidates would participate in a group discussion. This would lead to an overall recommendation to the full admissions committee regarding the quality of a candidate. In Europe, such methods were highly unusual, and were closer to corporate recruitment practices than those associated with academic selection. Indeed, some of the students found the questions on motivation, personal experiences, character traits and *imperfections* rather intrusive.[24] Again, the transposition of 'standard' Harvard procedures to the European context would require local adjustments.

The technical committee had established a number of guidelines regarding the target population and optimal intake. The objective for the first class was an intake of 60–70. This was no arbitrary figure: it corresponded to a section at the HBS. This was considered the minimum threshold needed to capture a meaningful level of diversity of nationality, of academic background and of experience. The aim was for engineers, accountants and economists to mix with lawyers and liberal arts graduates; for fresh-faced graduates to mingle with entrepreneurs and people with work experience. International diversity tended to enrich this variety of background and experience naturally, since each country had its own elite disciplines and itineraries, ranging for example from French *Grandes Ecoles* engineers to German chemists or Oxbridge classicists, but all requiring a complement of management education and benefiting from the international exposure. In terms of age, the anticipated intake would range between 21 and 28, and they should be graduates.

Notwithstanding these guidelines, the rallying call was diversity. For example, applicants falling outside the age brackets would be considered, as would non-graduates – and in more remote countries, where it was impossible to establish a pre-selection committee, candidates could be screened by well-briefed proxies, such as trade or cultural attachés – and in exceptional circumstances, be admitted on the strength of their file. As Giscard d'Estaing had written to Doriot, in their earliest exchanges: "The student body should include the widest possible variety of backgrounds, the overriding principle being: Never mind what they did before, as long as they did it well."[25]

One element of diversity which did not yet feature in the intake, was

---

[23] Doriot's correspondence, letter from Olivier Giscard d'Estaing, 20/10/58.
[24] See Michael Nagel, 'Profile of a European Business School,', The MBA, April 1967.
[25] Doriot's correspondence, letter from Olivier Giscard d'Estaing, 2/8/57.

gender. It was considered that European, and particularly French, business circles were not yet ready to accept women as senior managers. Judging by today's standards, this may seem a regrettable decision. But three contextual points are worth making. First, exemplar establishments such as HBS, HEC and *l'Ecole Polytechnique* did not accept women at the time. Second, this was such a 'blindspot' in that era, that no press article from the early years even raised it as an issue. Third, and most significantly, Insead was an incipient institution. Its reputation would depend on its tiny body of alumni making their mark quickly in as many sectors, functions and countries as possible. There were pressures, therefore, to opt for 'safe bets'.

By March 1959, the original deadline for applications, the number of candidates stood at 75. A month later, they had climbed to 108, nearly half of whom were French. By 20 July 1959, when the supervisory committee (including Doriot) got together, the tally of candidates had reached 130. Unfortunately, only 110 had completed the full application procedures. Of those, 75 had been admitted, more than were actually expected to start the course given the likelihood of 'no shows'. Accounts actually vary as to the number of applicants rejected. It could be that the numbers were somewhat inflated in order to give an impression of a tough school, not just for the benefits of outsiders, but also to 'condition' those admitted.

As Giscard d'Estaing had put it in an earlier note to Doriot: "This feeling of respect for the institution exists among French students who attend Harvard, but that is really a different entity, since the standing of the school is long established. Moreover, Harvard is located in a country whose business traditions are strong and dynamic."[26]

A show of selection stringency was therefore central to fashioning a reputation, and instilling a sense of pride among those admitted – '*pour encourager les autres*'. A similar element of 'bluff' surrounded the anticipated size of future intakes. The technical committee had envisaged intakes of between 150 and 200 students.[27] Doriot had written back advising them to revise their objectives, if only as an entry barrier: "Personally, I think you should say from 500 to 600, so as to give people an idea that you see big ... If you tell people that the school will be only 150, it might give them the idea to start another school somewhere else."[28] In terms of institution building, Doriot helped to make them conscious of the importance of bold growth projections as a key to attracting candidates, as a way of deterring rival initiatives, and as a kind of 'stretch objective'.

[26] Preliminary document discussing the European school, Olivier Giscard d'Estaing, 2/8/57.
[27] *Activity Report of the Technical Committee* (July–August 1958), 3.
[28] Doriot's correspondence, letter to Olivier Giscard d'Estaing, 1/10/58.

COURTING FUNDS

Although Insead can be regarded as an outgrowth of the movement towards European integration, it never aspired to be a part of Europe's institutional framework. Its mission was clearly articulated in the initial document written jointly by Posthumus Meyjes and Giscard d'Estaing summarising the aims of the school: "INSAD [as it still was] is a partner of businesses. That is where its funds, many of its instructors, and the course material will all come from... A close liaison with companies will be developed so that what is taught corresponds exactly to their needs .... [This] will contribute significantly to the success of INSAD."[29] A fundamental choice at the outset was that the financing of the school should be developed primarily from international free enterprise sources. The school would be answerable to business and would do its best to be market responsive, reflecting Doriot's wish that: "The school remain a bastion of defence for free enterprise."[30]

In terms of attracting funds from corporations, the school was up against two big problems: companies did not quite understand what the school was about or what they might get in exchange for their donations. Both of these difficulties echo the earlier observation that even where the Harvard model showed the way, there was additional work involved in transposing that 'solution' to a new environment.

The first problem was that corporate representatives were not altogether sure about the school's teaching methods. As Posthumus Meyjes wrote to Doriot in early August 1959: "From my travels in Europe I have noted that the 'Case Method' is often little known and almost always misunderstood ... It therefore seems necessary to undertake some kind of campaign to enlighten their minds and to explain to business people and university people in Europe, the nature of our teaching."[31] To curtail the amount of time spent explaining in person, Posthumus Meyjes proposed that the school's next brochure include copies of an article entitled "Because wisdom can't be told".[32] Posthumus Meyjes asked Doriot to see if it would be possible to obtain copyright clearance to reproduce the article.

The second problem concerned what might be in it for the companies. Again borrowing from the Harvard model, the school was hoping to lure students with its high powered placement possibilities, and to attract companies by giving them privileged access to these young high flyers. While 'on campus interviews' were an established practice in the US, over in Europe they remained a fairly radical proposition. One can imagine the reaction of corporate representatives: "Let me get this straight. We make a donation of

[29] *INSAD: Summary of the Objectives and Programme*, September 1958, 13.
[30] Doriot, G.F. (1976) *The Creation of Insead*, personal notes.
[31] Doriot's correspondence, letter from Willem Posthumus Meyjes, 6/8/59.
[32] Charles J. Cragg, 'Because wisdom can't be told' in *The Case Method at Harvard Business School* (edited by Malcom P. McNair, 1954).

several thousand francs and, in exchange, you allow us to interview your students before other companies?" Setting aside the unproved quality of the soon-to-be-admitted students, company representatives were shocked by the idea of *travelling* to meet applicants. The least they could expect, as they saw it, was that prospective recruits show a modicum of commitment: "If your students are interested in our company, it is not up to us to make the effort. Let them come, show some motivation. We will receive them, but we will never come to see them." Giscard d'Estaing remembers trying to explain: "You should not take it that way. It's a market economy and if you want talented managers then you need to grab them early." But it was a tough sell.

The very first corporate subscribers were motivated by a mixture of staunch belief in the idea and friendship for Doriot. They included Péchiney, Saint-Gobain and Compagnie Electro-Mécanique under the respective impetus of Raoul de Vitry, Arnaud de Vogüé and Paul Desombre. Their contributions encouraged others such as Air France, Rhone-Poulenc, L'Air Liquide and the French employers' federation (CNPF). But among the 17 companies which had pledged funding by September 1959, there was a conspicuous absence of non-French contributions.[33] Only Philips, the Dutch electrical company, enticed by Posthumus Meyjes, featured among the early subscribers.

Culturally, the idea of supporting a business school made more sense to the big US corporations with interests in Europe, than it did to most European companies. But the US companies were reluctant to commit until they could see some signs of interest from European companies or some evidence of the quality of the output.

This left the school pinning its hopes on the Ford Foundation, part of whose mission was to promote management education in Europe. Contacts with the Ford Foundation dated back to the earliest public discussions of the project in July 1955. At that time, the foundation's vice-president, Thomas Carroll, had commented: "If a promising proposal were to be developed, ... we should be glad to *consider seriously* contributing to its initial support" (highlighted in original).

The Ford Foundation's early interest in the school was nurtured by Doriot who took care to keep its president abreast of the project's progress. It was also sustained by occasional meetings, both in Europe and the US, between the representatives of the Ford Foundation and those of the Paris Chamber of Commerce. In March 1959, with the school now six months from its official launch, it was time to make official advances. Posthumus Meyjes wrote to Thomas Carroll, outlining the development of the project and alluding to an unspecified shortage of funds: "The further realisation of our

---

[33] The size of the French contribution served as a further justification for electing to establish the school in France.

projects makes additional financial help indispensable."[34] Again Carroll showed sympathy offering his "sincere congratulations on the impressive progress you and your associates have made".[35]

The following month in New York, Jean Marcou, president of the Paris Chamber of Commerce, met up with Thomas Carroll and Forrest Hill, both of the Ford Foundation. Reporting to Doriot on the meeting, Marcou commented: "I was very warmly received and they indicated that they would look very favourably upon our request for help."[36] An answer would be given in the coming weeks.

Shortly after the meeting, Marcou wrote to the Ford Foundation, spelling out the financial deficit in more detail. He showed that the school would be about 950,000 francs (around $190,000) short of its annual operating budget. This sum corresponded to the expected contribution of European companies outside France which had not yet materialised. Marcou officially requested the Ford Foundation's assistance in covering this shortfall for two years.[37]

LIVING WITH UNCERTAINTY

In April 1959, even with the starting line in sight, there remained numerous uncertainties and threats to the survival of the project. The foremost threat remained the lack of funds. While the school had been successful in attracting international patrons, persuading international corporations to contribute financially was proving a struggle. The accumulated funds plus the student fees covered just over half of the anticipated budget for the first year of operation.[38] The possibility of offering a 'reduced programme' was envisaged.

The situation was desperate enough for Giscard d'Estaing and Posthumus Meyjes to reveal separately the extent of their worries to Doriot. "The only real problem now is to know whether we open the school or not," wrote Giscard d'Estaing. "We are intensifying our efforts but we will only know for certain around 15th May."[39] A letter from Posthumus Meyjes dated the same day as Giscard d'Estaing's letter laments: "Given the considerable results achieved in all other domains of activity, it would be a great pity to have to renounce for lack of immediately available funds."[40]

The 15 May deadline mentioned by Giscard d'Estaing alluded to the impending decision by the Ford Foundation on whether or not to assist the school. On 12 May they received the bad news: "Our conclusion, I regret to say, is negative."[41]

[34] Doriot's correspondence, letter from Posthumus Meyjes to Thomas Carroll, 9/3/59.
[35] Doriot's correspondence, letter from Thomas Carroll to Posthumus Meyjes, 13/3/59.
[36] Doriot's correspondence, letter from Jean Marcou, 22/4/59.
[37] Doriot's correspondence, letter from Jean Marcou to Forrest Hill, Ford Foundation, 21/4/59.
[38] *Conference of European Community Chambers of Commerce*, 29/4/59, 3.
[39] Doriot's correspondence, letter from Olivier Giscard d'Estaing, 3/4/59.
[40] Doriot's correspondence, letter from Willem Posthumus Meyjes, 3/4/59.
[41] Doriot's correspondence, letter from Forrest Hill to Jean Marcou, 8/5/59.

Besides the continuing scramble for funds, there remained a question mark regarding the unusual request, for a school backed by the Paris Chamber of Commerce and ostensibly part of the French higher education system, to be recognised as a foreign non-profit association. With only a few weeks left until the opening date, one sensed a note of urgency in Giscard d'Estaing's letter asking when they could expect a reply from the Ministry of the Interior.[42] Once the school's legal existence was established, it would still have to register with the Ministry of Education. And what if the request were inexplicably turned down?

Another outstanding issue was the refurbishment work going on in the palace. As Giscard d'Estaing explained to Doriot in late August 1959, only three weeks before the scheduled start: "There are still heating problems in the palace, but the works should be completed in time."[43] At that time the staff were all working out of two offices – with access to a printing machine – loaned by the Chamber of Commerce in Paris. Everything would soon have to be transported to Fontainebleau by removal trucks. The issues ranged in scale, but they had in common their capacity to wreak chaos for the scheduled opening. Again, the school only had one chance to make an impressive start.

Setting aside these practical concerns, the school's top management was also beset by diffuse anxieties. There was no shortage of people predicting failure in more or less spectacular style. Doing the rounds in France, Giscard d'Estaing had encountered numerous objections. Was there really any need for such a school given that France already had a lot of commercial schools, such as HEC and ESCP, filling that role? Also management remained an unknown academic discipline and numerous sceptics maintained that it could only be learned by doing. Others still, argued that the school's international dimension was not really necessary. For example, Yvon Chotard, then head of the *Centre Français du Patronat Chrétien* predicted: "You won't succeed because either you have to create a school for Europe or you have to create a business school. This way you'll fall between two stools." Giscard d'Estaing replied: "On the contrary, it is like two blades of a pair of scissors. You cut the paper because you have the two blades coming together. One reinforces the other rather than damaging the other." As he saw it, creating 'just another business school' would have deprived Insead of its competitive advantage – whilst creating a school to 'train Europeans' would have narrowed placement possibilities. However fervently he believed this, such criticisms were confidence sapping. And there were other imponderables.

The earliest predictions had been that there would be no candidates as the entry requirements – good university degree, plus work experience, plus

[42] Giscard d'Estaing's correspondence, letter to M. Lefevre, 30/6/59.
[43] Doriot's correspondence, letter from Olivier Giscard d'Estaing, 24/8/59.

linguistic capabilities – were hopelessly restrictive. Time, relentless promotional efforts, including 125 conferences, plus a certain flexibility on requirements, had shown otherwise. The international demand existed. The problem now was that these 'rare birds' might choose to pursue other options. A 'drop out' rate had been built in to the number of places awarded, but given the newness of the school, was it not likely that others might drop out over the summer? For an established school this is not a serious concern. Accepted candidates are reluctant to give up the concrete advantages that the school would bestow – career prospects, a label, a recognised diploma, an alumni network. Insead offered none of these verified benefits. Its pulling power rested exclusively on the attractiveness of an idea – the promise of a business education with a European dimension, in an international ambiance.

Moreover, looking at it from the perspective of those accepted, why should they take the risk? They had been offered places once, so there was no reason to think they would be turned down if they renewed their application the following year. Wait and see how the school and its graduates fared. Already by mid July 1959, four of the 75 places awarded had been turned down. By late August, the figure had climbed to 11 – with many of the students asking to be reconsidered for next year – and it was anybody's guess how many would actually turn up on opening day.

As if 'natural wastage' was not enough of a threat, the French government had just passed legislation which threatened to decimate the first intake. Barely three weeks before the school was supposed to open, Giscard d'Estaing's hasty postscript informed Doriot of fresh bad tidings: "New legislation concerning deferment of military service means that it would be refused to all our students concerned – that is, 26 out of the 31 French students. We will go and talk to the Minister of Foreign Affairs to request an exception to this rule which would prove catastrophic in that it would reduce our intake to around 35 students."[44] Here again we see the capacity of external events to knock the fledgling venture off course.

A STEADYING INFLUENCE

Doriot responded quickly, providing ammunition with which to fight back. He suggested they bring to the attention of the French authorities the fact that young Frenchmen coming to HBS did benefit from a deferment. "It seems highly unfair that, after struggling to start a school in Europe so that young people can get graduate business training because they cannot all come to America, those who are attending the new school cannot profit from the same privilege as the ones who come to America."[45]

[44] Doriot's correspondence, letter from Olivier Giscard d'Estaing, 24/8/59.
[45] Doriot's correspondence, letter to Olivier Giscard d'Estaing, 3/9/59.

As was so often the case during the preparatory period, Doriot was the primary source of advice for Posthumus Meyjes and Giscard d'Estaing when real trouble threatened. Without his advice and support, the uncertainty surrounding the venture might have proved debilitating. The loneliness of their challenge is discernible in a letter from Posthumus Meyjes shortly after Doriot's return to the US: "Now you have left again, we feel how much we need you. For two months [June and July] we had the huge benefit of your advice, experience, encouragement; without them we feel diminished."[46]

Doriot was fully aware of his role as comforter and confidence booster, especially towards the young Giscard d'Estaing. "As the opening date comes closer, everybody must be under great stress," Doriot warned. "People will realise some of the shortcomings. They will realise that they did certain things wrong, and tempers will get short .... Remember that the ultimate goal is a successful school. Do not leave any stone unturned ... Again let me say that I understand what you are up against, but I know you can lick it, and I am glad you have the opportunity."[47] In his correspondence, Doriot was always conveying his high expectations – particularly of former students – and his faith in their ability.

When he offered them unsolicited advice, he always made sure that it was understood as a suggestion, not an instruction in disguise. There are two striking examples. First, in October 1958, he proposed to Giscard d'Estaing: "Perhaps a committee [of patrons] could be formed on this side of the ocean. What do you think is the best way to go about it from your standpoint? I want to be guided by your thoughts."[48] Similarly, as the launch date approached, Doriot volunteered to organise a press conference in the US, unless "you have any objection to our doing this" but reminding Giscard d'Estaing: "The dedication is the time to get the publicity going. Otherwise we could have very little to say to the press for some time."[49] Doriot also asked Posthumus Meyjes for 150 invitations to the inauguration which he might distribute in the US: "Most people will not go, of course, but it is a nice way to attract their attention to the school."[50]

Doriot's advice was judicious but never imposed. He worked tirelessly behind the scenes, promoting the school, recommending potential instructors, encouraging his friends and colleagues to take an interest, even answering letters from prospective students. He showed an unusual ability to walk the fine line between involvement and interference. As he once put it to Giscard d'Estaing: "I do not know what else to tell you, outside of the fact

[46] Doriot's correspondence, letter from Willem Posthumus Meyjes, 6/8/59.
[47] Doriot's correspondence, letter to Olivier Giscard d'Estaing, 28/8/59.
[48] Doriot's correspondence, letter to Olivier Giscard d'Estaing, 1/10/58.
[49] Doriot's correspondence, letter to Olivier Giscard d'Estaing, 31/8/59.
[50] Doriot's correspondence, letter to Willem Posthumus Meyjes, 19/8/59.

that I hope you will write often and make suggestions as to what we might do."[51]

THE END OF THE BEGINNING

On 24 August 1959, George von Peterffy, Doriot's assistant on loan to Insead, wrote to Doriot to announce the arrival of a first group of students: "They are off to Berlitz tomorrow and we won't see them again until 12th September. Thank God! We still have a little work!"

Von Peterffy went on to praise the efforts of those involved with the school, but he too had misgivings about its future: "Olivier is good! He has drive and vision and courage. He is Insead's most valuable asset. I know he is young and I'm sure he'll grow into the job much better than anyone I have met here yet. He and his people have accomplished a formidable amount in the year they have been here. But it is not enough! They need to be better yet. They cannot afford to be merely good. They've got to be outstanding if they want to lead."[52] Even people closely involved with the preparations had no idea whether they had done enough to succeed, or even survive.

In one step, on 9 September 1959, three days before the opening day, the accumulated books, cases, brochures, stencilled information and sundry equipment were moved from Paris to their sumptuous Fontainebleau quarters. Three trucks were enough to effect the removal of the incipient school. Two weeks earlier, on 28 August 1959, the French Minister of the Interior had finally approved the legal form requested – as a foreign non-profit association – thus giving the school its legal autonomy. And after visiting the Prime Minister, Michel Debré, Jean Marcou had been assured that the school would be added to the list of institutes eligible for national service deferment.

There was still an expected shortfall in the budget, but with the tuition fees coming in, there would be enough money to start the school. It would be a case of making do until fresh funds could be attracted. The big difference now, in terms of soliciting donations, was that the school would have a tangible 'product' and a 'process' to show off to visitors. Everything was set.

As conveyed by the first annual report, the opening day had all the predictability of a military exercise: "So effective was the planning and split second timing that Registration Day took place without the slightest problem."[53] In reality though, the sense of tension and vulnerability accompanied the preparations right up to the last moment. On the day of official registration, Saturday 12 September, those associated with the project were gathered in a corner of the palace waiting for the new students to arrive.

[51] Doriot's correspondence, letter to Olivier Giscard d'Estaing, 1/10/58.
[52] Doriot's correspondence, letter from George von Peterffy, 24/8/59.
[53] Insead Year Book: 1959–60, 28.

By lunch time, of the 62 students officially expected, only ten had shown up. As Claude Janssen recalls, "We had a rather uncomfortable lunch." The majority of students arrived in the afternoon – and a few turned up the following Monday.

Doriot received a cable from Claude Janssen, Jean Raindre and George von Peterffy on 12 September 1959 reading: "The ship is launched. 57 registered today. Opening ceremonies completed. All engines turning." In a longer missive, two days later, Janssen signed off: "It remains for us to thank you for starting up the whole idea and giving us the opportunity to contribute to an endeavour with so much future."[54]

THE ROOTS OF STRATEGY

It may seem odd to devote a whole chapter to a period lasting no more than 14 months. But the infrastructure decisions and policies that emerged from this short period were to condition much of what followed. Beyond the fact that many of the initial choices were to prove judicious and flexibility enhancing, they also help to explain subsequent strategic constraints and the direction of the school's development. The choice of location, the board structure, the practical orientation of the programme and the faculty, the legal status and funding policy, showing a determination to remain independent, the decision to specify international quotas in the constitution, the language policy and the selection process with interviews. These were all choices destined to facilitate or impede future options – and which would help to forge a distinctive identity.

In effect, by the time of the inauguration, the three pillars of Insead's philosophy were firmly in place: it was resolutely international, independent and close to business. These three dimensions were not unrelated. Why did Insead have to be independent? Because it was international. No government would take charge of the school, so it had to take charge of itself. And because the school had to find its own finance, it had to be practice-oriented and responsive to the needs of business. These remain the key drivers of Insead's culture and evolution.

Press articles in the early 1960s typically described the new school as a small-scale replica of the HBS. The association with Harvard was grossly flattering for Insead, but it also diminished the thought and effort which had gone into devising the new school. Firstly, it overlooked the international dimension of the initiative. This was no 'bolt-on' accessory, but a 'built-in' characteristic which influenced virtually all subsequent decisions, from the legal status of the school to its teaching methods, faculty composition and financing – not to mention all the selection policies. Secondly, it tended to

[54] Doriot's correspondence, letter from Claude Janssen, 14/9/59.

suggest that the task was mechanical: the template existed and it was simply a matter of transposing blindly from one context to another. This failed to acknowledge both the cultural adjustment needed in order to make the 'transfer' work – and the derisory means at the European school's disposal.

From obscurity to respectability

CHAPTER 3

Fighting above its weight

"To succeed in the world, we do everything we can to appear successful." François de la Rochefoucauld, *Maximes*.

AN IMPRESSIVE FACADE

Napoleon, that aggressive early European, might have seen the irony of it. The Fontainebleau palace had been one of his favourite haunts. In the *Cour des Adieux* he had bid farewell to his weeping generals before being escorted to the island of Elba. Nearly two centuries later, it had become the home of a European business school striving to eradicate national boundaries in a more consensual way.

On the eve of opening the school, Olivier Giscard d'Estaing had written to Doriot to reassure him about the move from Paris to the palace: "Our class room is ready, our library and cases are all set. We are all installed in our new offices and our school, but one day old, gives the impression of age-old permanence."[1]

The 62 students who finally enrolled for the first course hailed from 14 different countries.[2] Setting aside the predictable domination of Western European, and specifically French students, a sprinkling of other nations were already represented – Morocco, Hungary, and the United States – which augured well for the widespread appeal of the initiative.

The official dedication ceremony took place on 9 October 1959 in the *Salle des Colonnes* at the Fontainebleau palace. The international audience of 300 included numerous distinguished guests headed by Georges Doriot

---

[1] Doriot's correspondence, letter from Giscard d'Estaing, 11/9/59.
[2] The one-third limitation on students of a given nationality would almost have been observed had it not been for the high drop-out rate among non-French students who had been offered places. The school's first class of 61 students comprised 31 French students. The ruling would be enforced in future.

himself, Paul-Henri Spaak, general secretary of NATO, Etienne Hirsch, president of Euratom and Roger Grégoire, director of the European Productivity Agency. In his speech, Grégoire praised what he termed "this new cultural laboratory".[3] Jean Martin of the Paris Chamber of Commerce chose to conclude his address with the Chinese proverb: "If you are planning for one year, sow wheat; if you are planning for twenty years, plant trees; if you are planning for 100 years, develop minds."

When it came to Doriot's turn, he saluted the first American donation to Insead, which had not come from a corporation but from a personal subscriber, Thomas E. Congdon of Denver. He had attended Doriot's Manufacturing class back in 1942 as a Harvard student. He wrote to Doriot enthusing about his experience at HBS and hoping that his cheque of a few hundred dollars might contribute in some small way to helping Europeans to benefit from the same opportunity. It was a symbolic gesture, echoing the wider American philanthropy towards Europe, particularly in the domain of education, which characterised the post-war decades. It also confirmed the tremendous pulling power of Doriot – seventeen years after graduating, an alumnus from Denver had spontaneously come forward to give money to an institution with which he would have no further association.[4]

An even more impressive demonstration of 'the long arm of Doriot' came later that afternoon when Willem Posthumus Meyjes, the director general of the school, read out the telegrams from well-wishers. After reading messages from the queen of the Netherlands, the secretary general of OECE, and the secretary general of the Council of Europe, Posthumus Meyjes cleared his throat to deliver the last message with suitable aplomb. It read: "The President extends his congratulations to all those who have taken part in the establishment of this Institute which is destined to play a creative role in the economic affairs of Europe and the world,"[5] and was signed Dwight D. Eisenhower.

Behind the scenes, for several weeks, Doriot had been working on a former HBS alumnus, Wilton B. Persons, assistant to President Eisenhower, to suggest that the government officially recognise the opening of the school. He had sold it to them on the basis that the moral support of the US was important "so that young Europeans are brought up with a good conception of American ideals and the free enterprise system".[6] This argument had done the trick and when Eisenhower's unexpected message was read out it received an enthusiastic round of applause.

The high-profile inauguration gained wide coverage in the national press

---

[3] *La Liberté*, 16/10/59.
[4] This was not a one-off. There was a similar gesture from former student, Elmer Funkhouser, who spontaneously donated ten shares with a mean value of $56 to Insead via Doriot (letter from 23/12/64).
[5] Message from President Eisenhower via American Embassy to Willem Posthumus Meyjes, 9/10/59.
[6] Doriot's correspondence, letter to Wilton B. Persons, assistant to US President, 25/9/59.

of the six Common Market countries, but also featured in the international press, including the *Financial Times*, *New York Herald Tribune*, *Newsweek* and *Time*.[7] After such a fanfare, the only remaining problem was to deliver on the promise: in terms of quality of teaching, calibre of students attracted and cross-cultural learning.

THE PULL OF THE PLACE

To understand the attraction of Insead, we have to consider the mindset of the early participants. What moved them to come and study a nebulous discipline, in an unknown school, outside their home country for half of them? What persuaded them to endure the constraints of obligatory presence,[8] heavy workloads and residential accommodation, mostly in shared rooms with rudimentary facilities?

There is a rational answer to do with the distinctiveness of the programme. The study of business was still in its infancy in Europe. The proposed content of the programme was unusual in eschewing the staple ingredients of economics, accounting and law which characterised business education in Europe – and focusing rather on novel imported techniques such as market research, newer systems of cost accounting, quality control, statistical analysis and the wonders of organisational psychology. Europe's more orthodox universities and commercial courses were still some way from offering such programmes.

The eye-catching content of the programme included a business simulation game, offered from the very first year, in the middle of the second term and piloted by IBM. There was no computer on site, so it was a matter of punching cards which were then sent up to Paris overnight to be processed. Clearly this was all very *avant garde*. Unfortunately, the system had a nasty habit of crashing so that the painstaking calculations then had to be done by hand. It was perhaps symbolic of the underlying tension between the school's lofty aims and its fragile reality.

The programme was also designed to alert students to the risks and opportunities of foreign trade – how to launch a new product in a foreign market, how to raise capital most advantageously. As Giscard d'Estaing put it to a *Newsweek* reporter: "We are trying to teach our students to look at industries and industrial problems without visualizing national boundaries."[9] *Time* magazine also welcomed this forward looking approach: "Insead lifts its

---

[7] *Financial Times* (14/10/59), *New York Herald Tribune* (29/9/59), *Newsweek* (19/10/59) and *Time* (19/10/59).

[8] The Academic Standards and Regulations issued in 1959 clearly stipulated: "Absences from class will be authorized for such serious reasons as illness, death or serious illness in the immediate family, military orders and court summons." It then listed a number of circumstances under which absences might be tolerated "at the discretion of the Director of Studies".

[9] *Newsweek*, 19/10/59.

students out of long fixed European business habits by stressing practical problems, discouraging narrow specialization and insisting that they take a global view of every business opportunity."[10]

The teaching process was different too. The case method, based on the concept of learning by doing rather than learning by listening and reading, sounded like fun. At the time, only a handful of European institutions proposed the case method, notably CEI, IMEDE and CPA, but those were all fairly small programmes aimed at seasoned executives, not recent graduates. For many of those not prepared to cross the Atlantic, Insead was the only show in town.

But Insead also held a deeper emotional appeal. The first intakes had all been through the war, mostly as children or adolescents, but one or two of them had actually fought on opposite sides. Their determination to create a new Europe was based on the impassioned plea of 'never again'. Growing up in France, Germany and the Netherlands many of them had been encouraged by their parents or teachers to visit other European countries. They were European zealots and could see economic interdependence as a way of preventing the recurrence of such follies. The application forms of the first intake almost invariably refer to European unity. The following extracts, drawn from the first few alphabetical files, give a good flavour of their motivation:

Jean-Marie d'Arjuzon: "I believe in the fortune of Europe, both economic and political, and I want to contribute to it."

Yves Arzel: "Having travelled a lot, I believe strongly in the future of Europe. I am attracted by the school's fresh perspective. It is well adapted to the world we are entering and it constitutes the first real opportunity for Europeans to meet without frontiers."

Antony Belfield: "I have realised that the differences between the peoples of Europe should not constitute barriers between them. I firmly believe in the idea of a European Common Market and also of a United States of Europe. I would like to assist in the mammoth task of making it a reality."

The evidence suggests that attending Insead was not just a professional decision for these people; it was almost a political statement. And what outsiders viewed as the ultimate constraint, namely the trilingual requirement was, for early participants, at the heart of the school's attractiveness – a symbol of its European mission. This spirit of European reconciliation was still alive in 1975 when one former student, John Cutts, went to tell his father that he had applied to Insead. His father, who had fought in the war, simply replied: "Oh well, that's a good thing. It's important that there be no more wars in Europe."

[10] *Time*, 9/4/65.

Insead's unique selling proposition was therefore based on a combination of a noble cause and an apprenticeship in international business, an attractive reconciliation of the idealistic and the pragmatic. Henri Dougier (Class of '63) conceded as much in his 1959 application form, explaining that he has chosen the school: "because it combines the two dimensions along which I want to invest my energy: building and learning, combining my material aspirations and my desire to pursue a fulfilling endeavour." Or as Jean-Marie d'Arjuzon (Class of '60) later put it: "I think that we were seduced by an idea which was original and which opened horizons: towards the future and towards Europe."[11]

The fact that the school was new merely added spice to the experience. That spirit of adventure was evident right from the start, before the course had even begun. After meeting informally with the newcomers of the very first intake, Claude Janssen wrote to Doriot: "From talking with the students, I understand that they are very enthusiastic and have a strong sense of being pioneers and trailblazers."[12] They would need to be in order to stay the course.

A FOREIGN EXPERIENCE

Whilst commitment was high, few of the participants were quite prepared for what awaited them. It was a culture shock in more ways than one, even for the French students.

First, there was the bewildering novelty of interactive learning, which suited some participants better than others. As Giscard d'Estaing commented after only a few weeks of starting: "So far, we are meeting the normal reaction to the case system. Some of the students are enthusiastic, some find it difficult and different from what they expected and feel a bit lost."[13] Certain educational cultures or types of training had never exposed students to notions of class participation, open disagreement, much less the idea of challenging the professor. Some could not really see the point of learning from fellow students who were no more knowledgeable than themselves – and waited patiently for the right answer from the professor. The first graduate of France's prestigious *Ecole Polytechnique* to go through the programme reflected that: "*Polytechnique* graduates may find the case method more disturbing than others, for two key reasons: the lack of structure in the flow of the discussion and the absence of a single correct solution to the problem set."[14]

[11] Jean-Marie d'Arjuzon, speech for 'Launch of the Capital Campaign', Insead video, 29/9/95.
[12] Doriot's correspondence, letter from Claude Janssen, 14/9/59.
[13] *France Actuelle*, 1/12/59.
[14] Gauthier, M.-A., 'L'Institut Européen des Affaires,' *La Jaune et la Rouge*, 1/12/61.

Another feature of the learning process which took some getting used to was the emphasis on group work. Again the norms for working in groups varied widely between national educational traditions. Those with a more individualistic orientation were frustrated by the idea that their grades would rely in part on the efforts of their colleagues which, coupled with personality clashes and rivalries, led to disagreements within the groups. Friction was inevitable given the heterogeneity of the intake, but it was *reinforced* through careful manipulation.

The composition of each work group had been contrived to ensure maximum diversity. The key criteria were nationality and training, with additional consideration of differences in age, experience and even marital status. Thus, a typical group might oblige a young American linguist to work with an experienced German engineer or a French political scientist. Tensions were further fuelled by the pressures of daily case preparation, weekly group reports and quarterly exams. The aim, as Giscard d'Estaing had described it back in August 1957, was "to give students a foretaste of business life".[15]

Adapting to fellow students and to the learning approach under such pressures was not easy.[16] Additional pressure came from the deliberate policy of setting more work than the students could reasonably handle, thus forcing them to make trade offs – as they would later have to in business. Like most encounters with a new culture, the experience seemed highly stimulating at the start, but quickly lost its shine. Already by the third intake, a pattern was emerging: "Keeping up students' morale is one of the main problems. It starts high each year and climbs through mid-November. Then, by the first examination period in December, students tire and become discouraged by the lack of concrete results that is an inherent feature of the case method."[17] This description sounded very much like the classic U-curve[18] associated with adjustment to a foreign culture. The initial stage of elation and optimism (the honeymoon), is soon followed by a period of irritability, frustration, and confusion (the morning after), at which point some people bail out, while others make a gradual adjustment to the new environment (happily ever-after).

It is a pattern of adjustment experienced by Insead students even today, though less intensely for a number of reasons: first, Insead and the case method are better known, so students have a clearer idea of what awaits them; second, active learning methods are more widespread today, even in some of the 'hard' disciplines like engineering; and third, incoming students

[15] Preliminary document discussing the European school, Olivier Giscard d'Estaing, 2/8/57.
[16] Commenting on the experience at the time, one student explained: "The learning methods are completely new for most of us and require a huge effort of adaptation." (*Travail et Méthodes*, June–July 1969).
[17] *International Management*, June 1962.
[18] Lysgaard, S. (1955) 'Adjustment in a foreign society: Norwegian Fulbright grantees visiting the United States', *International Social Science Bulletin*, 7, 45–51.

have a lot more 'international exposure' than they once had, so working with 'foreigners' is less of a novelty.

Of the 62 who enrolled at the start of the first year, 52 finally received their diplomas. Three French students called up for military service had to abandon within weeks of starting, but would return to a later class – while the remaining seven students abandoned, were dismissed after the first term exams or else were not awarded their diploma at the end. These tough measures were deemed necessary both to set standards and to guarantee the quality of the output. Placing work groups under pressure was considered to intensify the cross-cultural learning and to accelerate adaptation.

FROM THE SUBLIME TO THE RUDIMENTARY

The school having been granted use of the Fontainebleau palace for one year only, it became fairly urgent to find alternative premises within a few months of settling in. In April 1960, an unexpected opportunity arose. For those who regarded the palace as an unlikely setting for a business school, Insead was about to go one better.

The 19th-century Carmelite priory was situated two kilometres away from the palace in nearby Avon. With the monastery ceasing its teaching activity, part of the premises had become available, comprising: two large classrooms, a dining room with kitchens capable of serving 200 meals, a 16-bed dormitory (with possibilities of partitioning!), and various rooms to serve as meeting rooms and offices. Giscard d'Estaing decided to visit the monastery accompanied by his architect friend, La Tour d'Auvergne. Their report, dated 23 April 1960, listed the pros and cons.

A key advantage was the possibility of grouping the library, print shop, restaurant and all the offices on a single site. Equally important were the financial arguments: a rental charge had not been settled but it was thought likely that it would be modest given the lack of alternative uses for the premises. The buildings were well heated and in a good condition so minimal refurbishment costs were envisaged. Moreover, a rapid calculation had shown that, with access to its own kitchens, Insead would save one franc on each meal served, resulting in a monthly economy of 3,000 francs (about $600). That such considerations even mattered shows to what extent money was short.

The chief inconvenience was the distance between the premises and the student residences in town, some 15 minutes away on foot.[19] Giscard d'Estaing noted that going back and forth several times a day might prove rather tiresome for the students, especially with the onset of winter. He also

---

[19] At the time the students were housed in two buildings near the palace, one a former hotel (Hotel d'Albe) and the other a former private mansion (Hotel St Honoré). They lived one, two, and in some cases three to a room. While the premises had seen better times, they nevertheless exuded a sense of *grandeur*.

thought that the location might seem rather depressing and wondered whether "the impression of calm emanating from these buildings might be excessive and might even prove morale-sapping".[20] On balance, these existential considerations were no match for the more immediate financial pressures. It would be character building.

One drawback which the report failed to mention was the potential harm to Insead's image as a leading-edge institution. But Giscard d'Estaing had already worked out a way of maintaining appearances. In a separate memo to Posthumus Meyjes he speculated: "We could perhaps maintain usage of the palace – or at least the class room and one reception room – for reasons of standing."[21]

And so it was that Insead moved into the *Collège des Carmes* while keeping one foot in the palace. The palace remained the first point of contact for people visiting the school or writing for information. Students receiving the Insead brochure saw photos of the palace and the student bedrooms, but no pictures of the *Collège des Carmes*. Logically enough, some assumed that the bedrooms were actually in the palace. They were in for a surprise.

Alumni recollections of the *Collège des Carmes* are not especially flattering.[22] Adjectives like 'beat-up', 'seedy', 'ramshackle' and 'decrepit' spring to the lips to describe the cold, uncomfortable and ill-suited premises. The library was housed in the disused chapel, with the books lined up against walls featuring religious frescoes; the restaurant was part of the monks' refectory; and the small print shop, dedicated essentially to case reproduction, was set up in a prefabricated building. One concession to modern influence was the refurbishment of the upstairs classroom along American lines with semi-circular tiers of seats. The classroom downstairs retained a more austere French-style design.

The good news was that the move would clearly allow some scope for growth. There was also an unforeseen benefit of switching to these monastic premises, in that it reinforced the pioneering spirit. The close proximity of students and staff generated a familial atmosphere, particularly at meal times where everyone sat side by side at long tables. The ascetic setting was more in keeping with Insead's true financial situation – and perhaps sharpened the students' sense of responsibility for putting Insead on the map. Soon after graduating, Michel Gauthier, of the second intake, wrote: "One thing is certain: the Institute will be what the former students make of it, and they are determined to participate actively in improving it and making a name for it."[23]

[20] Memo from Giscard d'Estaing to Posthumus Meyjes regarding the possibility of relocating to Fontainebleau-Avon, 25/4/60.
[21] Memo from Giscard d'Estaing to Posthumus Meyjes regarding the possibility of relocating to Fontainebleau-Avon, 25/4/60.
[22] Louis Malle, the French film director, had been a pupil at the school under the Occupation and thirty years later had drawn on that experience for his classic film, *Au Revoir les Enfants*.
[23] Gauthier, M.-A., 'L'Institut Européen des Affaires', *La Jaune et la Rouge*, 1/12/61.

Unwittingly, the experience at the *Collège des Carmes* forged a collective identity, a solidarity born of adversity – and perhaps set the pattern of commitment and self-help which came to characterise alumni involvement. Paradoxically, it is often among these alumni that the sense of nostalgia for the premises, or at least the experience generated by those premises, is the most acute.[24]

PAST PARTICIPANTS

Significantly, it was the students themselves who took the initiative of setting up the alumni association, electing Jean-Marie d'Arjuzon (Class of '60) as the first president and adopting the salamander as their symbol. There are various accounts of how the salamander actually came to be chosen. Whatever the precise details, the choice was directly or indirectly inspired by the fact that the first classes took place in the palace, and that the salamander was the symbol of the king, François I.[25] Yet the choice of the salamander is interesting. Famous in Renaissance legend for its valour and perseverance, reputedly capable of surviving in flames, it was at once distinctive, enigmatic and rooted in history. For a school trying hard to fashion a tradition, it made a suitable emblem.

In France, the notion of belonging to an alumni association was strongly anchored in the *Grandes Ecoles* tradition. About half of the first intake being French, it seemed natural for Insead to go the same way. However, the central function of French alumni associations was to help graduates find a job or to switch jobs. At Insead, the comprehensive placement service run by Dusan Radivojevic took care of this activity.[26] Insead's alumni association would essentially be involved in promoting the school and screening candidates for admission – and would later participate in fund-raising.

For an unknown school, striving to build up its reputation, with hardly any permanent staff and no research output, the alumni were one of its key mechanisms for reaching the market. In a business organisation, they would have been described as the front-line sales force. Their unofficial brief was to promote the school in their respective countries, to look actively for 'Insead material' in their professional entourage and to encourage those people to apply to the school. Surveys of the first three intakes confirmed that

---

[24] Jacqueline Tourlier-Pope recalls that for one of the early Insead students, the experience was particularly nostalgic, indeed bizarre, as he found himself studying in the same premises where he had once been a school pupil.

[25] The design currently used by the Alumni Association was copied from one of the carvings in the palace in 1979.

[26] As explained in the *Christian Science Monitor* (16/5/63): "Insead has created a placement service for its graduates that is unique in Europe. Although the practice is common in the United States, European businesses are not used to canvassing the campuses for promising graduates." It is worth adding that keeping the placement service internal, rather than handing it over to the alumni association, was the best way to retain some leverage over the financial contribution of recruiting firms.

participants came to know of Insead overwhelmingly through word of mouth, and often as a result of contact with alumni.[27]

A few of the early alumni took it upon themselves to write articles about the school. Michel Gauthier (Class of '61) publicised its original methods and mission in *La Jaune et la Rouge*, the review for graduates of *L'Ecole Polytechnique*, who would rapidly become a steady source of recruits. Brian Barrow (Class of '61) wrote about the school in the journal published by the American Chamber of Commerce in France,[28] Jean-Louis Lecocq (Class of '66) wrote about it in *L'Hermès*, a journal for French expatriates,[29] and Antony Pierce-Grove (Class of '66) wrote about it in *The Accountant*.[30] In 1965, Henry Dougier (Class of '63) launched a trilingual journal, *European Business Review*, which would later provide a natural outlet for some of the faculty's early publications.[31]

The other key role of the alumni was to serve on the pre-selection committees which vetted applicants for admission. As with the efforts to promote the school, one can ask oneself why alumni would devote their valuable time to such activities. The instrumental answer is that these were the levers which, over time, would enhance the value of the Insead diploma. By helping to improve the quality of the input, the alumni were protecting and fructifying their own investment. But there was also an emotional tie, evident in the well attended reunions and on-going links with the school – in spite of the geographical dispersion.

This raises an interesting paradox between Insead's comparatively short programme and the lasting relationships between alumni. A number of distinct ingredients probably contribute to this close-knit alumni network.

Firstly there is the initial experience. The intensity of the programme, the relative isolation of Fontainebleau, the fact that students often arrive with their partners and sometimes children lends a particular atmosphere. The students live in close proximity of one another, yet sufficiently far from Paris to force them to "make their own entertainment". National origins are cast aside with the students focusing instead on their homogeneity: their elite schooling, their career aspirations, and their cosmopolitan outlook which, for the early promotions, also meant their European idealism. The whole experience is hyped with a 'we're all in the same boat' and 'let's have fun in France' disposition, and easy camaraderie blooms. Social exchanges typically revolve around career options, denunciations of the school's administration, psycho-release stories about dreadful interviews, and anecdotes about the strange ways of the local population. It has something of the feel of an

[27] See *Annual Report*, 1961–62, 2.
[28] No. 170, 15/12/61.
[29] *L'Hermès*, June–July 1966.
[30] *The Accountant*, 29/4/67.
[31] In 1967, the journal was re-launched on a larger scale with the backing of Insead and other sponsors.

expatriate community – and the social bonds born of this experience are durable.[32]

On leaving Insead, the alumni population is more likely to maintain or build multiple ties by virtue of its high mobility. For one thing, there will immediately be a dual allegiance to a class and to a country, since the alumni association was geographically decentralised by Jeremy Leigh-Pemberton (Class of '61) when he took over as its president in October 1965. Over a career, Insead alumni also tended to move between countries to a greater extent than alumni of other schools which meant that they made contact with the alumni associations in different countries. Since Insead graduates typically moved into jobs with an international dimension, the possibility of calling up fellow alumni for briefing purposes quickly became an established practice. Such traditions have helped to foster a general sense of goodwill and continue to weave fresh links within the alumni network.

A PRESS MAGNET

Prior to the inauguration, Doriot had warned Giscard d'Estaing that there would be few opportunities to publicise the school for some time after the launch. In fact Doriot had underestimated the novelty value of the initiative: the incongruity of a business school housed in a palace and an old Cistercian monastery; run by a "forceful and svelte director"[33] who was a Harvard graduate barely older than the students themselves and also happened to be the brother of the French finance minister; and a quirky new teaching approach designed to produce fabulous 'Eurocrats', long before the term had become pejorative. It was simply too good a story to pass up. The unique difficulty facing the school was that it was not targeting a common press body, which meant translating press releases, cultivating contacts with journalists internationally, and generating stories of potential interest to different countries.

Visiting journalists were encouraged to talk to the students and to sit in on classes. This very open approach was in stark contrast with the prevailing ways of dealing with the press, typically involving restricted access to senior people armed with scripted answers to the questions posed. The trilingual classroom experience never failed to impress journalists. As one observer enthused: "The professor's French, precise, brilliantly clear, slices through the logic of the argument ... From a corner of the room, a young man casually throws in a question in English. The professor reflects for a moment and

---

[32] As Insead professor and former student, Gareth Dyas, likes to put it: "The closest thing to an Insead experience is another Insead experience. I can describe all the anecdotes about the differences back then, but there is more in common in what I went through as a student and what they go through today than there are differences."

[33] *The Sunday Times*, 21/3/65.

answers him, in English. In another corner, an argument begins, in German between two students each with his own interpretation of a contract. Good naturedly, the professor quizzes them in French. As the students walk off in groups into the grounds of the Fontainebleau Palace, the strangely exciting, trilingual discussion goes on."[34] For reporters and readers alike it seemed like a glimpse into the future of Europe.

Giscard d'Estaing made sure that the journalists never went away empty handed in terms of facts and figures about the achievements of the school. For instance, barely after the first wave of students graduated, the *New York Herald Tribune* noted: "For the school's first crop of graduates, three times as many graduates could have been placed in firms as were available."[35] What the school may have failed to specify was that half of the first graduating class went straight on to do national service, so perhaps the pool of available recruits was smaller than expected.

Early articles repeatedly mentioned that the school was open to candidates of any nationality, that 45 per cent of graduates were working outside their native countries and 80 per cent were employed by international concerns, which were fairly rare at the time. Effectively the school was setting itself up as a kind of 'obligatory stop-off' for anyone intent on an international career. Symbolically, the first 'year book' was multilingual, with the course outline in French, the director's message in English and the description of the alumni association in German. The early annual reports went to considerable lengths to trumpet the school's international credentials. They were packed with tables indicating the national origins of the students, the faculty, the board, the recruiting companies, the cases, and even the library books. It was a striking affirmation of the business saying: 'You treasure what you measure.'

The underlying news value of the Insead story was given a topical spin by inviting high-profile speakers to give talks to the students. In the early years, the speakers invited and the themes broached were heavily oriented towards European integration. René Mayer, former head of the European Coal and Steel Community (CECA), tackled the theme of supranational intervention in national economies;[36] Paul-Henri Spaak, secretary general of NATO, spoke on the problems of European and transatlantic cooperation;[37] John Pinder, managing editor of the Economist Intelligence Unit, discussed Britain's position regarding the Common Market;[38] and Valéry Giscard d'Estaing, then secretary of state in the finance ministry and the rising star of French politics, outlined the challenge of establishing a European budget.[39]

Other 'staged events' included the opening and graduating ceremonies,

[34] *The Lion*, April 1964.
[35] *New York Herald Tribune*, 19/12/60.
[36] Reported in *La Liberté*, 8/4/60.
[37] Reported in *Le Soir*, 21/10/60.
[38] Reported in *L'Economie*, 22/12/60.
[39] Reported in *La Liberté*, 27/1/61.

which provided regular opportunities to remind journalists about the distinctiveness of Insead.[40] The school also organised 'national days' when several speakers would be invited to present the social and economic characteristics of a particular European country. For example, Italian day elicited articles in *Corriere della Sera* (23/5/61) and *24 Ore* (26/5/61); and British day was picked up by *The Times* (25/5/62), *Financial Times* (25/5/62) and *The Statist* (25/5/62). As the faculty grew in experience, the school started to organise more ambitious seminars. In September 1964, Roger Godino in collaboration with George Steiner of UCLA/Stanford Research Institute ran a five-day seminar with 80 high-level participants to discuss issues of multinational long-range planning. The seminar's bold conclusions about the concentration of world industrial power generated considerable press coverage.[41]

In the course of 1965, there followed a number of one or two-day seminars: on Franco-German relations, on international research and development, on international co-operation and economic growth and, most appropriately, on relations between companies and the press – an area in which Insead was rapidly gaining expertise.

Of course, the school could not rely exclusively on journalists prepared to come to Fontainebleau; it also had to go out and make itself known. This task fell in large measure upon Olivier Giscard d'Estaing who spent much of his time on the road, projecting the image of Insead, lecturing, recruiting, raising support and funds. His May 1962 visit to Lebanon, for instance, where his grandfather had once been high commissioner (1927–30) generated large spreads in the middle eastern press.[42] Giscard d'Estaing also wrote several semi-academic articles on the challenges of building Insead,[43] as did Jean Martin of the Paris Chamber of Commerce.

But there were other ways of creating visibility. Within France, several company visits were organised, but there were also a variety of international trips. For instance, there were several trips to Berlin – including one in 1961 before the wall was built and another in 1963 to meet Willy Brandt, then mayor of Berlin. The school also derived increasing visibility from its language seminars in Germany for incoming students which, under the direction of Dusan Radivojevic, gradually became elaborate cultural introductions to Germany.

Perhaps the most spectacular initiative, however, was the 'graduation trip'.

---

[40] 'Twenty nations will be represented at the opening ceremony' ran the headline in *Le Parisien* (13/9/63) announcing the arrival of the fifth intake, now numbering 99.

[41] *Le Monde* (15/9/64) reported that: "In less than twenty years, 600-700 large companies will account for three-quarters of all industrial production." *The New York Herald Tribune* (12/9/64) reported the conclusion that: "size rather than nationality was the major guide to how a company was run".

[42] In *Beirut* and *L'Orient* (13/5/62).

[43] For example, in *L'Université Européene* published by the University of Brussels (1962) and in *La Revue Politique et Parlementaire* (November 1962).

From the very first year, the school organised an end of year coach tour for all the students which, over two weeks, took them through five European countries. The itinerary included stop-offs at the Council of Europe in Strasbourg, the CECA in Luxembourg, the Ford plant in Cologne, the Shell refinery in Rotterdam, Philips in Eindhoven, the Bell telephone company in Anvers and was rounded off with a graduation day at Brussels under the auspices of Etienne Hirsch, president of Euratom. This inaugural trip launched an Insead tradition and generated considerable local interest wherever the 'road show' alighted.

Of course, the trip had a serious educational and social purpose – to acquaint students with European institutions and companies, to impress on them the huge differences existing between cultures and the practical barriers to integration. Such events were not merely 'photo opportunities' or 'publicity stunts' – but they were organised, in large part by the students themselves, to achieve maximum impact in countries where the school sought visibility, through press conferences, official receptions and the invitation of renowned figures to hand out the diplomas. The point is that, more like a business than an academic institution, Insead took press relations seriously from the start.

FINANCIAL HEADACHES

While the Paris Chamber of Commerce had pledged financial support for the first year, a condition of its on-going support was that other sponsors should be found. Without this support, there was no guarantee of funding for the second half of 1960, which meant that in spite of the rash of enquiries elicited by the widespread press coverage, the second intake might have to be smaller than the first – a real setback for the school's reputation. As Giscard d'Estaing wrote: "M. Desbrière (the Paris Chamber of Commerce's treasurer) was categorical. He cannot see any way of increasing the intake for 1960–61, unless significant complementary funds can be raised."[44]

Commenting on the results of his recent fund-raising trips abroad, Posthumus Meyjes was pleased to announce sizeable donations from Royal Dutch and a Dutch shipbuilding syndicate, but lamented the poor showing of the German, British, Belgian and Swiss companies.[45] Nearly a year later, on the eve of another *grand tour*, he noted ruefully that: "On this side of the Atlantic, soliciting funds is an extremely long and painstaking process."[46]

In Europe, there was a deep-seated belief that education should be government funded. Companies which had already paid their taxes, saw no need to contribute 'a second time' to educational establishments. There was

[44] Doriot's correspondence, letter from Giscard d'Estaing, 7/12/59.
[45] Doriot's correspondence, letter from Posthumus Meyjes, 20/11/59.
[46] Doriot's correspondence, letter from Posthumus Meyjes, 19/10/60.

therefore no incentive, either economic or moral, to help fund the school.[47] But perhaps Insead was simply asking too much from these companies. The school's articles for members were designed to attract large donations, ranging between 5,000–50,000 francs (about $850–8,500), from big companies.[48] Maybe the school was missing out on a plethora of smaller donations. Thus, in early January 1960, an association[49] was set up to collect funds on behalf of the school from smaller companies, associations and professional unions willing to make donations of up to 5,000 francs. In its first year, the association yielded a revenue of some 25,000 francs, but never surpassed that annual figure in subsequent years.[50]

By March 1960, the financial situation was starting to look rather desperate. Significantly, in order to obtain large funds fast, Giscard d'Estaing did not renew the appeal to French firms, much less European firms; nor did he try the French or European authorities. Rather, he headed straight for the US. Within two weeks of arriving, he was able to announce a donation of twenty thousand dollars from IBM, enough to resolve the immediate financial crisis.

This funding allowed for a moderate growth in the second intake, which comprised 67 students, but the increase was deemed sufficient to justify two separate sections. To the outside world, Insead had doubled its intake, even if the number of students enrolled had risen only by five. Appearances would be saved.

Later that year, in November 1960, Insead's longstanding pursuit of the Ford Foundation finally bore fruit, producing a grant of $120,000 spread over three years. It was a welcome contribution, the only drawback being that it was tied to two specific objectives: the training of instructors from developing countries in management education; and the setting up of a research programme. Insead dutifully invited four 'would-be professors' (including one woman!) to sit in on the course alongside the students; and it established a research centre, headed by Paul Silberer. In reality, the body of available professors was insufficient to support a viable 'teacher training' programme; and few cases actually emerged from the research centre since the American professors supervising them rarely stayed in Europe long enough to assemble the documentation or work through the final drafts.[51]

Significantly, the Ford Foundation was not unduly put off by these

[47] As Doriot himself observed in a letter to Louis Cabot (25/8/60): "I found it very hard to get financial help for the school because European businessmen are not trained to give for schools."
[48] See letter from Posthumus-Meyjes to Georges Desbrière, President of the *Compagnie Française des Métaux*, 17/3/60.
[49] *L'Association pour l'Encouragement de l'Enseignement de l'Administration des Affaires.*
[50] The sums collected by the Association were: 25,000 francs for 1960, 23,000 for 1961, 20,000 for 1962, 10,000 for 1963, 19,000 for 1964, and 15,000 for 1965.
[51] From 'A proposal to the Ford Foundation on behalf of Insead', submitted by D.F. Berry, 1/4/71, Appendix 1.

failures and, in 1965, renewed its funding of Insead, to the tune of $150,000 over five years, to fund a joint research programme with HBS in 'The Management of International Enterprises'. That this generosity coincided with the years of the 'Cold War' is not without relevance, and illustrates the influence of external events on the development of Insead. As argued by Gemelli, the Ford Foundation's role in Europe was not purely altruistic: "It was part of a grander vision of the 'diplomacy of ideas' in strengthening the cultural and ideological unity of Western civilization through the development of higher education in research and training, which concerned management education as well as the social sciences."[52]

Even with these substantial grants, Insead remained a precarious operation with little to spare between revenues and outgoings. In December 1960, Insead earned the right to collect a French education tax direct from companies, known as the *taxe d'apprentissage*. It did not represent much money, but with Insead's high fixed costs, it provided a little extra discretionary income. Recalling the limited resources at his disposal, Giscard d'Estaing observes: "I remember George von Peterffy (formerly Doriot's assistant at HBS) coming to see me in the second year to say that I should buy an overhead projector. I told him that no professors had asked for one and that anyhow I did not have the money to do it. He grew furious, telling me that we were hopeless and that it was ridiculous that we had no money. In the end, he managed to get an overhead projector donated by the firm which manufactured them." Self-help was the order of the day.

Quite possibly, Giscard d'Estaing's caution regarding undue expenditure was driven by the fact that no one really knew whether the school was solvent or not. In 1963, Jean Marcou, the chairman of the board, called in Lee Remmers, a former student who had stayed on as a research assistant in finance, to 'look into' the school's accounting system. Remmers protested that he had no experience in setting up accounting systems, but it was to no avail. Dipping into the accounts, he was in for quite a shock. There was a ledger in which transactions were recorded, but there were no counter entries; a statement of cash in and cash out, but no balance sheet or income statement. All the calculations were done by hand.[53] Describing the existing system to a couple of people, to get advice, Remmers was told he had to start from scratch.

Remmers arranged for an inventory of what physical assets the school owned – chairs, desks, a car for ferrying professors to and from the airport –

[52] Gemelli, G. (1994) 'American influence on European management education', in *Management, Education, and Competitiveness: Europe, Japan and the United States*, R.P Amdam (ed.) London: Routledge, 1996, 38–68.

[53] When Remmers shopped around for mechanical accounting equipment, the suppliers he called had never heard of Insead and, based in Paris, were initially unwilling to come down to Fontainebleau to give advice or set things up. Again, it is a reminder of Insead's visibility outside certain very restricted circles.

and attributed a nominal value to them, then depreciated them immediately 100 per cent. Looking at the bank deposits, creditors and debtors, he established a balance sheet. "Fortunately," he recalls, "the assets were bigger than the obvious liabilities." Getting the people entering the data to apply the new double entry procedures proved another headache. Typically they would forget to make a counter entry so, during the first year, the accounts would only balance after much trial and error – sometimes never.

The anecdote borders on the comical, but shows to what extent this remained a shoestring operation. Over the first years, Posthumus Meyjes or Giscard d'Estaing would occasionally secure larger donations, but these provided only brief respite. Lack of finance was the key bottleneck to growth and the main topic of the correspondence with Doriot. There were other constraints too, such as lack of classroom or student housing facilities, and indeed of permanent staff, but all of these could have been fixed with deeper coffers. Insead was a prisoner of its strategic independence. When reading Giscard d'Estaing's correspondence, the image that comes most readily to mind is the cartoon figure of the train driver feverishly picking up rail track from behind and laying it down in front of the runaway locomotive.

MUDDLING THROUGH

Mindful of adding unnecessarily to the high fixed costs, the school's recruitment policy for professors remained cautious. For the first eighteen months, Gilbert Sauvage, lured from the *Bureau International du Travail* in Geneva, was the only professor who was close to full-time (he also taught at *Sciences Po*). Sauvage ran the 'Cadre Européen' course which was central to the image of the school; and being fluent in German, Italian and English, he also travelled a lot to promote the school overseas. Many of the leads he initiated – for instance, in Eastern Europe and Canada – were not followed up for lack of resources, but were 'rediscovered' later when the school started actively prospecting further afield. Besides this external role, Sauvage and his wife also played an unsung internal role receiving students at their house and welcoming new professors – providing a vital social glue at a time when the professors were in perpetual motion and students could easily feel abandoned.

It was Sauvage who, in February 1961, collected Salvatore Teresi from the airport at Le Bourget in his convertible to bring him down to Fontainebleau. Teresi had an unusual background, having already helped set up a business school in his native Sicily (ISIDA[54]) before heading off to Indiana to complete an MBA. He had gone on the recommendation of the American professors – Clewett and Waterman – who, in 1955, had acted as consultants

---

[54] ISIDA – *Istituto Superiore per Imprenditori e Dirigenti d'Azienda* in Palermo.

to the nascent ISIDA, and subsequently helped out with the launch of Insead. Business education in Europe was a very small world at the time. It was their suggestion that Giscard d'Estaing recruit Teresi, a recommendation largely based on his organisational ability. Initially put in charge of the marketing course, within six months Teresi was asked to coordinate the whole programme.

Besides the three full-time professors – Giscard d'Estaing, Teresi and Sauvage – faculty meetings were also attended by course assistants, mostly recruited from the previous year's students. They administered the courses and supported a core of dedicated individuals – including Roger Godino, Paul Silberer, Peter Smith, Maurice Teper and Stefaan Cambien – who, though part-time, became pillars of the school throughout the early 1960s. These professors were progressively joined by others including Lee Remmers, Guy de Carmoy and Theodore Weinshall.

For several years, Insead also benefited from the experience of a succession of visiting American professors, starting with Robert Masson and George von Peterffy from Harvard. To attract experienced American professors, Insead had to rely on outside finance – the Ford Foundation, the European Productivity Agency or sponsored chairs. And few of these professors stayed for more than one academic year.

The rest of the teaching staff were visiting instructors from business. Besides their strong practical orientation, they also guaranteed Insead a useful external visibility within their firms or with their business clients. Reliance on visiting faculty was such that one of Giscard d'Estaing's routine concerns was checking that incoming flights had arrived and, with no motorway access at the time, ensuring that the professors would show up without getting lost. The completion of a motorway linking Paris to Fontainebleau in 1962 proved a major boon for those visiting professors. It was also a relief to the course assistants who had to step into the fray whenever professors failed to show up.

The proportion of visiting faculty drew criticism from certain external observers. For example, in response to a favourable article on the school, Pearson Hunt of HBS wrote a letter to the *Economist* commenting that: "The large turnover provided by 50 visiting professors has resulted in confusion rather than a well integrated series of related material ..." and going on to question whether "the size of the permanent staff was adequate to provide the academic help that students sometimes need".[55] While he had exaggerated the numbers of visiting faculty, inflating them with the guest lecturers, his criticism was not altogether unfounded.

There was also disquiet from within. The results of a questionnaire survey organised by the alumni association among the first three intakes had raised

[55] Letter to *The Economist*, 4/5/63; Giscard d'Estaing's response appeared in the edition dated 22/6/63.

a number of 'severe criticisms' of the teaching dispensed. Though conceding the need for this type of feedback, Giscard d'Estaing was angered at not having been consulted on either the contents or the distribution of the report: "It is very difficult for a young institution to obtain a reputation for high quality," he complained. "I therefore disapprove strongly of the decision to disseminate criticism of the school throughout Europe, without any real control over its consequences."[56]

Arguably, the faculty body, and therefore the curriculum, lacked consistency. Some of the professors engaged had limited experience with the case method. As Salvatore Teresi recalls: "Nearly all the professors were under 35, and many of us were rather like sorcerer's apprentices." The variable quality of the teaching was not helped by the fleeting contacts between visiting instructors. Jacqueline Tourlier-Pope[57], recruited in May 1963 with responsibility for administration, personnel and finance, was also asked to coordinate the contents of each course to make sure that there were not too many overlaps.[58]

But the problems did not just stem from the professors and curriculum. The students were also difficult – very demanding, yet with widely differing expectations, experience bases and linguistic capacities. Even for veteran American professors, teaching them was 'no sinecure' as Robert Masson put it.[59] One or two American professors who neglected to adapt their material or their approach, fared particularly badly, failing to engage their mainly European audience. Others succeeded, but 'knew they had been in a fight'. After his first class, Robert Masson commented: "I now make my first report after teaching two classes in the second Insead program. I wrote General Doriot ... and gave him my enthusiastic appraisal of their quality, obvious seriousness, and active response in my first class. In fact, I can say that I never have had a more active and meaningful discussion of a case in all my experience."[60]

Given the many implementation difficulties and the lean faculty body, there was a danger that the professors would be constantly caught up with fire-fighting and never have time to reflect on medium- and long-range issues for the school. Posthumus Meyjes had seen this risk coming and, in November 1959, had invited a number of interested outsiders to form a *Comité de Perfectionnement* to assist the school in its development.[61] Those

[56] Letter from Giscard d'Estaing to Jean-Marie d'Arjuzon, president of the Insead alumni association, 6/2/64.
[57] Jacqueline Charmont at the time.
[58] When recruited she had caused quite a stir by demanding a salary which, though moderate, exceeded that of Olivier Giscard d'Estaing.
[59] Letter from Robert Masson to Vernon R. Alden, Associate dean HBS, 7/10/60.
[60] Letter from Robert Masson to Vernon R. Alden, Associate dean HBS, 7/10/60.
[61] Letter from Posthumus Meyjes to the members of the former Technical Committee to invite to join the new committee (16/11/59).

enlisted included Jean Martin of the Paris Chamber of Commerce, Claude Janssen, Robert Goetz (head of the *Centre d'Administration des Entreprises*), Heinz Rudolph of the European Productivity Agency, Pierre Petot of the CPA, and Elio Pesso of the OECE. From December 1959 onwards, the committee met with Giscard d'Estaing every two months or so to discuss growth in intakes, reforms in faculty composition, admission procedures, language requirements or the curriculum, and any new project proposals or developments. For the school, it was a cheap way of generating strategic reflection on its development – and started a tradition of creating committees to provide the support, advice and expertise not available internally.

PROMOTING STANDARDS

In early 1962 Posthumus Meyjes let it be known that he planned to retire at the end of the next academic year, in June 1963. Olivier Giscard d'Estaing seemed an obvious successor. The post of director-general would allow him to dedicate himself fully to what he did best – cultivating contacts with the outside world – while delegating responsibility for the faculty and students to someone else. Roger Godino was approached to become director of faculty, a position which he accepted part-time, three days a week. Looking back on the division of responsibilities, Godino describes his role as a kind of 'interior minister' contrasting with Giscard d'Estaing's role as 'minister of foreign affairs'.

The appointment of Godino to shoulder Giscard d'Estaing meant that the school would be piloted by two former Harvard students, with the standards and professionalism of their alma mater still very fresh in their minds. Writing to Doriot, soon after taking on the job, Godino noted: "We have to realise that we are moving from a small-time operation into an industrial-scale operation with all of the structural and organisational problems that entails."[62]

One of the on-going preoccupations was the need to improve standards. That issue was brought to the top agenda by an article which appeared in late September 1962, just as Godino was about to take on his new role. The opening paragraph noted: "An impressive car park awaits visitors: 3 Mercedes 190 SL, 1 AC Bristol, 2 Triumphs, 1 MG, 1 Jaguar ... These cars do not belong to chief executives, but to young people with an average age of 27."[63] As Godino recalls: "The implication was that it was a kind of finishing school for rich kids." This reputation was partly inevitable in that trilingual candidates, in those days, tended to come from well-to-do families who had lived or travelled in several countries. Moreover there was a risk in attending an unknown school, which family backing went a long way to attenuating.

---

[62] Doriot's correspondence, letter from Roger Godino, 31/10/62.
[63] *Les Echos*, 28/9/62.

Dispelling this reputation could partly be achieved by tightening up on admissions standards and testing procedures throughout the course as recommended by the *comité de perfectionnement*. But it was also a question of establishing a different climate and set of expectations from the start. In his addresses to incoming students at opening ceremonies, Godino issued a dark warning: "I am very happy to see you here today – and all I can say is that you won't all be there when we reach the end of the year. I will monitor your levels in each course and those who are not up to standard will have to leave before Christmas."

In reality, there was not much of an increase in the numbers of students eliminated, which remained at around half a dozen each year. However, the workloads intensified and there was more continuous testing. Of course, this had repercussions on the social climate within the school. As one American student commented in 1964: "It's about as different from an American campus as you could imagine ... closer knit and with a stronger sense of urgency; more dedicated but less fun and far, far less social. We have too much work to do."[64] As another journalist concluded, after outlining the workload and pressures piled on students: "With all of this in a five-and-a-half day per week schedule, Paris might as well be 400 miles away rather than just 40 miles."[65]

The continuous testing was particularly anathema to the European students who were accustomed to relaxing through the year and cramming right at the end. Indeed, in 1965, there was even a student strike in protest over a surprise test sprung by an economics professor.[66] The strike lasted three days, and was resolved by an agreement that no warnings were necessary for non-technical tests, but that technical tests needed to be announced in advance. One of the ironies of this episode was that Gareth Pooley, the second youngest student in that intake, who made a speech to try to calm the situation, was mistakenly identified as one of the ring leaders of the strike. The minutes of a faculty meeting held during the strike proposed dealing with the whole incident by simply expelling Pooley. Had this solution been implemented, Insead would have been deprived of one of its future pillars, better known as professor Gareth Dyas.

In addition to increasing the intensity of pressure on students, Insead also went to some lengths to publicise the difficulty of getting onto the course. For instance, in November 1962, the *Daily Telegraph* announced: "Any

[64] *The Lion*, April 1964.
[65] *The MBA*, April 1967. A journalist writing in the *Sunday Times* (21/3/65) noted that: "From September to June there is little chance for relaxation. Most of the students I spoke to had only been to Paris once or twice in the last six months."
[66] The decision to strike can perhaps be seen as a typically European way of protesting, particularly in the mid-1960s. There is an interesting contrast with the students of HBS, in the 1920s, who registered their discontent by noisily cheering for the opposition at football games. (J. L. Cruikshank, *A Delicate Experiment*, 1987, p. 97.)

graduate of any nationality may apply for the course, and applications exceed places by about six to one."[67] This ratio of six to one kept popping up, for example in *Management* (March 1963, 108) and *The Statist* (3/9/65). In truth, the ratio of applications to admissions was nearer two to one, even in 1965.[68] There seemed to be a confusion between the number of enquiries about the school and the number of formal applications – the consequence being that Insead seemed almost as tough to get into as Harvard. Yet a measure of *trompe l'oeil* is critical to any new venture. Unlike most business schools, Insead did not bask in the reflected glory of a prestigious university or official body. Self-promotion was therefore the only way forward.

The school also started to publish the list of those admitted in *Le Monde*.[69] This practice is typical among the most prestigious *Grandes Ecoles* which are schools with entrance exams. Insead has never had an entrance exam. But again, the idea was to emphasise the selectivity of the school – as well as its international dimension since those selected were listed by nationality. Beyond trumpeting the fact that Insead was hugely oversubscribed and successful, it was also designed to encourage self-selection and push up standards. If candidates think it is a 'tough' school, then those who look upon it as a finishing school are less likely to apply. To some extent, Insead was working on the old principle that saying it would help to make it so.

Quite apart from improving standards, Godino was well plugged into US academic circles, having attended both MIT and Harvard, and he set about leveraging those connections. In 1962, he was already testing the water with Doriot about creating an international advanced management programme.[70] In 1964, Godino organised the first high profile international seminar for outside companies, thanks to his links with Stanford Research Institute. He was also behind the joint research project with HBS which led to the second grant by the Ford Foundation. But perhaps his most important contribution, in the course of his frequent contacts with the US, was to initiate the move towards a professional faculty.

Godino succeeded in getting Harvard to accept the idea of training management professors for Insead. So it was that, starting in 1966, a number of Insead alumni, who had stayed on for a year as research assistants, were sent to Harvard to complete their doctorates. Amongst the first to go were Gareth Dyas and Heinz Thanheiser. For the school, there was a double benefit. They went to Harvard to obtain their doctorates but they also attested to the quality of Insead's one year programme.

---

[67] *Daily Telegraph*, 2/11/62.
[68] The official statistics for 1965–66 show 232 applicants and 133 admissions.
[69] See for example, *Le Monde*, 1/8/64; or Le Figaro, 18/7/66.
[70] Doriot's correspondence, letter from Roger Godino, 31/10/62.

BUILDING FOR GROWTH

Within days of the school's launch *Time* magazine was announcing to its readers that Insead's ultimate goal was 800–900 graduates a year.[71] The school later revised its projections and settled on a figure of 500 as its standard objective. For example, *The Economist* cited Insead's plans "to expand the school to take first 200, then 500, with students coming from countries all over the world".[72]

Another aspect of 'thinking big' can be seen in the announcement, from the start, that the school would build its own premises. Already in early 1960, the local Fontainebleau newspaper was headlining the fact that: "Insead intends to build premises capable of accommodating 500 students".[73] The school was never coy; it had no qualms about publicising the high salaries offered to its graduates,[74] broadcasting its ambitions, or compressing the estimated time needed to achieve its aims – intakes of 500 students were only achieved in the mid-1990s. Again, we sense in these predictions the idea that if repeated often enough, they may actually happen. The point is that Insead did not plan on staying small for long. Today, we might call it strategic intent.[75]

In order to negotiate Insead's continued presence in the palace, Giscard d'Estaing had needed to show that the school was actively planning to move out – which is why the local press had already picked up on the plans for purpose-built premises in early 1960. Yet this alleged 'architectural project' remained entirely hypothetical without the context of a site – and until the project could be formalised, there was no way of knowing how much it might cost.

Although remaining in Fontainebleau was both convenient and helpful for marketing purposes, there was no actual obligation to stay put. Conscious of the potential impact of the school on the region, both economically and in terms of intellectual and international prestige, the mayor of Fontainebleau, Paul Séramy, worked hard to find a solution. The town of Fontainebleau is a small island surrounded by a huge forest. There are no possibilities of extending the boundaries of the town without trespassing on the forest which is protected by the state. This posed quite a challenge, until Séramy managed to purchase five hectares of land adjacent to the forest. This was not the proposed site, but rather land which could be re-wooded, in order to then trade it for five hectares of the forest itself. This way the

---

[71] *Time*, 19/10/59.

[72] *The Economist*, 30/3/63.

[73] *La Liberté*, 29/4/60.

[74] In November 1961, *Business* told its readers: "Firms tend to offer INSEAD diplomees salaries 10 to 15 per cent above what they would normally offer to graduate trainees". 18 months later, the figure had risen significantly: "The school insists that companies pay the students approximately one-third more than comparable management." (*Christian Science Monitor*, 16/5/63.)

[75] G Hamel and C K Prahalad (1989) 'Strategic intent', *Harvard Business Review*, May–June, 63–76.

boundaries of the forest would be slightly altered, but the forest would preserve its surface area. It was a neat solution which was formally approved by the state in December 1963.[76]

Giscard d'Estaing then asked his architect friend, Bernard de La Tour d'Auvergne, to conceive a set of buildings for the school. In his early 30s, La Tour d'Auvergne was imaginative and had received numerous prizes for his designs, but was somewhat inexperienced on large projects. To make the choice of architect more acceptable to the local authorities, he was asked to work with Rogatien de Cidrac, the chief architect of the palace. The initial design proposed, a drab four-sided structure, was turned down. Given a freer hand the second time round, La Tour d'Auvergne came up with a much more interesting concept with its own distinctive style – using modern materials, like aluminium and bricks, but squat and with lots of mirrored glass so as to be in harmony with the forest. The existence of the model was reported in the local Fontainebleau paper, *La Liberté*, in July 1962.[77]

The centrepiece of the structure was a huge entry hall leading to the five amphitheatres which branched off from a hub. Somehow reminiscent of the *Champs Elysées* leading up to the *Place de l'Etoile*, the idea was that there should be room for people to circulate yet points of convergence to force them to meet. The buildings were not luxurious in terms of the materials used – there was no marble or brass for instance – but there was the luxury of space. With an estimated cost of 8 million francs (roughly $1.6 million) for the premises, the question now was where to find the money.

Initial attempts to raise the funds from corporate donors or the Ford Foundation proved fruitless – and without shareholders or collateral there was no way of borrowing the money. Eventually, the Paris Chamber of Commerce offered to purchase the land on behalf of the school. In January 1964, Jean Martin signed a cheque for the five hectares of forest previously earmarked by the Fontainebleau authorities for the new Insead premises. The land would be leased to the school at no rent for 40 years.

As for the buildings, the school was helped out by the French authorities, which granted a subsidy of 2 million francs and arranged a 6 million franc loan from the state agency, the Caisse des Dépôts et Consignations at a rate of interest normally reserved for community projects. The loan guarantees were provided jointly by France's chambers of commerce (Assemblée Permanente des Chambres de Commerce et d'Industrie), the regional council of Seine-et-Marne and the town of Fontainebleau.[78] It would be fair to say that the government's help was rather unexpected given the school's previously distant relationship with the French authorities – and while Paul Séramy's support in front of the *Assemblée Nationale* was certainly voluble,

---

[76] See articles in *Le Parisien Libéré* and *La Liberté*, 9/12/63.
[77] *La Liberté*, 27/7/62.
[78] The French National Assembly voted the bill through on a second reading on 17th December 1963.

there was also opposition to the proposal.[79] The French satirical paper, *Le Canard Enchaîné*, was quick to speculate on this sudden burst of state generosity, musing on the school's privileged access to prime minister Georges Pompidou via the finance minister, Valéry Giscard d'Estaing.[80] It is also worth noting that the 2 million franc grant came from the ministry of foreign affairs and not the education ministry which might in return have expected some say in the running of the school.

The ceremony for the laying of the first stone took place on 26 October 1965. Typically, it was a high profile affair with Michel Maurice-Bokanowski, the industry minister, inaugurating the proceedings. The construction work was completed in time for the September intake of 1967. Ironically though, Giscard d'Estaing did not accompany the school into its new premises, deciding it was time to move back into industry in the course of 1966.

Besides his relentless efforts to improve and promote the school, Giscard d'Estaing had overseen its fragile development from a tentative project into a going concern. Intakes had more than doubled, reaching 163 by the time the school moved into the new buildings, with a third section having been introduced in 1964. Giscard d'Estaing instilled an ambition for growth – the new premises being its most obvious manifestation – which has come to characterise the school's breathless development. Evidently, Giscard d'Estaing had internalised Doriot's early advice that the school should "grow fairly fast because it will display a vitality which is important".[81]

A SELECT FOLLOWING

In Autumn 1964, an article in the *HBS Bulletin* assessed Insead's progress: "After only five years, it is not, to be sure, an absolutely unqualified success; and not entirely without problems ahead. But for all of that it is a reality, with some fine backing, a growing reputation, and five years of invaluable experience."[82]

The school had clearly awakened significant interest in certain circles, but for the most part it remained very much of an unknown quantity, as reported in the American review, *The MBA*, in early 1967: "Until now, the school has been regarded with an air of suspicion either as a young men's finishing school, as a French school of diplomacy, or as a part of NATO. It has frequently been mistaken for the executive training school in Switzerland called IMEDE."[83]

[79] See *La République de Seine-et-Marne*, 30/7/67.
[80] *Le Canard Enchaîné*, 13/4/64.
[81] Doriot's correspondence, letter to Giscard d'Estaing, 3/11/59.
[82] *HBS Bulletin*, September–October 1964.
[83] *The MBA*, April 1967.

Nevertheless among its growing number of followers, the school did count some key opinion leaders. For example, Insead had quickly won favour with the emerging breed of multinational companies as witnessed by the sponsorship of four professorial chairs as early as April 1962: Procter & Gamble for sales-marketing, Péchiney and Saint-Gobain jointly for production, IBM for quantitative techniques and McKinsey for business policy.

McKinsey's backing is particularly noteworthy in that it was both early and forceful. In May 1960, a letter from Ewing W. Reilley of McKinsey to Doriot asserted: "We want to help [Insead] in every way we can. This will include recommending to the other members of the McKinsey Foundation that the Foundation contribute to the support of the school ... Also we will be glad to participate in the work of any committee and to undertake to raise funds from our clients and other business friends."[84] By 1962, McKinsey was contributing more to Insead than to any other school, even in the US.[85]

Warren Cannon, president of the McKinsey Foundation, recalls his first meeting with Giscard d'Estaing which perhaps goes some way to explaining McKinsey's early involvement with an unknown school: "The school's main offices were then in one of the wings of the palace. The palace itself was a magnificent building, although at the time it had not yet been renovated. So the housing was regal, but the offices themselves were about as unimpressive as I could imagine. The floor was covered with an ancient rug of some sort that was in a state of advanced disrepair, and Giscard d'Estaing's telephone was one of those ancient models with a separate mouthpiece and ear piece – the sort you see in museums. What's more, the classes were in a former nunnery, the faculty was non-professional and they were offering a ten-month programme. But there were some people with real vision and imagination involved. Somehow I was impressed by their sheer audacity."

Equally encouraging was the recognition of IBM. Giscard d'Estaing had been invited as guest speaker at the IBM conference for the heads of European operations. After Giscard d'Estaing had described Insead to the 80 participants, Arthur Watson, president of IBM World Trade, asked them to "contribute 'whatever they could' to the development of Insead".[86] Watson went one step further in August 1960 when he agreed to head up the US advisory committee for Insead designed to promote the school and raise funds for it in the US.[87] Watson was succeeded at the head of this committee by such distinguished figures as Armory Houghton, former chairman of Corning Glass, Harold Blancke, chairman of Celanese, then Harold Geneen CEO of ITT in 1966. The British magazine, *The Statist* (3/9/65), applauded

---

[84] Doriot's correspondence, letter from Ewing W. Reilley, McKinsey, 9/5/60.
[85] Confidential report by Giscard d'Estaing, 14/12/62, p. 5.
[86] Reported by Giscard d'Estaing in a letter to Doriot, 7/12/59.
[87] Letter from Doriot to Giscard d'Estaing, 31/8/60.

the school's "vigorous policy of self-help", adding that this was "the first of a series of national committees to help guide Insead through its expansionist phase".[88]

This high level American interest in the school can be attributed to the fact that companies with multinational interests at that time were predominantly American: "In 1964 the US had 55 companies each with annual sales of one billion dollars or more. There were only eight such concerns in West Germany, six in the U.K. and one in France."[89] Only later, as the European companies started to expand operations beyond their own national borders did they begin to believe in the school and its 'products'.[90]

Besides the companies, the school's other 'clientele' were of course the students, and here the changing composition of the student intake was an important yardstick of the school's expanding reputation. For example, the presence of two American students in the first intake demonstrated that the school was already perceived to be offering something distinctive. The US being well endowed with centres of business learning, this was a first test of Insead's appeal in the most sophisticated and demanding of 'markets'.

On the other hand, the presence of only one Briton in the first intake, and just two in the third intake, was significant for other reasons. It betrayed a lingering view in Britain that business was not a real profession or at least not one that could be taught; coupled with widespread apathy regarding the idea of European integration. Numerous articles in the British press bemoaned the lack of interest on the part of either British students or industry. *Business* headlined: "No Britons Among Europe's Future Leaders?"[91]. *The Economist* went further concluding that: "The almost total lack of interest in INSEAD by British industry shows that Britain's failure goes wider than the Brussels debacle."[92]

If the prevailing climate in Britain had muted potential interest in the school, events elsewhere in the world had pushed other students to discover Insead sooner than might have been expected. For example there were refugee Czech and Hungarian students in each of the first three intakes. One of these was Georges Szanto (Class of '62) who, having graduated, went on to take over responsibility for the school library – and later changed his name to Sandeau. By adding a documentation service to the development of conventional library activities, he gave the library an external visibility it would not otherwise have enjoyed.[93] More surprisingly perhaps, under his

[88] *The Statist*, 3/9/65.
[89] *Financial Mail*, 29/7/66.
[90] In a letter to Doriot (3/3/63), Giscard d'Estaing outlines the geographical breakdown in donations to the school for 1962: 55% came from France, 40% from US and a mere 5% from the rest of Europe.
[91] Business, November 1961, 96–99.
[92] *The Economist*, 30/3/63.
[93] At the time, there was no research output to speak of, so the creation of a journal called '*Management Documentation*' was an important way of reinforcing Insead's image in academic circles.

management, the library regularly turned in a moderate profit by charging corporate subscribers for its various services.[94]

Other landmark arrivals include the first Indian and Pakistani students in 1962, the first central African student in 1963 and the first Japanese student in 1964. As Salvatore Teresi recalls: "I remember our first Japanese participant, Masaru Yoshimori, very well. He had been sent by his company. It was a great victory for us that they should send him over. When he arrived he came to my office to tell me that he had jaundice and was very worried about the time he would lose through illness. But he managed to catch up – and in the end, he finished towards the top of the class. He was quite unique."

By the time the school moved into the new buildings, the proportion of French students had dropped to 26 per cent and the spread of nationalities represented in the student body had risen from 14 to 24 – including 17 representatives (11 per cent) from Central and South America, Asia and the Middle East.

IGNITING THE GROWTH ENGINE

This launch phase of the school is characterised by a huge disparity between the school's pretensions and the resources at its disposal; between its public image – complete with impressive board,[95] palatial address, press coverage, high fees, oversubscribed places – and its actual workings. It is not a school which started out discretely and worked its way up. It began rather as a bluff upscale: the chassis of a Rolls-Royce with a two-horsepower engine.

Physical expansion was severely limited by financial constraints, but growth in reputation and visibility had more to do with resourcefulness than resources. The period 1959–1966 was marked by extensive and imaginative promotional activities – with lots of press activity, high visibility trips and conferences. Even seemingly mundane activities like the pre-Insead language course and the school's documentation service were astutely developed to increase visibility.

For seven years, and with financial pledges from companies rarely guaranteed for more than one year, Giscard d'Estaing and his team of part-timers managed to convey a sense of permanence and ambition – sustaining that illusion until the new premises were finally ready, a dramatic symbol of the school's progress and ambitions.

That they were able to pull it off is all the more surprising given that Insead was not held together by the types of glue that bind most business schools. There was no permanent faculty to ensure continuity, no university

---

[94] See *Seine-et-Marne Matin*, 27/4/65.

[95] Including Raoul de Vitry and Arnaud de Vogüé who had been instrumental in gaining business support for the school and who remained on the board throughout the 1960s.

hierarchy or government to provide backing or direction, no single culture or common language for easy complicity or to constitute a natural coalition. So what was the binding force? Perhaps, like the students, the faculty felt they were 'doing their bit' for Europe, or perhaps they simply valued the chance to have an impact on an emerging institution. Talking to pioneers such as Roger Godino, Peter Smith or Lee Remmers, it becomes clear that the school engenders a strong proprietary instinct among those associated with it. They see it standing for something, feel part owners of it and care intensely about what happens to it.

At the root of the school's rapidly acquired credibility, notably with firms, was its ability to deliver a reliable output – that is, graduates. This was the catalyst which brought recruiters to campus, attracted donations, boosted applications, drew faculty and triggered a virtuous circle. The quality of the output was largely a function of the admission system, which was distinctive and well adapted to the learning objective. Insead was unique in Europe in decentralising selection and interviewing candidates individually so as to assess their ability and motivation – based on "scholastic record, extra-curricular accomplishment, working record, and aptitude for leadership".[96] Such criteria and methods were closely aligned with those used by businesses.[97]

Of course, the best selection system in the world is no use unless suitable candidates can be attracted. Insead stimulated demand by offering a type of education for which there was a latent call and then boldly publicising its successes, citing stiff competition for places, high salary expectations and multiple job offers. Such details may have been considered slightly vulgar at the time, but Insead had neither a captive audience nor a university to advertise on its behalf.

The school was unusual in being well connected to big American corporations offering quick responsibilities and exotic careers to mobile managers. In addition, Insead clearly had a European vision which matched that of its students. Candidates were lured by the promise of prosperous careers as well as the educational content and European calling of the school – and the ability and quality of those students was confirmed by visiting professors from leading US schools who found them comparable to their own students.

For their part, the companies were less concerned with the learning dispensed. Many were simply buying an elaborate prospecting and selection system. By its capacity to gather in one place a group of bright, mobile,

---

[96] *France Actuelle*, 1/12/59, 3.
[97] It is worth reiterating that the students were often surprised by the selection procedure. As one student explained to a journalist at the time: "It can be pretty disconcerting, especially for us Europeans who are not accustomed to answering direct questions about ourselves, our personality, our character and so on." (*Travail et Méthodes*, June–July 1969).

multilingual graduates, including a growing number with work experience, the school was providing a unique service to international companies – irrespective of the knowledge imparted over the year. As *Newsweek* put it: "The institute's entrance requirements are so high that most firms would be quite happy to employ the students whether they attended the institute or not."[98]

That is unfair in that it suggests there was little substance. In fact, there was significant added value, but much of it did not emanate from the formal instruction. The students matured enormously as a result of the intense cross-cultural experience they underwent. Again this highlights the role of admissions as a competitive weapon: the idea that by bringing together the right mix of people – in terms of diversity, ability, international exposure – they would learn from each other. It was a type of learning which was not easily measurable, manifesting itself in faculties like adaptability and openness, rather than codifiable know-how. Yet that did not make it less real; nor less deliberate as an objective. As Giscard d'Estaing expressed it at the time, the approach was intended to foster "psychological flexibility, a state of mind which cannot be learned in textbooks but which is acquired via multiple and varied interaction".[99] The psychological development of the students was a stated learning goal from the outset[100] and explains why the study groups were organised to accentuate differences.

Clearly, it could all have fallen apart if the school had not also delivered in terms of formal business education – but that was not the decisive factor at the time, either for the students or the companies. Even with its defects, the teaching dispensed was still far better than the alternatives then available in Europe. Those pioneering professors, with their loose contractual affiliations to Insead, had the huge merit not to blow a good idea. And the rapidly increasing demand, both from candidates and recruiting firms, told them they were on the right track.

[98] *Newsweek*, 10/6/63.
[99] *Entreprise*, 28/4/62.
[100] As noted by Giscard d'Estaing in a 1962 speech: "This European training is accompanied by a psychological development which is not the least of the learning goals."

CHAPTER 4

Here to stay

"Now, here, you see, it takes all the running you can do, to keep in the same place. If you want to get somewhere else, you must run at least twice as fast." Lewis Carroll, *Through the Looking-Glass*, 1872.

STABILITY BECKONS

When Olivier Giscard d'Estaing had first mentioned his intention to move back into industry, the choice of a suitable successor had preoccupied Doriot considerably. Writing to Claude Janssen in August 1965, he remarked: "This problem of Insead is of very great importance, and if a good job is not done on it, you and I will regret it for many years to come. Insead is still so young that a poor selection might mean mediocrity or failure of the school."[1] The following month Doriot reiterated his point: "I am worried about Insead. This is an important turning point. The school is still quite young and needs very very good leadership."[2] It evoked the concern of a parent for a delicate child and underlined the frailty of the school at this juncture.

After long talks with Giscard d'Estaing, Janssen wrote back to Doriot telling him: "We think that at this stage of Insead's development, the school needs and can find someone with a solid experience. It is now in a phase which apparently requires an organiser rather than a promoter."[3] The small committee, headed by Jean Marcou, the chairman of Insead, eventually selected Philippe Dennis. A one time naval commander, Dennis had gone on to run L'Air Liquide's human relations department and then its Japanese subsidiary. Giscard d'Estaing had first met him in 1961 when trying to raise funds for the school and Dennis had been instrumental in securing the support of L'Air Liquide.

[1] Doriot's correspondence, letter to Claude Janssen, 12/8/65.
[2] Doriot's correspondence, letter to Claude Janssen, 2/9/65.
[3] Doriot's correspondence, letter from Claude Janssen, 18/5/65.

Though endorsed by Giscard d'Estaing, the choice of Dennis was not obvious in that he had no direct experience of business schools, as Doriot would have wished.[4] On the other hand, he did bring other potentially valuable attributes. As noted by Giscard d'Estaing, he was obviously enthusiastic about the challenge, he enjoyed travelling, and expressed himself comfortably in public – important qualities for the school's chief spokesperson.[5] Dennis was perfectly European, speaking French, English and German fluently and joking with journalists that he would be first in line for the European passport, whenever it came out.

He was also judged to be accommodating enough to handle the strong personalities – Roger Godino and Salvatore Teresi – who would be working with him.[6] Moreover, as a former director of human relations, he was expected to help instil a more professional approach to the administration of the school. The school looked set to enter a phase of what might be termed 'structuring and consolidation'.

That feeling was reinforced by the move onto the new campus, in June 1967. The elegant premises symbolised Insead's dramatic progress and projected "an aura of permanence and confidence".[7] Visitors to Insead's new campus were invariably impressed by the 'ultra-modern atmosphere' and the most advanced classrooms in Europe. Many of the learning principles developed over the previous seven years were now 'set in stone': there were large converging spaces in which people could interact randomly; there were also small circular crucibles whose brick walls did not reach up to the ceiling so that groups could work in isolation but with a constant hum of background activity; and there were state-of-the-art classrooms. Journalists enthused over the fact that classrooms had been designed to "encourage dialogue and interruptions over blackboard monologues".[8] They applauded the acoustics, the lighting, and the layout, right down to details like the winding blackboards. The classrooms even boasted ventilation systems!

Such a level of material comfort for students was unprecedented in Europe – and was in striking contrast with the dire conditions which prevailed in French universities. Back in the mid-1960s, Europe was still rebuilding its schools, roads and bridges and feverishly putting up high-rise blocks to house people. In France, it was the period of the housing crisis. Insead's new premises were almost brazen in such a context. Micheline Dehelly,[9] in charge of student admissions at the time, recalls that the new buildings made things a lot easier: "Receiving candidates at the old *Collège des Carmes* was hard

---

[4] The choice of Dennis was significant in that it was the first major decision on which Doriot was not consulted.
[5] Doriot's correspondence, letter from Olivier Giscard d'Estaing, 7/1/66.
[6] Doriot's correspondence, letter from Claude Janssen, 23/12/65.
[7] *International Management*, April 1968.
[8] *International Marketing*, March 1969.
[9] Micheline d'Arcangues then.

The Palace at Fontainebleau   *Georges Doriot*

Inauguration ceremony of Insead at Fontainebleau Palace on 9th October 1959: W. Posthumus Meyjes, Director General, G. Doriot, J. Marcou, Chairman of the Paris Chamber of Commerce and Industry (CCIP) and Chairman of the Board, J. Martin, Vice President of the CCIP and President of the Executive Committee

Inaugural speech of Georges Doriot in the Salle des Colonnes

Jean Marcou, Chairman of the Board, 1959–1969

Jean Martin, President of the Executive Committee at the Inauguration

Jean Marcou with Olivier Giscard d'Estaing, Director

Willem Posthumus Meyjes, Director General, 1960–1963

Students of the first intake

Guests and students in the Cour Ovale

Temporary entrance notice

Olivier Giscard d'Estaing, Director General, 1963–1966

Executive meeting: O. Giscard d'Estaing, W. Posthumus Meyjes, P. Silberer, C. Janssen

Opening ceremony of the first post-graduate programme

Entrance notice

Among the first lecturers: R. Morin, P. Silberer, A. Reiff, P. Smith, S. Teresi, O. Giscard d'Estaing, J. Miller, F. Allender, G. Sauvage

Faculty meeting: O. Giscard d'Estaing, S. Teresi, P. Silberer, G. Sauvage, P. Smith

Peter Smith, Finance Professor

Lectures at the Palace, 1960–1961 intake

Touring Europe (1961–1962 intake in Berlin)

1962 official visit of the US Ambassador in France; O. Giscard d'Estaing, J. Gavin, J. Martin, W. Posthumus Meyjes, G. Sauvage, in front of the Palace gates

Seminar co-directed by R. Godino and G. Steiner from UCLA/Stanford Research Institute, hosted by Prince Bernhard of the Netherlands and sponsored by McKinsey, represented by W. Cannon; among the French authorities, P. Lemoine, curator of the Fontainebleau Museum and P. Séramy, Fontainebleau Mayor, respectively on the right and on the left of the Prince

Roger Godino and Olivier Giscard d'Estaing during the 1964 opening ceremony at the Palace

Jean Marcou welcoming Paul-Henri Spaak, Secretary General of NATO

Speech by Etienne Hirsch, Chairman of Euratom, at the Collège des Carmes in Avon in November 1962

Official inauguration of the new buildings, on 23rd May 1967 with A. Bettencourt, Minister for Industry, J. Marcou, P. Dennis, Director General

Olivier Giscard d'Estaing alongside a model of the future buildings

O. Giscard d'Estaing, J. Marcou, M. Bokanowski, Minister for Industry, R. de Cidrac, official Palace Architect, for the laying of the first stone on 26th October 1965

Insead new campus entry

John Loudon, Chairman of the Board, 1969–1982

Main court of the new campus

*Philippe Dennis,
General Director,
1966–1974, with
Lee Remmers,
Finance Professor*

*Salvatore Teresi,
Marketing Professor,
later to become
Director of Cedep*

*First Stanford – Insead executive programme: R. Godino, P. Dennis,
E. de Rothschild, P. Bond, Associate Dean of Stanford*

Dean Berry,
Dean,
1971–1976

German Day,
Dean Berry and
Ambassador von
Braun

Spyros Makridakis, Operational
Research Professor

Dominique Héau, Business Policy Professor

Pierre Cailliau, Director General, 1974–1982

1977 visit of the Ambassadors of the Philippines, Malaysia, Indonesia, Singapore and Thailand to prepare a seminar for the South-East Asian Countries Association with Henri-Claude de Bettignies

Guy de Carmoy, European Environment for Business Professor, with 1978 students Jean Mallebay-Vacqueur and Will Hutton

Uwe Kitzinger,
Dean, 1976–80

With Roy Jenkins, President of the Commission of
European Communities, and Pierre Cailliau for the
opening of the Residences in September 1979

With Giovanni
Agnelli, President
of Fiat, Guest of
Honour at the
MBA opening
ceremony in
September 1976

André Laurent,
Organisational
Behaviour Professor

*UK Alumni Group Annual
Dinner, in November 1979 in
London : The Guest of Honour
is John Freeman, Chairman of
London Weekend Television:
D. Berry, D. Montagu,
Chairman of Orion Bank and
Chairman of the UK Friends of
Insead, P. Cailliau, J. Freeman,
U. Kitzinger, and Lord
Armstrong, Chairman of
Midland Bank*

*December 1978 Development meeting in New-York : Robert McNamara,
President of the World Bank, John Loudon and Phil Caldwell, President of
Ford*

*R. McNamara, J. Loudon, G. Doriot, P. Caldwell, P. Cailliau, W. Cannon,
Director of McKinsey, at the same occasion*

Heinz Thanheiser,
Dean, 1980–1982

G. de Carmoy, C. and A. Rameau, D. Héau, J. Story, European Environment
for Business Professor

First scholarship
recipients admitted to
the MBA programme
in September 1980,
following the
campaign launched
by Uwe Kitzinger to
increase the number
of women in the
programme:
D. Ponter, F. de
Mulder, A. Fowler,
A. de Wilde,
J. Tyrrell, C. Blondel

Patrice Triaureau, Finance and Administration Director, John Loudon

Gareth Dyas, Strategy Professor, Heinz Thanheiser

P. Cailliau, C. Janssen, J. Loudon, H. Thanheiser, C. Rameau during the ceremony of departure of Pierre Cailliau

going. Candidates arrived in a courtyard and the first thing they saw were the kitchens. In the new buildings, it was plain sailing."

With the change of premises and the recent arrival of a former naval officer as director-general, the school seemed to be heading for a period of increased control and more sedate development. Indeed, one could reasonably expect a certain complacency to set in after several years of struggling for survival. Surprisingly, this did not happen.

THE LIGHT BRIGADE

One of Dennis' priorities, coming into the job, was to secure a core of "home-grown professors to chair each of the seven basic courses".[10] In early 1967, Dennis and Godino sensed that the prevailing "free-swinging system", with only two full-time professors, was "running into trouble now that the total student body is around 140".[11] The problem was that the school could not afford to wait until its own doctoral students returned from Harvard – and in any case, they might not, or else they might do so only briefly.

Insead faced serious obstacles in its aim to recruit high-quality, full-time faculty. Some of these obstacles stemmed from the school's geographical and academic isolation, but there were other deeper problems. The school could not offer tenure, nor even proper contracts – budget uncertainties meant that the school could only propose one year contracts. Nor could the school offer academic prestige, association with distinguished business school professors, active research programmes, high salaries or remunerative consulting opportunities. Finding professors would not be easy and, given the prevailing terms and conditions, those attracted were unlikely to be mainstream academics.

A surprise first catch was a Briton, David Hall. Godino had met Hall when both had been invited to teach at the new management school in Cape Town in the summer of 1966. He subsequently invited Hall to come to Insead for a year. Hall, a Harvard DBA, had some qualms about coming to an unknown school, where the research possibilities would be severely limited, and he would be the only full-timer with a doctorate. But he was swayed by the international aspect of the school – and the fact that he would be a full professor which was two rungs up from his current position in Canada.

Claude Rameau's recruitment was even more haphazard. He was attending a cocktail party for alumni[12] while working as a consultant in early 1967. Roger Godino sounded him out in a typically roundabout style, asking him if he knew 'anyone' who might be interested in teaching managerial

[10] *International Management*, March 1967.
[11] *International Management*, March 1967.
[12] Claude Rameau was a graduate of the class of '62.

economics at Insead. Godino was increasingly occupied by his ski resort project at Les Arcs[13] and was trying to reduce his teaching load. Rameau did not react immediately, but on reflection thought that it might not be such a bad idea. As Rameau recalls: "I thought to myself, I'll give it a try for a year. Plus at Insead there are lots of useful corporate contacts, so it might help me to find a different job. I was just married and wanted to do a bit less travelling." When he went over to Dennis' house to discuss conditions, the only sticking point was the salary. As a consultant, Rameau was earning twice what was on offer to an assistant professor. They eventually found a compromise whereby Rameau actually took on two posts simultaneously: apart from his teaching work, he would also develop cases, though the output would not be measured. As with the lightning 'promotion' of Hall, it would be fair to say there was a certain flexibility in the recruitment procedures.

A similar pattern later followed with the appointment of Henri-Claude de Bettignies. Again, there was no formal application or interview process. De Bettignies was returning to France after five years of research and lecturing in Japan. The two men had previously met at a conference while Dennis had been head of L'Air Liquide's Japanese subsidiary. They had kept in touch as a result of a shared interest in human resource issues and Japan. In this respect, Dennis did offer the school an extra-European dimension which, for once, did not emanate from the US. His openness towards the Far East – the legacies of which are evident today – was highly unusual at the time.

A number of former Insead graduates were also co-opted into the permanent core, notably Lee Remmers (Class of '62), who had essentially never left, Jean-Pierre Schmitt (Class of '65), Joe Bissada (Class of '65) and Dominique Hellé (Class of '68) – adding to the core of pioneers which included Guy de Carmoy, Gilbert Sauvage, Gerhard Dahlke and Peter Smith. Faculty members were officially encouraged to devote one quarter of their time to freelance consulting activities, partly to stay close to business realities, but also to give them a competitive salary.

This gradual build-up of full-time professors, which included some visiting professors on sabbatical, had several repercussions. For a start, it provoked questions about the curriculum. With Teresi, a marketing professor, as programme director, the weight of marketing had tended to grow unchecked. Now there was a counterweight, including Hall in organisational behaviour, creating a certain pressure to rebalance the disciplines. After some discussions, this culminated in a redesign of the curriculum.

The full-time presence of professors also changed relations with the

---

[13] Godino's Les Arc initiative has an interesting association with Insead. The idea was matured with the help of Insead successive intakes of students who studied various aspects of this hypothetical venture. When Godino finally launched the resort, he took on several former students as managers, and the story became a very successful case study, written by Gareth Dyas, and used on the entrepreneurship course.

students, both formally and informally. For example, group work and class participation had been key aspects of the learning process from the outset. But now, it became possible to accord these official recognition in the student grading system.[14] In more general terms, it became easier for professors to monitor the progress of individual students – and to keep in touch with the student body via the introduction of section leaders.

In informal terms, the nature of the relationship between professors and students was modified by the recruitment of a group of young professors, several of them former alumni, who were very close in age to the students. That changing relationship was discernible in the annual cabaret and, more particularly, in the creation, in 1969, of a student magazine called *Play Boss* In it, the professors were caricatured and affectionately lampooned. As noted by Dennis at the end of the academic year: "It occasionally required a philosophic distance to swallow the sarcastic comments aimed at some of us."[15] But these barbs were actually signs of an increasing complicity.

The constitution of a permanent faculty triggered something else too. It helped spread the burden of responsibility for generating revenues. Until then, this had been the unenviable task of the director general and occasionally the director. The part-time professors were not so acutely concerned by the tenuous existence of the school. They all had other jobs to fall back on. The new professors did not; and they knew that their job security relied in part on their own efforts to help generate revenues. It was their problem too. Professors could not elicit donations from companies, but they could organise courses for practising managers – and it seemed that the demand existed.

GETTING DOWN TO BUSINESS

Short courses designed to update the knowledge of alumni had been planned from the start as an integral part of Insead's mission – a kind of after sales service to recruiting firms. However, lack of space and resources had meant the idea had to be deferred. Now, in the new premises, space was no longer a constraint, especially over the summer months. This opened up the possibility of on-campus seminars, not just for former students, but open to all managers. The only problem was that the school did not have sufficient faculty or prior experience in developing and running such courses. In this new domain, it lacked credibility.

What the school did have, in the shape of Roger Godino and Salvatore Teresi, were two tireless entrepreneurs. In the summer of 1967, Teresi linked up with the British Marketing Council, with its 'captive' membership, to

[14] See *Cahiers de l'Association Nationale des Docteurs en Droit*, October-December 1968.
[15] Philippe Dennis, preface to the Year Book, 1970.

provide a three-week course in international marketing for 40 managers. The following summer, Godino achieved a long-standing objective, setting up an Advanced Management Programme in partnership with Stanford University. A total of 75 senior executives attended the four-week course.

Philippe Dennis' prior experience in corporate human resources made him particularly receptive to these initiatives. He had little difficulty taking a 'customer perspective'. Indeed, at the time of his recruitment he had expressed his desire to add middle and top management programmes to Insead's development activities.[16] Dennis was also in favour of anything which eased the school's financial burden.

These courses helped to create a climate in which such initiatives from professors were not simply accepted, but expected. In the summer of 1969, Henri-Claude de Bettignies launched a two-week course on 'The Managerial Challenge of International Business' in conjunction with colleagues from Harvard and MIT. In early 1970, Claude Rameau helped set up an ambitious nine-week 'International Executive Development Programme' targeting middle managers in association with Columbia. Even those who seemed less entrepreneurially inclined, like David Hall and Lee Remmers, got drawn in: Hall organised a 10-day course entitled 'Effective Executive Leadership' using T-group methods; while Remmers, together with a Stanford colleague, ran a week-long course focusing on the 'Financial Management of Multinational Companies'.

The school had initially been launched to target postgraduate students requiring a business complement to their education. But it had quickly become apparent that, in contrast to the US, the larger educational need in Europe lay in the post-experience market. The school was well placed to spot and respond to these needs; its international character corresponded more closely to the emerging realities of business; and it set Insead on a different strategic course from its US counterparts.

This rapid introduction of executive programmes would not have been possible without outside help. The school became very good at leveraging its network of international contacts. From a US perspective, Insead was not especially credible, but the US schools were keen to 'internationalise' and there was not an abundance of suitable partners on the European scene. Certainly, Insead had no 'big name' professors to put alongside the seasoned professionals from Harvard, Stanford or MIT. But Insead could offer international expertise and it traded hard on this commodity to pull in partners for its various programmes.

For Insead, the association with foreign institutions and academics yielded numerous benefits. The credibility of the specific courses was boosted by having US professors on the billing. In terms of institutional image too, the

---

[16] Doriot's correspondence, letter from Olivier Giscard d'Estaing, 7/1/66.

ability to entice prestigious partners – particularly the Stanford 'joint-venture' – confirmed Insead's growing reputation: a school defines itself by the company it keeps. But the participation of US professors also achieved something more substantial. It helped accelerate the school's apprenticeship in executive education.

Teaching experienced managers is best learnt by doing – and without their international colleagues, the Insead professors would not have had the chance to try, at least not at such a demanding level. But equally important was the possibility for Insead professors to observe their international colleagues up close for a sustained period: to see what they taught and how they taught it, and to gain insights into programme design. The initial differences in teaching scores – the Insead professors averaging 2.5 out of 5 versus 4.5 for the Stanford professors – underlined the difference in experience. But within a few years the gap was closed – and once acquired, this know-how spread rapidly across Insead's small faculty, facilitated by the fact that they taught on each other's programmes and that they were in constant contact, not spread over a large campus. It made for a relatively painless ride along the executive education learning curve.

The professors were not the only ones taking initiatives. Under the guidance of Georges Sandeau, and with the blessing of Philippe Dennis, Insead's library was going from strength to strength. By 1968, it possessed the richest European collection of books on management: 8,500 in all![17] More significantly, Sandeau had built up the documentation centre into an outstanding facility, which had the added merit of generating income – and which threatened to upstage even the executive development initiatives in terms of press coverage. The centre continued to publish *Management Documentation*, distributed to thousands of corporate subscribers and described by the *Financial Times* as "a useful fortnightly digest of selected business articles which have appeared in specialised journals".[18] In January 1968, the centre installed a brand new data retrieval system which allowed rapid access to documents. The centre was considered so advanced that it even laid on its own specialist training courses for business documentalists.

Not to be outdone, Dusan Radivojevic, who organised the intensive language seminars in Berlin for students needing to brush up on their German, had also branched out. In 1969, in response to demand from firms, he organised an annual two-week language-cum-business briefing in Germany for senior executives with an interest in the country. The aim here is not to exaggerate the scale of such initiatives, but to show that everyone was 'in on the act', trying to propose services or to respond to the needs of business. The emerging culture encouraged such activities.

[17] Noted in *Spectacle du Monde*, January 1969. For the sake of comparison, it is worth mentioning that the management library at Columbia had amassed 200,000 volumes (*Le Monde*, 24/12/67).
[18] *Financial Times*, 13/6/67.

Insead's visibility was further helped by its publishing efforts which, though modest faced little competition in Europe. For example, the school developed a series of programme texts written in French by the faculty and sent out to participants before they arrived. The series, entitled 'Insead Management',[19] was launched by Guy de Carmoy and Claude Rameau. In the late 1960s, French books on management were pretty rare, so the simple texts sold well, finding an eager audience beyond the incoming students.

Similarly, Henri Dougier's journal, *European Business*, re-launched in 1967 under the Insead banner, won some unexpected plaudits, receiving the McKinsey award in 1968. *Harvard Business Review* and *California Management Review* were the only previous recipients of the award.[20] As Warren Cannon observed soon after: "Insead has been unusually fortunate with the Review. It has attained a recognition that sponsors of several older and far better financed journals must surely envy. It may well have pre-empted a position in European management literature that almost certainly would have gone to some other graduate business school in the United Kingdom or on the Continent."[21] Again, Insead was pushing out in various directions – and some of the bets were paying off.

For Insead, the late 1960s emerged as a period of opportunity exploration which spilled over beyond faculty circles. There was a strong entrepreneurial drive. As Claude Rameau recalls, the prevailing ethos was very much one of '*pourquoi pas?*' (why not?) – an amusingly negative formulation of what the Americans would call 'can-do'. The school was not encumbered by strong scholarly pretensions so it could more easily respond to unmet organisational needs. Few opportunities were ruled out 'on principle'. This gave the school flexibility and made it different from other academic institutions which remained impervious to evolving business trends.

RISING TO THE CHALLENGE

Insead was not evolving in a vacuum. There were numerous external influences – both opportunities and threats – driving its development. Perhaps the most talked about of these influences was what Jean-Jacques Servan-Schreiber described as the 'American Challenge'.[22] Until the publication of his widely acclaimed book, the success of American corporations in Europe was often attributed to superior technology and financial muscle, both stemming from greater wealth of natural resources. While acknowledging these 'auxiliary' factors, Servan-Schreiber proposed a more uncomfortable explanation: "The American challenge is not basically

[19] The publisher was *Editions d'Organisation*.
[20] Letter from Philippe Dennis to Edmond de Rothschild, 17/9/68.
[21] W. Cannon, "Planning the Future of Insead", internal report, May 1968.
[22] J.-J. Servan-Schreiber, *Le Défi Americain* (Paris: De Noël) 1967.

industrial or financial .... It involves our capacity for organization: the ability to work under different conditions, to take advantage of an enormous market, to know how to make profit from it and adapt to its needs. Europe's lag seems to concern *methods of organization* above all."[23]

This argument aroused a momentous debate on the relative weight of the 'management gap' versus the 'technology gap' – and provided a tremendous fillip for the cause of business education. Alongside this critical change in perceptions, there were also more concrete changes afoot which further boosted the demand for management development. In the mid-1960s, European firms were fast moving away from functionally centralised structures towards divisional structures. This had important repercussions on managerial competencies: "The need for generalist skills, previously required only of the top managements of functionally specialised structures, is multiplied as new positions, such as group manager and division managers, are created."[24] And below that, positions like product and brand managers were appearing. Managers at many levels were therefore in need of training to develop new skills. So this was good news for Insead.

Less good news, was the fact that competition was hotting up. A decade after its founding, Insead faced a tougher academic environment, one in which its competitive advantage was eroding. Some of the business schools in the US were starting to internationalise, both in terms of course content and in terms of student body. For instance, by 1967, the proportion of foreigners in Columbia's intake was up to 15 per cent.[25] More worrying though, was the increasing competition in Europe. In addition to the Swiss-based schools, IMEDE and CEI, there was IESE (in Barcelona), and two major graduate business schools newly established in Manchester and London which had "impressive full-time faculties, international student bodies, although predominantly English, and a strong European orientation in the curriculum".[26]

Another threat to Insead's distinctive appeal lay in the depressing reality of European construction. Progress towards economic union was painstakingly slow, and there was still considerable resistance to strong political unity. So, while persisting with the three language entry requirement, one also sensed a subtle broadening of emphasis in pronouncements regarding the school's mission. In Autumn 1968, Philippe Dennis noted that: "Insead now has much more of an international vocation than a strictly European one."[27] The following summer, Dennis wrote: "Faithful to its international vocation, with a European focus, Insead is

[23] J.-J. Servan-Schreiber, *The American Challenge* (US edition) 1969, 168.
[24] G. Dyas, and H. Thanheiser, *The Emerging European Enterprise* (London: Macmillan) 1976, 318.
[25] *Le Monde*, 24/12/67.
[26] Warren Cannon, 'Planning the future of Insead', Internal Report, May 1968.
[27] Internal report by Philippe Dennis, no title, October 1968.

confident of bringing a modest but essential contribution to the construction of a unified global economy."[28] While remaining strongly rooted in Europe, Insead was keeping its options open.

STUDENT MOVEMENT

In the late 1960s, Insead's student body and student expectations were evolving in various ways. Perhaps the most significant change in the student body was the arrival of women on campus in 1967. When they applied for admission, Hélène Ploix and Marie-Solange Perret were kept waiting "the board not having decided yet on female candidates".[29] Following a board resolution in February 1967, both women were offered places.[30]

The following year, Philippe Dennis proudly announced: "We are not closed to any nationality, gender, colour or religion. Openness to gender is very recent. Our predecessors were not much inclined to introduce women to Insead; at the end of a long battle, and for the first time last year, we took in two women, who not only succeeded well, finishing up near the top of the class, but who also went on to find very interesting positions."[31] In another interview he explained that: "Women used not to be admitted to the institute, the top management considering that they represented an 'unprofitable investment', either because they might have difficulty finding a position on graduating, or else because they might leave the company quickly to start a family."[32]

For these "business school suffragettes" as Claire Guédron[33] (Class of '69) dubbed this generation of women, there were few concessions. Insead was not a particularly comfortable place to study. Gender, like nationality or training, was 'just another' differentiating factor which could be put to use in composing heterogeneous work groups. So it was that the four women in the 1968 intake were placed not just in separate work groups, but in four separate sections.

While the women's movement may have had an indirect impact on the school, the student revolts of May 1968 had virtually none at all – other than making it difficult for visiting professors to make their way down from Paris and panicking the foreign students when they saw the tanks rolling past the school towards Paris. Some were afraid they would be caught up in a revolution and a Danish student even moved his whole family back to Copenhagen. Philippe Dennis reassured them by telling them that they were

[28] *Travail et Methodes*, June–July 1969.
[29] Letter to Hélène Ploix from F.P. Staddon, Admissions Office, 3/1/67.
[30] It was not exactly a mass entry, but proportionately, this was said to be comparable to the number of women admitted to HBS (*Spectacle du Monde*, January 1969).
[31] *Cahiers de l'Association Nationale des Docteurs en Droit*, October-December 1968.
[32] *Spectacle du Monde*, January 1969.
[33] Cited in *Vision*, February 1971. Claire Guédron became Claire Pike and, in 1978, rejoined Insead.

free to leave when they wanted, at no penalty to themselves, and to return when things had calmed down.

The riots, which eventually mobilised nearly half of France's working population, were motivated by an amalgam of grievances relating to censorship, discrimination and centralisation. But if we consider the specific demands of the French students down in the streets one can probably understand why they left Insead students unmoved. The chief complaints were about overcrowded classrooms, old fashioned teaching methods and the fact that they were not listened to. At Insead, the quality of the facilities, the interactive nature of the instruction and the existence of section representatives pre-empted such complaints. There were not even any graffiti on the walls to suggest latent resentment.[34]

This period saw another important example of Insead students being 'untouched' by outside events. It concerned the Arab-Israeli conflict in 1967. As later reported by the *Financial Times*: "During the Six Day War the Arab and Israeli participants got together and organised a dinner followed by films of life on each side on which the other side commented."[35] Young institutions need their myths and this demonstration of international tolerance quickly passed into the Insead folklore.

While the students remained tolerant towards one another, they were growing increasingly demanding towards the school. Partly this was because the school was becoming more demanding of them, accumulating entry barriers: the three-language requirement was maintained although the German content of the curriculum was fast disappearing;[36] the need for prior work experience was reinforced;[37] for those concerned, it had become obligatory to have completed military service; and the Princeton test was introduced.[38] In spite of continually raising the selection bar, the intakes continued to grow rapidly.[39]

All this tended to push up the average age of the students as well as their expectations. Older students, who had already embarked on careers, together with better qualified students who had perhaps turned down places at good US schools, were more acutely aware of the opportunity cost of attending Insead. The school itself was now a respected institution so it had fewer

---

[34] The events of May 1968 did have one practical consequence on Insead students: end-of-year graduation trips were increasingly ambitious affairs, and the planned trip to New York had to be re-routed via a military airport as the civilian airports were all blocked by strikes and petrol shortages.

[35] *Financial Times*, 8/5/70.

[36] See letter from Philippe Dennis to Dusan Radivojevic (20/7/70) explaining that: "There is little chance of any German case discussions in the coming year."

[37] Between 1965 and 1970, the proportion of students with at least 9 months of work experience grew from 20 per cent to 60 per cent. *International Management*, May 1971.

[38] Officially known as Admission Test for Graduate Study in Business, and better known today as the GMAT. This additional requirement reduced the number of applications from 568 for the 1969 intake to 509 for 1970.

[39] Between the 1966 intake and the 1970 intake, enrolments had gone from 139 to 224.

excuses. When members of the administrative services had known the students individually, problems with the administration had been easier to sort out. Lapses, on both sides, which might have been forgivable in the cosy atmosphere of the *Collège des Carmes*, seemed less forgivable in this less personal context. Inevitably, the student culture was changing. Back in the early years, the students had felt like builders of an institution. With the new premises and the growing numbers, this sense of participation in an adventure was eroding. Now they came more as consumers as evidenced by the content of their application forms (1969 intake):

> *Rolf Abdon*: "I believe firmly that Insead will give me a better international outlook and considerably improve the possibilities of being useful in the administration of an international business."

> *Jean Andersen*: "To get into top management, an engineer needs generalist training; an understanding of social, legal and financial issues, as well as technical ones. Such training is required by more and more large European companies."

> *Alfred Baillet*: "Insead's training will improve my chances of success by providing me with a tool that very few possess."

Another factor in the changing outlook of students was the intensified demand from recruiters which even outstripped the growth in the student body.[40] By 1970, there were almost more companies (203) than graduating students (206). Moreover, each company had several jobs on offer and some of the students were already 'spoken for' in that they were returning to family or sponsoring firms. As one journalist put it in May 1970: "This year I was told that about ten times as many interviews had been arranged as there were participants. There seemed no doubt, in the minds of the latter at least, about who was really interviewing whom."[41]

AT THE CROSSROADS

In the autumn of 1968, by most visible indicators, Insead was progressing well. It had an expanding student body; it was steadily building up its permanent faculty (now up to 12); and it was multiplying the number and scope of its courses for senior and middle managers. It was also growing increasingly self sufficient. As Philippe Dennis put it: "The Paris Chamber of Commerce has reduced its absolute contribution, and even greater its relative contribution, to the running of the school since the business community

[40] Between 1967 and 1970, the number of recruiting firms visiting the campus more than doubled (93 to 203). In the same period, the number of graduating students went from 134 to 206.
[41] *Financial Times*, 8/5/70.

took up the relay."[42] For all these signs of health, there was a growing sense of unease from some quarters.

In May 1968, Warren Cannon had written an internal report entitled 'Planning the future of Insead'. The report raised several questions about the future of the school: should it continue as a single independent entity or should it seek institutional relationships with other European schools, formal affiliation with a European university, or the patronage of a multinational organisation such as OECD? Also, should its programmes be directed towards or away from the special interests of large multinationals? And should it expand significantly into post-experience education or should this remain a marginal activity in relation to the postgraduate programme?

The report drew particular attention to the school's lack of long-term planning on various fronts. For example, an active research programme had been one of the school's major objectives from its inception – the aim being to "contribute to the economy of Europe, improve the quality of instruction, attract outstanding students and scholars, and enhance the status of the Institute", yet such a research programme "remains a still-distant goal".

Similarly, the number of permanent professors was becoming respectable but they were still somewhat lacking in terms of "maturity, distinction, and fields of specialization". The school's scheme of sending former students to the US for doctoral training could "not possibly yield a mature and distinguished faculty short of many years". Given that the professors were a critical determinant of future effectiveness and considering the lead times involved in developing such a faculty, the need for long-range planning was "nowhere more apparent and urgent" than in this domain.

Finally, in terms of organisation and administration, the school's structure still reflected "the needs and possibilities of a young, experimental, marginally financed institution". Through its various councils and committees, the school continued to rely on the "unpaid services of many interested and highly qualified individuals" whose "activities extend deeply into the day-to-day operation of the Institute". This relatively elaborate support structure was necessary to compensate for the school's inability "to support the full-scale administrative apparatus one might expect to find in a graduate school of this size". The dedication of the likes of Micheline Dehelly, Gerrit Kohler, Dusan Radivojevic or Jacqueline Tourlier-Pope could not make up for the inadequacy of resources at their disposal.

Underpinning all these shortcomings was a common financial denominator. Unless the school could dramatically increase its income, it could not hope to engage in meaningful development on any of these fronts. The report urged the school make a careful assessment of its real needs, however large, and to project seven to ten years into the future.

[42] *Cahiers de l'Association Nationale des Docteurs en Droit*, October-December 1968.

Warren Cannon was not the only one sounding warning bells. John Loudon, former chairman of Royal Dutch Shell, who had been enticed onto the board by Philippe Dennis, in June 1967, also voiced his concerns in private meetings with Dennis and Cannon. After a long meeting with John Loudon in October 1968, Dennis wrote to chairman of the board, Jean Marcou, to convey Loudon's thoughts. Loudon felt that the school could pursue one of two routes: "Either we continue on the financial front to painstakingly eke out small sums of money – which would allow Insead to struggle along – or else we look for 'big money' which would allow Insead to become the best business school in Europe." Loudon also felt that "too many of those on the list of board members are unfortunately too often, just names on a list".[43]

Loudon's proposed solution was an 'executive committee', comprising four or five high calibre people with a genuine commitment to Insead.[44] Doriot, who was still very much in touch with developments at the school, sensed that this might be too few: "If two or three of them are sick or cannot attend a meeting because of bad weather, you are not going to have many meetings."[45] Doriot thought that a nucleus of 8 to 12 people would be more appropriate.[46]

Loudon also considered that if the school wanted to approach people for money, they would have to know what the Institute planned to become in the future, and that implied "an urgent need for a long term plan".[47] Like Doriot, Loudon was adamant that "Insead is at a crossroads".[48] It echoed Warren Cannon's earlier conclusion in his confidential report: "What the directors of the Institute do today will greatly affect what they can, and cannot, do in the years ahead."[49]

It is significant that most of this 'forward thinking' was done by people outside the school, notably Cannon, Loudon and Doriot. It shows to what extent even oversolicited people were drawn by the originality of the school. It also suggests that those on the inside were fully occupied trying to make ends meet on a daily basis.

There seemed to be general agreement that in order to make a significant move forward in terms of size, prestige or excellence the school would need to plan ahead. The question was how without more income? As Dennis lamented in November 1968: "Right now, I cannot see how we will manage

[43] Letter from Philippe Dennis to Jean Marcou, 10/10/68.
[44] Letter from Philippe Dennis to Georges Doriot, 9/10/68.
[45] Letter from Georges Doriot to Philippe Dennis, 17/10/68.
[46] Doriot's abiding influence was visible in other ways too. He orchestrated reciprocal arrangement between Insead and Harvard whereby Lawrence Fouraker, dean of HBS, sat on Insead's board between 1970–77, while Claude Janssen was invited to sit on HBS's visiting committee from 1972–1978.
[47] Reported in a letter from Philippe Dennis to Warren Cannon, 10/10/68.
[48] See letter from Philippe Dennis to Georges Doriot, 9/10/68.
[49] Warren Cannon, 'Planning the future of Insead', Internal Report, May 1968.

within five years to increase our income so as to meet our needs. Thanks to a massive fund-raising effort, we managed to double our revenues between 1965/66 and 1968/69. But one senses a certain exhaustion on the part of the European companies. Tuition fees can not go up much; they were raised 30% just this year. The alumni are still too few and too young to bring an important contribution. Benefits from the special programmes are helpful but only represent a tiny fraction of the needs. I am wracking my brains to see how to get out of this situation."[50]

Dennis' response consisted essentially of trying to get the European countries which benefited the most from the school to pull their weight financially. Germany was the foremost culprit. Its contributions represented around a fifth of the tuition costs incurred by the German students. Dennis wrote to influential German figures urging them to remedy the situation. For example, in September 1968, he wrote to the Paris representative of the *Bundes Deutsche Industrie*: "We have 43 German participants this year ... which is almost the size of the French contingent. Once again this raises the issue of German contributions to Insead."[51] In a report, the following month, Dennis commented on this imbalance: "Unless we find a way of reversing the position, Insead is condemned to struggle along, and will be prevented from becoming a great institute."[52]

Other than trying to exert moral pressure on countries or individual companies which took out far more than they put in, the school seemed unsure how to proceed. Yet, a solution was at hand. Almost unconsciously, the school had developed a listening capacity, a degree of flexibility and responsiveness which distinguished it from all of its rivals. And as the saying goes, luck favours the well prepared.

INDECENT PROPOSAL

The idea of a possible collaboration between Insead and a group of companies led by L'Oréal, the French cosmetics company, first surfaced in late 1968. Philippe Dennis was invited to lunch by François Dalle and Guy Landon, respectively president and vice president of L'Oréal. The company had been an early supporter of the school, regularly taking on its graduates and even sponsoring a marketing chair since 1966. Over lunch, Dalle evoked the considerable problem L'Oréal faced with its management development. Sending managers to the US for development was costly and therefore viable only for small numbers of senior executives.

What L'Oréal really needed was to develop managers in large numbers so as to help the company internationalise rapidly. Having found no European

---

[50] Letter from Philippe Dennis to Georges Doriot, 20/11/68.
[51] Letter from Philippe Dennis to Dr. F. Riedberg, 18/9/68.
[52] P. Dennis, Internal report, October 1968, 2.

organisation capable of meeting their needs, they were turning to Insead for assistance. The numbers concerned were too large for Insead's existing executive development courses to handle, so a new solution would be needed. A further meeting was arranged for 19 December 1968, where Guy Landon, whose initiative it was, made a more detailed presentation, this time with Salvatore Teresi present.[53]

Landon described the three ambitious objectives of the speculative development programme. The goal was to change attitudes, to acquaint managers with advanced management techniques and to improve human relations – it was perhaps a tall order for the proposed duration of two 15-day sessions. Landon envisaged a first wave of some 80 senior executives, half of them French, and then a second wave of around 300 middle managers. Landon urged Dalle to approach two or three like-minded French company heads, notably Antoine Riboud (BSN) and Renaud Gillet (Rhone-Progil), to join L'Oréal in this initiative. The idea was not just to share the financial burden. It was also to avoid the kind of in-breeding sensed by Landon when visiting the management training facilities of certain multinationals.

While enthusiastic about the project, Dennis immediately sensed a potential problem. An all-French consortium would clash with Insead's international image. In particular, it might vex dedicated international supporters like John Loudon, Warren Cannon or Robert Hankey. Dennis immediately pressed Landon to contact Swiss, Belgian or Italian companies to participate in the consortium, with a view to starting up an English-speaking programme later. Whatever objections the board might raise, Dennis felt confident that it would view favourably the "contribution to material facilities (amphitheatres, library and so on) which would surely accompany this initiative". He also considered that the risk to Insead's image would be slight "provided the initiative is not fully integrated into the Insead programmes". It would probably be "a management development centre with its own budget, but using our professors and instructional resources."[54]

It is a testament to Insead's independence, ambition and lack of 'academic complexes' that the idea was even entertained. The educational sector at the time was notoriously unresponsive to requests from the business community. Co-operation was tantamount to 'selling out'. While Dennis was clearly attracted by the financial aspect of the proposal, he could also see that it would make a difference to the school in terms of scale and visibility. Writing to Warren Cannon soon after, he noted: "It would allow me to have a much bigger faculty, do some research, have a larger library, and so on."[55]

Since money seemed to be no object, logistical difficulties such as classrooms, meeting rooms, and residential accommodation could easily be

[53] Memo from Philippe Dennis to Jean Marcou, 19/12/68.
[54] Memo from Philippe Dennis to Jean Marcou, 19/12/68.
[55] Letter from Philippe Dennis to Warren Cannon, 29/1/69.

resolved. The main problem would be finding suitable professors and designing a programme. In the weeks that followed Salvatore Teresi worked hard, in conjunction with Landon, to refine the concept. One obvious difficulty, for example, was the proposed duration of the training. It was too short to achieve any lasting change, yet L'Oréal could not afford to 'lose' key managers for lengthy periods, especially in large numbers.

Already by February 1969, when Dennis re-contacted Jean Marcou, the project had evolved somewhat.[56] A Swiss and a Belgian firm had agreed to join the quartet of French firms to establish the *Centre Européen d'Education Permanente* (Cedep).[57] By this stage, it had become clear that the likely throughput warranted the construction of purpose-built facilities and the Fontainebleau municipality confirmed that three hectares of land on the edge of the existing campus would be available for purchase.[58] Moreover, the proposed training period had multiplied eightfold, with executives now spending a total of 16 weeks in training, spread over more than two years.[59] This idea of eight residential periods at three-month intervals was critical. At a practical level, two-week absences were considered less disruptive to a manager's job than a prolonged absence of three months. From a learning perspective, the 'sandwich' structure would allow the executives to reflect on and try out ideas between training periods.

So the proposal was presented to the faculty. Their reactions were fairly negative. David Hall, as chief crusader for Insead's academic respectability, considered that the initiative would lead the school astray. As he saw it, this project was different from the existing executive courses in that the school would be explicitly working for particular companies. Whereas individual executives were fairly powerless, companies could exert considerable pressure on the school. Thus, professors would be forced to relinquish their academic freedom and become 'mercenaries'. Hall was right, there would be additional constraints; but there would also be additional opportunities. The learning would not all be one-way. In fact, one of the main arguments for accepting the proposal was that it would help professors to experiment with learning methods, to develop case material, to get close to real business dilemmas, and to produce leads for research and consulting. Today such learning, embodied in concepts like 'grounded theory',[60] is perfectly legitimate. Back in the late

---

[56] Memo from Philippe Dennis to Jean Marcou, 14/2/69.

[57] Yves Dunant, head of the Swiss firm Sandoz, was a member of Insead's board, and Antoine Bekaert, head of the Belgian firm Bekaert, was a close friend of François Dalle's. Besides L'Oréal, the three French firm founders were Rhône-Progil, BSN and Gervais-Danone. BSN and Gervais-Danone eventually merged, a process considerably facilitated by the close relations and common training of their managers who had jointly attended Cedep programmes.

[58] Letter from Philippe Dennis to Jean Marcou, 14/2/69. As with Insead, the land would be purchased by the Paris Chamber of Commerce and leased to Cedep.

[59] Whereas the timing and spacing of the residential periods have been slightly modified since then, the basic structure has remained unchanged.

[60] Glaser, B. and Strauss, A. (1968) *The Discovery of Grounded Theory: Strategies for qualitative research* (London: Weindenfeld and Nicholson).

1960s, no one considered proximity to business as academically enriching.

Finally, the argument which really swung it for the faculty was that it would allow the growth in faculty numbers to be financed from external sources. In order to meet the projected teaching loads, the school would virtually have to double its body of professors. This was a source of considerable anxiety: how would the school manage that process and where would it find those professors? It was also a one-off opportunity.

Surprisingly, for a project which was set to double the size of the physical plant, the proposal elicited no real opposition from the board when presented in November 1969. As one former board member recalls: "It was seen by some as an unfortunate financial necessity." Others felt that the swing towards European-based companies might help to redress Insead's skewed reliance on US multinationals.

Once the proposal received the official go-ahead from the board, Salvatore Teresi decided to give up his teaching activities at Insead to devote himself full-time to the project. Teresi set to work on a fully integrated concept, where the structure and content of the course, the process for designing the course, and even the buildings in which the course was taught, would all concord.

To determine what should be taught and how, seven small committees were established. These were highly innovative in bringing together professors from Insead, big names from the US business schools – including Wickham Skinner, Robert Hayes, Pearson Hunt and Mason Haire – and company representatives. It was an unprecedented '*ménage à trois*'. At the time, even in the US, no one ever consulted the companies. Teresi hired a house not far from campus where they could work undisturbed. A key principle to emerge from these discussions was the idea that groups should be thoroughly mixed by function, hierarchical position and age. This was a real novelty for European companies which were traditionally very hierarchical and where training was typically 'streamed' to avoid discomfort in front of bosses or subordinates in a learning situation.

Quotas were established to guarantee a certain heterogeneity within each group attending the course. There were several influences behind this decision. First, the principle of diversity had already proved a useful accelerator of learning in Insead's one-year programme. Second, 'mixing' corresponded to the corporate objective of creating cross-boundary connections and constituting a 'critical mass' of managers who might serve as catalysts for change throughout the company. Third, the wider social context was ripe for such initiatives. Following the large-scale protests of May 1968, the idea of allowing everyone to participate in the evolution of an organisation was very fashionable. It was considered progressive to constitute a forum where people of different ranks could talk to each other, exchange ideas and information, and even use the informal '*tu*' form of address!

The design for the buildings also reflected those democratic principles. Landon together with Teresi, a trained architect, had some clear ideas about what they were looking for. They worked very closely with Bernard de La Tour d'Auvergne, who had previously designed Insead. Consequently, although the same building materials were used in both cases, the new premises would have a very different feel inside – much cosier, less formal, more like a club. Building work started in May 1970 and was completed within a year.

IN READINESS FOR CHANGE

In parallel with the Cedep proposal, Dennis faced two delicate leadership issues on which he solicited Doriot's advice in September 1968. The first concerned the dean of faculty, Roger Godino, who was increasingly side-tracked by his external interests. In the short term, this had forced Dennis to take on some additional tasks and to find someone else to run the faculty meetings instead of Godino, who was still officially dean. More significantly, though, it meant finding someone to replace Godino full-time: "This poses a difficult problem as I cannot think of a European capable of taking on the position. Europeans with a knowledge of running a business school are rare. It is not insoluble, but it is difficult to resolve ... Of course, one solution would be take an American, but this might provoke an allergic reaction from a large number of European companies."[61]

In many ways, the lack of suitable replacements was a tribute to Godino himself. His growing absences had left a void in the school's academic leadership. Right through to the mid-1960s, he had been the prime force driving for improvement in teaching and admissions' standards. More significantly still, it was Godino who had set in motion the agreement whereby Insead students were sent to the US to pursue their doctoral studies. It concerned only half a dozen students but it constituted a critical break with the prevailing values. At the time, the board was still obsessed with hiring practitioners and part-timers.

Dennis' other leadership preoccupation was the imminent retirement of Jean Marcou as chairman of the board. Marcou had been central to the launch of the school. He had taken the initial risk, pushing the project through while head of the Paris Chamber of Commerce, and he had helped find sponsors. Since taking on the chairmanship of the school, he had followed developments at the school closely, coming down to attend functions, to talk to the students and to meet with Giscard d'Estaing on a regular basis. He even sat in on some meetings of the admissions committee.

By far the most desirable candidate to replace Marcou was John Loudon.

[61] Letter from Philippe Dennis to Georges Doriot, 23/9/68.

If Insead had existed in 1930, this Dutchman, fluent in five languages, with a law degree, might well have studied there. Having transformed the Royal Dutch/Shell Group in his thirty-five year career there, he now served on numerous boards and was chairman of the advisory committees of Chase Manhattan Bank, Ford and Shell. His international business aura was hard to match. He was one of the very few Europeans to be taken seriously in the US. Since joining Insead's board, he had already proved his commitment to the school and his determination to see it develop.

While keen to help, Loudon was not particularly taken with the idea of another chairmanship. As Dennis told Cannon: "He fully agrees to be a member of the new executive committee of Insead, but I think it will take some persuasion to decide him to head that committee [and by implication the board]."[62] Dennis subsequently told Doriot: "[Loudon] does not seem at all inclined to take the post, saying it requires someone younger."[63] Effectively, Loudon had already reached an age, 64, at which it was customary to retire.

When Dennis finally persuaded Loudon to assume the chairmanship, confirmed by the board in June 1969, it represented a real coup. It promised to invigorate the role of the board. It also promised to attract a new generation of board members, this time drawn from the international business community rather than from international public bodies. In this respect, it would help the school to remain close to business. Noting the shift from visiting practitioners towards full-time professors, Claude Janssen had written to Doriot: "Though perfectly capable of running the school and developing it, the arrival of permanent professors may mean that the school progressively cuts itself off from the realities of business. The appointment of a chairman who is more in touch with international affairs, will help prevent the school from turning into a traditional university."[64]

Loudon quickly set about constituting the 'executive committee', he had previously suggested to Dennis. Prior to Loudon's arrival, Dennis had complained to Doriot that finding people willing to take an active role on the proposed executive committee was proving very difficult, especially finding suitable representatives from Germany or Britain.[65] With Loudon taking over, new doors suddenly opened. Over the summer of 1969, nine people were persuaded to commit themselves actively to the school.[66]

---

[62] Letter from Philippe Dennis to Warren Cannon, 30/10/68.
[63] Letter from Philippe Dennis to Georges Doriot, 20/11/68.
[64] Letter from Claude Janssen to Georges Doriot, 25/9/68.
[65] Letter from Philippe Dennis to Georges Doriot, 20/11/68.
[66] The members were: Sven Bernström, Warren Cannon, François Dalle, Philippe Dennis, Yves Dunant, Olivier Giscard d'Estaing, P. Goedkoop, Jean Martin and Patrick Reilly.

THE LOUDON EFFECT

Among his many board positions, Loudon also happened to be the only non-American trustee on the board of the Ford Foundation – and for Insead, this remained the most likely source of major funding.

Consequently, when Warren Cannon returned to petition the Ford Foundation on Insead's behalf, it was a rather different proposition. Cannon's initial contacts suggested that the Foundation would look very favourably upon a grant request provided the school were willing to recruit a professional educator as its next dean of faculty – and the dean's responsibility would be to build up a professional faculty. Philippe Dennis, who by autumn 1969 was feeling over-stretched, Roger Godino having now left, was firmly in favour.

The first executive committee meeting, which was set to become the school's strategic decision-making body, was convened for November 1969. The issue of recruiting a new dean was at the top of the agenda. Even with the reduced membership, not everyone was convinced that this was the course to follow.

Some felt that only practising managers could teach the practical art of management and were worried that the school might become over-academic. Others feared that the acquisition of professional educators would result in a heavy and inflexible financial burden. But perhaps the most sensitive issue was that there would be an increasingly American presence in what was meant to be a distinctively European institution. After much debate, this was conceded as an essential step in the continuing development of the school. It remained to find the right incumbent.

The executive committee initially set its sights on Jim Howell, then assistant dean at Stanford. As discussed by the executive committee, in November 1969, the sales pitch to the prospective candidate was simple: "We are offering something which is not available anywhere else: a perfectly international school and the chance to make his mark on a spectacular development."[67] Apparently, these arguments were not as convincing to outsiders as they were to insiders. After some deliberation, Jim Howell opted instead for the *Wissenschaftliches Zentrum* in Berlin.[68] Others were approached but, as Dennis explained to the dean of HBS, "either the candidates were not good enough, or one or two candidates, for different reasons could not accept".[69]

Meanwhile, David Hall, in charge of the human relations course, had taken it upon himself to try to persuade an American professor, teaching at London Business School, to reconsider the post. The professor in question

[67] Minutes of the Executive Committee, 24/11/69.
[68] Letter from Philippe Dennis to James Howell, 23/3/70.
[69] Letter from Philippe Dennis to George Lombard, Dean of HBS, 30/4/70.

had already been sounded out by Warren Cannon the previous summer but had shown little interest in the job. Now, with the prompting of Hall, he had clearly changed his mind.[70] After some reflection, he agreed to take the position of dean on a part time basis for the academic year starting in September 1970, assuming full functions the following year. Predestined for such a calling, he was the aptly named Dean Berry.

During this time, Warren Cannon had pursued discussions with the Ford Foundation, single-handedly but with the implicit support of Loudon. As Cannon recalls: "Marshall Robinson, representing Ford, could have been very tough with the University of Arkansas, say, but not with John Loudon's Insead. On top of that, Marshall himself had considerable enthusiasm for Insead. He was very academic in orientation. I think he deplored the use of lay faculty and hoped that the money would help rectify that."

By the time Berry accepted the deanship, Cannon was able to report to the board that the foundation was envisaging a global grant of one million dollars, over four years, though several conditions remained to be negotiated.[71] So by June 1970, the school had a professional dean, a chairman of international stature, and a reinforced decision-making body in the shape of the executive committee. It also had a pledge of support from the Ford Foundation on one side and, through Cedep, the support of half a dozen dynamic European companies on the other. Things looked all set to move.

In anticipation of the influx of new faculty, the school would need to add to the existing buildings. The original premises had been conceived with visiting professors in mind, and were therefore ill-adapted to the future needs. It was not only the office space which was lacking. The library desperately needed to be relocated if it wanted to continue its expansion. And this was even more urgent for the printing and case reproduction facilities, whose employees were currently forced to work in "truly acrobatic conditions".[72] Such was the need, that when Dennis requested formal authorisation to build the annexe (North Wing),[73] construction work was already under way. To finance the work, the school borrowed money against guarantees provided by the town of Fontainebleau and supportive firms.[74] In many ways, it was a tribute to the progress under Dennis that barely three years after moving into the spacious new premises, the school was bursting at the seams.

[70] See letter from Philippe Dennis to John Loudon, 6/2/70.
[71] Minutes of the Board Meeting, 22/6/70.
[72] Letter from Philippe Dennis to Baron Edmond de Rothschild, 16/2/70.
[73] Letter from Philippe Dennis to Henri Courbot, president of the Paris Chamber of Industry and Commerce, 22/7/70.
[74] See minutes of the Ordinary General Meeting, 14/6/71.

THE SEEDS OF INNOVATION

In the space of 12 months, between July 1966 and July 1967, Insead acquired a new director-general and a new set of premises. Together these seemed destined to foster a predictable development. Contrary to what might have been expected, the few years preceding the designation of a professional dean, in June 1970, turned out to be a period of significant innovation. With relatively few professors, with inadequate administrative resources, and without a dean of faculty for much of the time, the school managed to grow in scope as well as scale. So what enabled this to happen?

Numerous contributory factors have been mentioned. First there was the external context. Within the business community there was a growing awareness of the benefits of management training – and a widespread perception that America's economic lead was attributable to superior business education. European companies were also divisionalising and internationalising, both of which fuelled demand for Insead's polyglot generalists. So the context was ripe, boosting demand for the one year programme as well as the management development programmes.

But what made Insead's professors respond to this market need? Partly it was a matter of profile. Few of those attracted to Insead were mainstream academics. Therefore, they were perhaps more inclined to take risks; and without the distractions of research, they were willing and able to invest their energies elsewhere. Many of them had been in business before, understood the needs of managers and felt they should respond to them. Moreover, their initiatives were rarely contested by a leader who was too busy trying to perform two jobs to interfere with theirs. Dennis' main concern was that the initiatives should ease the financial burden and, if possible, help visibility. So there was space to be innovative.

The bottom line, of course, was that they had to be innovative to survive. Independence was a founding characteristic of Insead's constitution which was good for flexibility, but left the school with a chronic financial weakness. The incoming faculty quickly realised that unlike other schools or universities, Insead lived from hand to mouth. They could not relax because money was needed, not just for growth, but to make the repayments on the new buildings and to pay their own professorial salaries. So even those who were not particularly inclined towards the needs of business found themselves caught up in the movement. Some were born entrepreneurial, others had it thrust upon them.

This convergence of means, opportunity and motive finds its crowning achievement in the creation of Cedep. This idea did not come from within the school, but the school had sufficient available land to entertain the idea of such a centre. The proposal was hugely unexpected and particularly timely, given Insead's soul searching about how to bulk up quickly. But that

does not mean it was lucky. By the time the idea came along, at the end of
1968, Insead had become a kind of lightning rod for unlikely opportunities
– indeed L'Oréal would never have approached the school unless it were
known to be open to such ideas.

There is a French saying that a starving stomach has no ears, but Insead's
experience seems to contradict that folk wisdom: it was precisely its hunger,
a consequence of its institutional independence, that made the school listen
very hard.

From respectability to prominence

CHAPTER 5

A faculty for renewal

"While it is all very well to talk of 'turning points', one can surely only recognise such moments in retrospect. Naturally, when one looks back to such instances today, they may indeed take the appearance of being crucial, precious moments in one's life; but of course, at the time, this was not the impression one had." *The Remains of the Day*, Kazuo Ishiguro, 1989.

A DECEPTIVE CHALLENGE

The conditions surrounding Dean Berry's part-time appointment as dean designate, from July 1970, seemed ideal. He had the full backing of the board and the director-general, and his engaging manner quickly won over the faculty.[1]

The school itself seemed to be full of possibilities, radiating "an air of something new, something happening or about to happen".[2] Not beholden to any one agency or nation, it was free to determine its educational stance. Its mongrel heritage and institutional flexibility made it perhaps the only school capable of keeping pace with developments in international business and politics. The school had acquired considerable expertise in managing a complex process of cross-cultural learning. It had an established reputation in Europe and market demand for its students and executive programmes was high. It had aesthetically pleasing buildings and there was room for expansion. Its precious intangible assets included an enthusiastic and entrepreneurial body of professors and administrative staff; an impressive international board; and the active support of geographically dispersed alumni associations.

---

[1] As Philippe Dennis put it in a letter to James Howell: "He has made the very best of impressions, on John Loudon, Warren Cannon, etc ..., also on the Faculty here ... and on me." (23/3/70).
[2] *Management Today*, July 1972, 73.

Working on a part-time basis for a year, as dean designate, would allow Berry to get to know the key players, to settle in to the Fontainebleau area, and to make up his mind about the strategic challenge ahead. He had not only time, but money. In July 1970, the Ford Foundation had agreed to give him $20,000 in order to study the management education needs in Europe for the coming decade and to prepare a five year plan for Insead. There was every reason to hope that the full grant of one million dollars would be accorded once this long-range plan was approved.

Berry also had a well-defined mandate: to oversee "an explosive development of the school: in terms of professors, research and programme contents".[3] As dean of faculty, he would not have to worry about administrative or budgetary matters, external relations or fund-raising which would be the responsibilities of Philippe Dennis, the director-general. The challenge therefore seemed straightforward enough. Also, with everyone behind him, it must have been difficult to imagine how he might fail.

As expected, Berry's report to the Ford Foundation in April 1971 highlighted a fundamental problem. Dramatising a little to convince the Foundation to do something he wrote: "A reasonable summary would conclude that there has not been previously a large enough, well qualified, full-time staff to develop modern curricula, to do professionally acceptable research, or to build an educational institution ... It seems fair to state that the School has succeeded because there was an unmet market need, because the students have been superior and because enough visiting professors have been employed to carry the weight of the programme."[4]

The solutions seemed obvious: the school needed money in order to build up a professional faculty and to develop more venturesome teaching material and research. That was precisely why Berry had been recruited and, from his comments to journalists before coming on full-time, he clearly relished the challenge: "I suppose also I'm some kind of managerial opportunist. The school was in the process of making a permanent faculty, and that's a once-and-for-all opportunity. The guy after me won't get it. People make commitments to this type of situation."[5]

What Berry could not fully anticipate were the difficulties of attracting the right kind of new faculty in sufficient numbers. Then, having attracted them, he would have to manage, develop and retain them; he would need to find ways to meet their demands and limitations; and he would have to cope with their inevitable repercussions on the culture and running of the school. In short, upgrading the faculty would upset everything. With hindsight, Berry's 'once-and-for-all opportunity' had all the makings of a poisoned chalice.

The same could perhaps be said for John Loudon. Within a few months

[3] Letter from Philippe Dennis to John Loudon, 1/12/69.
[4] D. Berry, *A Proposal to the Ford Foundation on behalf of Insead*, 1/4/71.
[5] *Management Today*, July 1972, 75.

of taking up the chairmanship of the school, Loudon, who was based in London and the Hague, realised that he would need an executive vice-chairman, who should be resident in Paris, to assist him. Doriot suggested he approach Claude Janssen, who had stepped back a little from the school since his intense involvement prior to its launch. Janssen officially took up the position in June 1971.

This signalled a change of style in the chairmanship. In contrast with his predecessor, Loudon did not plan to get involved in the internal running of the school or to be very present on campus. Partly, this was a consequence of his physical location. But also, he had not accompanied the school through its infancy and was not viscerally attached to Insead as Marcou had been. Loudon was also marked by the Anglo-Saxon business culture, where authority was more easily delegated than in the French business culture. Loudon saw his likely contribution to the school much more in terms of improving its international visibility and strategic vision. He clearly had every intention of adopting a 'hands-off' style. But circumstances were set to dictate otherwise.

SETTING THE BALL ROLLING

Berry's analysis and recommendations of the management education needs in Europe met with widespread approval. In March 1971, he made presentations in four locations – Amsterdam, Frankfurt, London and Fontainebleau – to invited audiences of professors, company heads and consultants. This constituted an important exercise in visibility and academic leadership. In Europe, at least, Insead was seizing the opportunity to point the way.

From the separate report submitted to the Ford Foundation, it was clear that Insead suffered from piecemeal financing which engendered short planning horizons inappropriate to educational investment. As Berry put it: "Financial commitments tend to be small, annual and legally non-continuing."[6] Reacting to events month by month created an uncertainty which discouraged individuals from committing to tasks with longer payoffs. Impressed by Berry's report, the Ford Foundation agreed to a grant of one million dollars over four years. There was just one catch. The first instalment would be without strings, but the whole would have to be matched by Insead one and half times.

'Matching grants' were fairly standard practice from US foundations. The aim was not to create a dependency but to encourage self-sufficiency. Such measures embodied a deep-seated American belief that people or institutions deserved help to the extent they were willing to help themselves. But for

[6] D. Berry, *A Proposal to the Ford Foundation on behalf of Insead*, 1/4/71, 13.

Insead, this clause would create additional problems. The school's fund-raising had always been conducted by the director-general, pretty much unassisted. In order to benefit fully from the Ford grant, the school would need to set up a formal fund-raising structure and to increase its fund-raising income by two-thirds.[7] This was assuming that costs stayed fixed. Yet the recruitment drive, in anticipation of the needs of Cedep, was poised to send costs soaring.

APPEALING TO DISSIDENTS

Trying to recruit new professors, Berry faced the same challenge as his predecessors, with the added difficulties of setting the quality bar higher and recruiting in larger numbers. Insead was still not credible academically: it had no PhD programme, no academic status or tradition, few research programmes, or sabbaticals. As one business school professor put it: "If there were nine other academics of high standing there, and I mean world-class, I'd go there like a flash. There aren't, and the only conceivable way of getting them there would be to tell each of them that the other nine were coming."[8] In a sense, that is exactly what Dean Berry did. Of course, there was no way that Insead could attract established stars, but with a bit of dressing up, it could entice prospective stars.

Each year, Berry toured the top American schools, interviewing mainly European doctoral students. His task was helped by European efforts to send potential management teachers to the US and Canada, sponsored by national foundations such as FNEGE in France, FUI in Belgium and DAAD in Germany.[9] Having previously contacted these future academics by mail, Berry was able to tell them that Insead was already attracting top talent. Spyros Makridakis and André Laurent had joined the school in 1970 and with two Insead-financed Harvard DBAs, Gareth Dyas and Heinz Thanheiser, morally obliged to return, the faculty was gaining a semblance of academic credibility.

New recruits would be joining a faculty which was international and young, as embodied by the much travelled Berry who was only 38 when he took the deanship. The setting was idyllic, particularly for those with young families. Berry was proposing an environment which was stimulating, interdisciplinary and opportunity rich – and if it was research they were interested in, he would see to it they were given the resources. Claude Faucheux's appointment, in September 1970, as full-time research coordinator, constituted a statement of intent. Berry sold prospective faculty

[7] *Management Today*, July 1972, 75.
[8] *Management Today*, July 1972, 74.
[9] Respectively *Fondation National pour l'Enseignement de la Gestion des Entreprises, Fondation Université-Industrie, Deutscher Akademischer Austausch Dienst.*

a compelling vision of what Insead could be like, carefully adjusting his sales pitch to the desires and circumstances of each candidate. The fact that a little-known school ended up grabbing far more than its share of available talent, in the toughest possible labour market, was a tribute to Berry's power of persuasion.

For the school, these recruits were long-term bets. As Berry later expressed it: "They were long on promise but short on authority."[10] But equally, those recruited, like David Weinstein, Charles Wyplosz or Dominique Héau, were taking a big professional risk. That is how the school ended up with a cohort of bright but atypical recruits all in search of 'something different'. They had already demonstrated their dynamism by leaving their home countries to study in the US. On completion, many did not want to remain in the US – but nor were they keen to return to national universities. They were happy to be thrown together in an international institution. In a sense, Insead became a haven for cultural misfits.

In the isolated context of Fontainebleau, their collective difference was reinforced. The rural setting, initially conceived to promote the learning process of the students, fostered a similar sense of community among the growing faculty body. A rich social life developed which tended to reduce status barriers between students and faculty, between faculty and senior executives, between faculty and administration or indeed between the dean and the faculty. There were departmental picnics; there were regular cocktail and dinner parties; and there were themed or fancy dress parties thrown by students and attended by the younger faculty. There were also formal social events such as the annual ball, the cabaret or sports matches which encouraged intermingling and promoted solidarity.

The new faculty were also ambitious and quickly realised that if they wanted to keep their career options open, they had to create something worthwhile at Insead. Although they held doctorates, there was a temperamental affinity with the entrepreneurs of the previous generation.

The downside was that these 'budding stars' had higher salary expectations than their predecessors – and since Berry was accountable to Dennis, this immediately posed boundary problems. Berry wanted full authority to negotiate their terms and conditions and sufficient leeway to capture these 'rare birds'. Dennis wanted to limit expenses and to run a tight ship.

For all their potential, the other problem raised by the incoming faculty was that they generally had little or no teaching experience – as well as lacking any real contact with the business world. These shortcomings were rather an inconvenience in the environment they were about to enter.

---

10 Claude Rameau's retirement, Insead Video, 9/9/93.

FROM TEACHING TO LEARNING

By the time Cedep was inaugurated, in June 1971,[11] the number of permanent faculty was 31, double what it had been just 18 months previously. Most of Berry's new recruits did not have the right profile to start teaching at Cedep, either in terms of experience or linguistically as the programme was exclusively in French for the first two years. So the challenge of launching Cedep would fall to Insead's more established professors, like de Bettignies, Rameau and Remmers.

As the final preparations were made to receive the first group of Cedep managers, anxiety levels were running high, starting with Landon and Teresi who had worked hard to bring the project to fruition. Insead's professors had only ever taught executives with the assistance of US colleagues; and those courses were of limited duration. At Cedep, if they messed up the first modules, they faced the prospect of dragging the same group along for over two years.

As *The Times* saw the initiative, it represented "the most revolutionary form of management education European business has seen so far."[12] To everyone's relief, the recipe worked from the start, for the companies, the participating managers and the professors.[13] This can be attributed to three key factors. Firstly, considerable preparatory work had preceded the launch. As Claude Rameau recalls: "The mere fact of talking to people in those firms, of trying to identify their needs, of trying to develop more specific material, including one or two new cases, facilitated things enormously. Goodwill was established early on and that triggered a very positive momentum." Secondly, through their exposure to successive waves of executives from the same companies, the professors teaching at Cedep quickly acquired an intimate knowledge of those companies from a variety of angles. Possession of privileged information gave them credibility and established a climate of trust. Thirdly, the participating executives turned out to be much more tolerant than expected. Far from shooting down the professors, they wanted them to succeed. Salvatore Teresi recalls: "The executives tried to help the professors, because they were 'their professors', just as Cedep was 'their school'. So they protected them and helped them improve."

Cedep therefore provided a benign learning environment for the incoming professors, as well as an educational laboratory where new approaches could be rapidly tested out and refined. In this way, Cedep helped to establish a teaching style and content with a distinctive flavour, less derivative of the American orthodoxy. It was partly through their involvement with the consortium companies that Insead professors learned to dialogue with firms,

---

[11] The official inauguration on 18th November 1971 was presided by Valéry Giscard d'Estaing, then French Minister of Economy and Finance.

[12] *The Times*, 11/5/72.

[13] Minutes of the Executive Committee, 14/2/72.

to listen to and respond to their needs. There was also the apprenticeship to case writing. The Cedep companies not only demanded European cases, they also supplied a ready source of case material. Until 1971, case writing was not an Insead speciality – Insead professors were primarily teachers. Between 1970 and 1975, 120 new cases were developed courtesy of Cedep. A whole new wave of instructional material with a distinctive European flavour swept across the campus.

Yet an underlying tension was also emerging as the number of Cedep teaching sessions grew and increasing numbers of faculty were solicited: Cedep needed first-rate teachers, while Insead wanted to recruit faculty with a strong research potential. The two profiles were not always compatible – or at least, not affordable.

TUNING IN ON A NEED

The Cedep experience marked Insead's educational philosophy in another important respect. Insead imported the notion of 'critical mass', earlier developed by its professors in discussions with the consortium companies. The idea was that Insead's executive education should not just be geared towards individuals. It could also help a company transform itself by training a cross-section of its managers. This paved the way for Insead's diversification into tailor-made programmes.

Back in 1972, when Insead launched its first customised programmes under the impetus of Claude Rameau, no one else was doing it, even in North America. The idea that a business school should work for a single company was rather frowned upon. At Insead, this debate had already taken place prior to the launch of Cedep so the threshold of resistance was lower.

Dean Berry was academically inclined, but he was also pragmatic. He realised that the path to academic respectability might require some compromises. He had little difficulty grasping the numerous merits of the proposed Management Development Unit (MDU).[14] First, Berry had a large number of faculty members with no executive teaching experience, and limited research or consulting contacts, especially in their new environment. The MDU would provide a mechanism to help broker relationships between professors and companies, to help professors learn to communicate with executives and get close to the realities of business. The MDU would provide opportunities for action research without financial burden to the institute.[15] And the teaching would be more stimulating than conventional executive teaching as the demands from the companies could vary greatly in thrust and scope.

Moreover, given the strong demand from companies, which soon

[14] Later renamed Company Specific Programmes (CSPs).
[15] Insead Four Year Plan: 1974–1977.

outstripped the available supply by a factor of four,[16] Insead could pick and choose its contracts. This gave the school a rare possibility of leverage over companies. It could favour those firms which offered the most interesting research sites, which made heavy use of executive programmes, which employed Insead graduates or supported the school. In other words, it could reinforce its long-term relationships with certain firms.

Another advantage, as pointed out by Rameau to the board in June 1973, was that it allowed the creation of 'ad hoc' teams of professors on each contract. This "avoids excessive departmentalisation at Insead".[17] It is interesting that this became an explicit objective of the MDU. These interdisciplinary clusters favoured intellectual development; they could also be a lot of fun, contributing decisively to the social cohesion of the faculty.

In this respect, Insead always differed from the typical business school culture, characterised by Rob Goffee and Gareth Jones[18] as 'fragmented'. Business schools are organisational oddities, in that they can function perfectly well while being weak on both sociability and solidarity. Typically, there is a low level of interaction among faculty; and there is no particular affinity for the institution which employs them. This was never the case at Insead. The faculty was small, cosmopolitan and isolated which tended to stimulate interaction. The teaching opportunities were diverse and required constant reconfiguration of people and renewal of competencies. Unlike most scholars, Insead's faculty developed an equal attachment to the institution which employed them as to their occupational group. Collegiality was required and reinforced by the activity mix.

BACK TO BASICS

At the board meeting in June 1972, Dennis revealed that for the first time in several years the school would record a deficit.[19] Given that the school had no endowment, retained earnings or shareholders[20] to fall back on, and a line of credit from the bank amounting to 500,000 francs,[21] such news tended to make board members nervous. Already Loudon and Janssen had felt increasingly compelled to scrutinise the accounts and financial forecasts.

Dennis explained to the board that this was mainly the result of the increase in faculty numbers and the corresponding need to reinforce secretarial and printing services. But there was also a question of operating efficiency. The school had no centralised control of purchasing, no system of

---

[16] Insead Four Year Plan: 1974–1977.
[17] Minutes of the Board Meeting, 18/3/73.
[18] Goffee, R. and Jones, G. (1996) "What holds the modern company together?" *Harvard Business Review*, November–December, 133–148.
[19] Minutes of the Board Meeting, 19/6/72.
[20] Insead's status as a non-profit organisation meant that it had no shareholders.
[21] Letter from Dean Berry to Peter de Janosi, Ford Foundation, 26/2/74.

cost accounting, nor even a proper budgeting process, "only forecasts and extrapolations made and held by the director general".[22] In its rapid expansion, Insead had outgrown its existing accounting and budgeting systems so these would need to be rebuilt. As Berry later commented: "This was something I never bargained on ... but in a managerial sense everything else has depended on that."[23]

As Berry saw it, better cost control lay not just in systems, but also in structure. So, in late 1972, he proposed to the executive committee a reorganisation based on delegated authority and cost centres. The proposal was approved and implemented in January 1973. Three associate deanships were created, with Lee Remmers taking responsibility for the postgraduate programme, Claude Rameau in charge of executive education, and Will Straver heading up administration.[24] In the new structure, all three reported directly to Berry who assumed full responsibility for faculty matters, planning and administration – thus allowing the director general to devote himself entirely to fundraising and external relations. This redefinition of responsibilities between Dennis and Berry was symbolised by the replacement of the direct reporting line with a dotted line, indicating the need for regular consultation.[25] Henceforth, Berry would report *directly* to the board within the scope of his responsibilities.

Besides managing costs better, the other way to balance the budget was to improve fundraising. In February 1972, the long range planning committee had signalled that it was "imperative that the Institute recruit as soon as possible fund-raising staff to assist the Director General in his efforts".[26]

Dean Berry asked Jacqueline Tourlier, who had been in charge of administration, to set up a fund-raising operation. Though a novice to fund-raising, she had high internal credibility which was considered more important.[27] To prepare her for the task, she was sent off on a three-month tour of the top US schools, meeting up with her future counterparts at Harvard, Stanford, MIT, Chicago, Northwestern and Columbia. The choice of schools is significant in that it reveals Insead's aspirations. It wanted to learn from and benchmark against the best. Tourlier gained both know-how and numerous introductions from her visits and came back with a better understanding of how to proceed. Unfortunately, the fund-raising climate she returned to had "never been less promising".[28]

As mentioned in previous chapters, there was no tradition of charitable

[22] Minutes of the Executive Committee, 3/12/73.

[23] Letter to A. MacDonald, McKinsey, 5/3/74.

[24] Appointing an academic to head up the administrative side of the school was not well received either by the administrative personnel or by the board. The experiment was short-lived and was not repeated.

[25] Approved by the Executive Committee (5/2/73). See letter from John Loudon to Philippe Dennis, 13/2/73.

[26] Report of the Long Range Planning Committee, 14/2/72.

[27] See letter from Dean Berry to Claude Janssen, 17/1/73.

[28] Letter to Peter de Janosi, Ford Foundation, 26/2/74.

giving in Continental Europe, except for religious or medical causes, nor any tax breaks for donors. Moreover, businesses were not keen to give in order to cover operating deficits – which was Insead's situation – they wanted to see their money creating something, not just plugging a hole.[29]

As for the alumni, a staple source of funds for US schools, they remained too few and too junior in their organisations to have a significant impact. The 'Salamander Fund', created by Michel Gauthier in 1969, to encourage their contributions was of symbolic importance – but little pressure was put on alumni to make donations, for fear of losing their active input and support on other fronts, like interviewing of candidates. To cap these fund-raising difficulties, a huge energy crisis was about to hit the industrialised countries.

In early 1974, Berry wrote: "Given the recent economic uncertainty, we are quite clear that our fund-raising effort this year is going to be highly selective."[30] Tourlier found herself trying to identify and target those firms which were the least affected by the oil crisis.[31] She quickly established an Affiliation Programme destined to secure more continuous funds – and within 18 months 54 companies had signed on for three years as affiliate or associate partners. This was an important step forward in stimulating the school's more systematic contacts with businesses which was precisely the intention of the 'matching grant'. But it fell a long way short of the full 'matching' target.

The Ford Foundation had very strict regulations as to which sources of income could count for matching purposes.[32] For example, the annual contribution from the Paris Chamber of Commerce and Industry and the 'goodwill' contribution from Cedep would not count. So fund-raising efforts had to be multiplied. Even Dean Berry was drawn in to some extent. In March 1974, he wrote a letter to numerous US corporations soliciting help. The opening sentence underlined Insead's still faint visibility in the US at the time: "I have the difficult job of introducing you both an idea that we think worthy of your financial support and at the same time, probably, introducing the institution in back of it."[33] Berry was not particularly thrilled at having to engage in such activities, but he viewed it philosophically. Writing to a friend in February 1974, Berry explained that he would "probably have to spend two or three long trips in the States doing some fund raising. Oh well, when you lose your virginity you might as well make a good job of it!"[34]

---

[29] Letter from Dean Berry to John Loudon, 25/5/73.
[30] Letter from Dean Berry to Jacques Sigall, director of research at Eurofinance, 5/2/74.
[31] See minutes of Executive Committee, 18/2/74.
[32] Letter from Dean Berry to Peter Pliem, 31/7/74.
[33] Circular letter sent to company presidents, 12/3/74.
[34] Letter from Dean Berry to H. W. Boyd, professor at University of Arkansas, 8/2/74.

MAKING A STAND

Given the prevailing financial anxiety within the school, there was constant pressure to reduce costs. One measure taken was to freeze faculty salaries, though with inflation running at around 8 per cent, this amounted to a pay cut. Another option was simply not to renew faculty contracts. Renewal decisions, like recruiting decisions, were determined by Dean Berry along with a select band of senior people, including Salvatore Teresi, Peter Smith, Guy de Carmoy and Claude Faucheux. From the junior faculty point of view, this was a fairly shadowy committee – some saw it as a kind of cabal. The decision-making process was not arbitrary, but it was unilateral and the committee's workings were rather opaque.

In early 1973, three contracts were not renewed. It did not look particularly good. One of those not renewed had refused to grade the papers of a senior faculty member and this was assumed to have been held against him. Another casualty was Manfred Kets de Vries who had experienced various run-ins with members of the selection committee. He recalls how the news was announced to him: "I was called into Dean Berry's office and he seemed quite embarrassed. He talked and talked and talked, and I had no idea what was going on, until I finally realised that he was firing me. Firing is all right but I needed some reasons and none were given. So I got upset and wrote a memo to the whole faculty complaining that there was no due process."

The memo prompted a faculty meeting and the faculty rebelled against what was happening. There was talk of striking. Spyros Makridakis, with his impeccable research credentials, was particularly outspoken saying that it was an unacceptable way of proceeding: whatever the justification for these decisions, they opened the way for abuses where people could be thrown out simply because they happened to end up on someone's blacklist. This collective stand, in the face of perceived unfairness, showed a growing solidarity, but it also forced the faculty to articulate some of its beliefs and values. Dean Berry had some sympathy for their protests and set up a six-person committee, including Gareth Dyas and Spyros Makridakis, the main drivers of the insurrection, to look at the issue of evaluation.

Reluctantly, the committee agreed not to go back over the three cases – Kets de Vries would return in style some years later – and worked instead on a new evaluation process. The task force proposed a system which relied exclusively on peer evaluation, with three of these to be appointed by the dean and three to be elected by the faculty, and specifying the election procedures.[35] The aim was to make the evaluation process more systematic, explicit and professional.

---

[35] See Task Force Report on Recruitment and Evaluation, 10/4/73.

The choice of evaluation system was an affirmation that Insead should remain a fairly non-hierarchical place – and for many years this was borne out by the systematic election of junior professors to represent the faculty on the committee. For example, Paul Evans and Jean-Claude Larréché, both former Insead students, returning from their doctoral studies in 1974, were elected in their first academic year.

In terms of performance management too, the creation of the evaluation committee was a vital step forward. It gave a new transparency to the promotion process, provided a powerful instrument for signalling the strategic orientation of the school, and made the professors responsible for 'cleaning their own stables' – being turned down on the basis of peer recommendation was a more painful proposition than a summary rejection by a remote authority. As some saw it, it poisoned the atmosphere. Ultimately though, it was the first evidence of the faculty starting to assert itself.

The following year, in 1974, the committee went on to formalise the criteria for promotion. The 'faculty guidelines' established that individuals would be appraised on three dimensions: teaching, research and institutional contribution. Significantly, these guidelines placed research output on an equal footing with teaching performance; but they also formally enshrined the idea that commitment to the institution was expected and would be recognised.

TENSIONS COME TO A HEAD

For structural reasons, Berry's relations with Philippe Dennis had never been frictionless. From the start, Berry's brief had been to enhance the academic reputation of the school and to take charge of its long range planning. This entailed recruiting high quality faculty, developing research and teaching materials, and generally spending money. On the other side of the equation, Dennis was responsible for filling the coffers and keeping the institution solvent. It was Dennis who had to answer to the board if expenses happened to exceed revenues and, given Insead's shaky accounting systems, he often received little advance warning.

The reorganisation of responsibilities, at the start of 1973, did not help matters. With Berry assuming responsibility for administrative affairs too, he quickly became enmeshed in shorter-term operating problems. There were too many people reporting directly to him. Many were new to the job and lacked the experience to handle issues by themselves. Moreover, there was no one to buffer him from a growing faculty who considered him their only direct, professional superior.[36] Writing to Claude Janssen, he lamented: "My new job is one hundred per cent as a manager. The amount of time I devote

---

[36] Letter from Dean Berry to John Loudon, 25/5/73.

to my academic job (courses, students, research, teaching etc.) is negligible."[37]

Dennis himself felt somewhat put out. Not only had Berry usurped some of his responsibilities, but he discharged some of them rather expediently. There was also a difference of style: with age, and perhaps in reaction to Berry's sometimes cavalier approach, Dennis' formality became more apparent. Dennis often felt insufficiently consulted on important issues and this led to disagreements, some of which became public. When questioned by Loudon about reported infighting, Dennis replied: "Berry and I both feel that, within a dynamic organisation, a certain amount of friction is very productive."[38]

By October 1973, however, their relationship was showing increasing signs of strain, as revealed by a memo from Berry to Dennis: "I do believe that discussions about this sort of thing are matters we can communicate with each other personally rather than through memoranda. When one receives a memorandum it is necessary to respond in the same mode ... So my first reaction ... is a sincere plea to sit down and discuss matters like this rather than to exchange memoranda 40 meters around the corner."[39] But communication between them did not improve.

Loudon and Janssen, who had been increasingly solicited to arbitrate between the two parties throughout 1973, were growing tired. The unscheduled meetings between Loudon, Janssen, Dennis and Berry had started taking place in late 1972, and the frequency of those meetings had escalated. Similarly, the quarterly meetings of the executive committee, scheduled for Mondays, were now systematically preceded by intense Sunday afternoon sessions with Dennis and Berry to try to get to the bottom of some of their difficulties, notably the financial mess. The situation was becoming untenable for all concerned, especially after the recent faculty unrest, the reorganisation and the installation of major new systems. It had created a rather nervous organisation. In December 1973, the executive committee met to make a decision.

Dennis and Berry were asked to leave the meeting while the committee deliberated. The two protagonists (antagonists) each went round in circles in their own offices, knowing that one of them would have to step aside, but they had no idea which one. Berry had a strong vision which he wanted to push through. And there was no knowing how the faculty might react if he were removed. On the other hand, anti-American feeling was quite strong in France at the time so it was tempting to replace him with a European. It was a critical test of the school's aspirations and resolve. The executive committee, under the influence of Loudon, ended up backing Berry, originally appointed by Loudon. Conversely, Dennis, who had been

[37] Letter from Dean Berry to Claude Janssen, 12/11/73.
[38] Confidential memo from Philippe Dennis to Claude Janssen, 10/5/73.
[39] Memo from Dean Berry to Philippe Dennis, 23/10/73.

instrumental in bringing John Loudon to the school and who had fought to establish a professional dean, felt somewhat betrayed. His resignation was officially announced in January 1974.

Loudon was neither overbearing nor authoritarian by nature, yet he was capable of decisive action, perhaps more in accordance with the norms of business than those of academia. So as to avoid plunging the school into further uncertainty, Pierre Cailliau, then head of European human resources at Shell, was rapidly named as Dennis' replacement by the board. The procedure was not strictly in accordance with the articles,[40] and the faculty was profoundly shocked to find Cailliau imposed without even token consultation.

Even Berry, who might have regarded this as a vote of confidence from the board, was not entirely satisfied. Officially, he would be named dean of Insead, as opposed to his previous position as dean of the faculty. Henceforth, he would sign faculty employment contracts and salary increases. But in practice it changed very little. Cailliau remained accountable to the board. Berry found himself in the same position as before, except that now he was dealing with someone who had the ear of John Loudon.

Fortunately, Cailliau proved rather more accommodating than his predecessor. His relaxed temperament and willingness to listen made it easier for him and Berry to discuss the fuzzy boundaries of their mutual responsibilities. Berry also took care to warn Cailliau of the challenge which faced them: "I feel that our primary task, given our organisational structure is not to let divisions creep in between us that can be exploited opportunistically by others. Even this structure can work given our co-operation to make it so."[41]

To introduce Cailliau to the workings of a business school, Berry arranged for him to meet senior people at both Harvard and MIT, telling them: "I think Pierre would like to know mainly how a first-class American business school is run, what its long term development capacity is, and how it collects funds for that purpose."[42] Berry was perhaps hoping that Cailliau's role would not extend much beyond his administrative, financial and fundraising responsibilities – leaving the more strategic issues to Berry himself.

A few months later, in August 1974, Cailliau sent Berry a draft of his new contract for comments. In his response, Berry noted his concern that neither he nor Cailliau were members of the board – and were in fact "prevented by statute from being represented on the Board. The idea that an external Board which knows little or nothing about the Institute and governs us without our participation is an anathema to me .... Moreover, I disagree with the principle

---

[40] As pointed out by Paul Delouvrier, Chairman of Electrité de France, at the following Board Meeting, 10/6/74.
[41] Letter from Dean Berry to Pierre Cailliau, 4/3/74.
[42] Letter from Dean Berry to William Pounds, dean of MIT, 6/3/74.

of being Deputy Director General of the Institute and not being involved in the choice of my boss."[43] Berry, like the faculty, was flexing his muscles.

THE SAME BUT DIFFERENT

From the outset, Berry had understood that the school needed to tread a fine line: it had to aspire to the standards of the best US schools, but it also had to cultivate its uniqueness. In many ways, Berry's new faculty recruits, non-Americans with US doctorates, epitomised that objective of 'selective imitation'. But the school planned to distinguish itself in other respects: in terms of strategy, course content and research activities.

Strategically, the school had to strive to make its mark but, given its limited resources, needed to pursue a different route from its transatlantic rivals. As Berry saw it, Insead needed to become a hub, on two levels. First, institutionally, the school's independence made it an ideal cooperator and coordinator within a network of nationally bound European institutions.[44] Insead was unusual in having established two successful 'joint ventures', with Stanford and Columbia. It could leverage this expertise with local institutions. Insead's lead, in 1973, in setting up a European consortium of European schools to take over the running of the International Teachers Program from Harvard was a good example.

Second, the school could create 'internal hubs', that is problem-centred research centres providing a meeting place for interested scholars. Once knowledge and materials were generated, short programmes could be run, and some aspects of the programmes could be imported into the curriculum.[45] The research centres proposed in Berry's 1971 report included one on 'new venture management' and one on 'east-west trade', meaning trade with the Eastern bloc countries. Back then, the idea of a centre focusing on relations with Asia remained a twinkle in Henri-Claude de Bettignie's eye.[46] Nevertheless, the choice to look east rather than west was another manifestation of Insead's distinctiveness.

Berry was conscious that it would be a long time before the school was large enough to create a broad distinctive stamp directly on the market. But he did feel that it could aim to provide such an effective model that others would feel compelled to imitate it. It was a neat concept: Insead would achieve "impact through emulation".

[43] Memo from Dean Berry to Pierre Cailliau, 8/8/74.
[44] "Our autonomy is our strongest asset when it comes to co-operation. And we intend to build a substantial part of our future growth on inter-institutional co-operation." D. Berry, *A Proposal to the Ford Foundation on behalf of Insead*, 1/4/71, 16.
[45] See D. Berry, *A Proposal to the Ford Foundation on behalf of Insead*, 1/4/71, 28.
[46] De Bettignies had first raised the issue of developing a centre dedicated to Asian studies in the late 1960s. Dennis had been receptive to the idea but felt that the school needed to build up its disciplinary foundations before dispersing itself further.

Clearly, the content of the school's programmes also needed to evolve. In the 1960s, Europeans had been happy enough to be exposed to a diluted version of American business education. But by the 1970s, there was a greater consciousness of the limitations of applying American models and practices to the European environment. As Berry asserted in his 1971 report: "Because the European culture is vastly different in its values and processes, ... schools must deliver a European education, distinctive in both form and content. Europe will no longer accept a European business education system that simply produces indigenous managers who can fit American patterns."[47]

The idea was that Insead would no longer be derivative but would attempt to develop its own 'take' on management. In the 1974 long-range plan, the thrust of this distinctive 'take' had become more explicit. It concerned two niches which had the peculiarity of cutting across all the courses. Course content would incorporate aspects of cross-cultural behaviour and multinational problems as a matter of routine; and course delivery would be designed to advance the state of educational design and technology.[48] These were areas in which the school had a head start and planned to excel.

To achieve this, the school needed to start doing its own research, rather than simply adapting or disseminating the research of others. This meant developing facilities and a culture where such activities were possible. The library, for example, was satisfactory for teaching purposes, but was "totally inadequate for modern research purposes, and inappropriately organised for study or reference".[49] The acquisition policy was totally decentralised which had led to a "very uneven collection".[50] Georges Sandeau, the head librarian, had focused on developing the documentation centre. This had become an activity in itself which was well run and commercially viable, but which was not really serving the needs of the immediate users, that is the faculty. It was efficient but inappropriate. The activity was no longer compatible with where the school was heading – nor with its new priority which was respectability rather than just visibility. Discontinuing the documentation services and releasing Sandeau, as part of a small wave of economic redundancies in late 1973, sent a strong signal about Berry's determination to build up the school's research capability. It also won him few friends on the administrative side of the school.

Later, in 1975, when *European Business* ran into trouble, the school made no effort to salvage it, although it had served the school's visibility in the past. Indeed, Berry even thought that the school should withdraw its name from the editorial board. He considered that the journal had changed its objectives

[47] D. Berry, *A Proposal to the Ford Foundation on behalf of Insead*, 1/4/71, 14.
[48] Insead Four Year Plan: 1974–1977, 27.
[49] D. Berry, *A Proposal to the Ford Foundation on behalf of Insead*, 1/4/71, 25.
[50] Insead Four Year Plan: 1974–1977.
[51] Memo from Dean Berry to Henri-Claude de Bettignies, 1/9/75.

and forfeited its academic credibility.[51] For Berry, it was a matter of pruning activities which were not especially compatible with the future strategy of the school or which diverted scarce resources from research ends.

In terms of developing a research culture, Berry made heavy use of Spyros Makridakis, a leading light in decision sciences, as an emblem of the new orientation. Makridakis was publicly praised, unburdened of part of his teaching load, allocated research assistants and encouraged to attend conferences. Quite apart from written output, professors were urged to join editorial boards and supervise doctoral theses, as ways of reinforcing the school's academic presence.

Yet there were limits to this new-found research orientation. When Robin Hogarth published a working paper on the psychology of identical and non-identical twins in a specific research setting, it generated sarcastic comments, both on campus and at board level. It came to represent the excesses of academic research and for many years served as an anecdotal reminder that Insead's research mission, as expressed in 1974, should be "interdisciplinary in nature, problem-solving in design, and real world in orientation."[52] The reality of the situation, in 1974, was that Insead spent three times more faculty man-hours on administration than it did on either research or course development.[53] Under Berry, academic values were more espoused than internalised, but it was an important first step.

LETTRES DE NOBLESSE

Another aspect of managing the tension between comparability and differentiation concerned the pressure to adopt the Master of Business Administration (MBA) label for the postgraduate programme. When Dean Berry arrived, the proposal had already been floating around for several years. Back in June 1969, the board had discussed the merits of such a measure but deemed it premature.[54] Meanwhile, out in the field, many alumni were calling their qualification an MBA as a shorthand way of indicating its merit.[55] In March 1975, Berry resumed the situation in a memo to Cailliau: "It is clear that the alumni would like it. It is clear that the students would like it. It is clear that the faculty would like it ... I believe we ought to move."[56]

After canvassing interested parties, notably the top US schools and Insead's chief recruiting companies, no one had raised any objection to the proposal. This was an important mark of external recognition. Even though Insead was not extending its duration, the programme had built up sufficient

[52] Insead Four Year Plan: 1974–1977, 34.
[53] Insead Four Year Plan: 1974–1977, 41.
[54] Minutes of the Board Meeting, 18/6/69.
[55] See comments by Jorgen Friisberg ('62) to colleagues on the Executive Committee, 21/4/75.
[56] Memo from Dean Berry to Pierre Cailliau, 3/3/75.

credibility to rate on a par with established two-year programmes. Since there were also legal implications, it was Cailliau who finally decided, in June 1975, that the school would officially call its diploma an MBA.[57]

This raised questions about whether to award an MBA degree retroactively to alumni. Gilbert Sauvage, now head of alumni relations, argued that it was: "Of course, Insead's teaching has improved over 15 years. It has grown in rigour and been enriched by new techniques ... But in relative terms, the Insead graduates of 1962 or 1963 are surely comparable to the MBA graduates today."[58] It would also prove a modest source of additional income, with alumni being charged 250 francs for the delivery of a new diploma.[59]

In many ways, the new appellation capped a number of structural changes to the one-year programme, driven essentially by Lee Remmers. For example, the course had been broken down into five periods, with exams or evaluations at the end of each one and five faculty members acting as period coordinators – the aim being to bring more flexibility to the curriculum and to ensure better integration between courses.[60] Electives had also been introduced. From the student perspective, this changed both the content of the learning and its character, in that participants now made up their own 'menu'. From the faculty point of view, electives often provided an easier introduction to the classroom experience, allowing novices to teach in their area of speciality to smaller groups. Another development was the introduction of the 'normal curve' for grading purposes, in response to four years of student complaints about the existing system.[61] The intention was to iron out the variability of grading between faculty, especially among visiting professors. There was also a progressive move away from cases as the prime vehicle for learning, with increasing emphasis on project work and business games. And even the teaching of cases evolved towards a more European style, with the professor giving a short lecture or debrief at the end. The teaching approach of many professors became a synthesis of American and European methods.

During this period, the one-year programme itself was not at its healthiest. For the first time since the school opened, enrolments stagnated – the 1976 intake was slightly lower than the 1970 intake. Partly, this was the result of lack of funds for expansion and increasing internal competition for resources, including teachers. For example, the exponential growth in Cedep teaching requirements meant that by December 1974, 21 of Insead's 42 permanent teaching faculty were doing their full teaching load at Cedep, and 14 were

---

[57] Minutes of the Board Meeting, 16/6/75.

[58] Memo from Gilbert Sauvage to Dean Berrry, 20/5/76.

[59] To an established business school, this sum might seem derisory. In the case of Insead, it would probably harvest as much as the planned campaign targeting the alumni, launched in the spring of 1976, and aiming for a contribution of 300 francs per head. (See minutes of the Board Meeting, 8/12/75.)

[60] Minutes of the Board Meeting, 16/6/75.

[61] See minutes of the Conseil de Perfectionnement, 23/10/70 and 2/12/70.

contributing in various degrees to the Cedep teaching.[62] With the more experienced professors sent off to confront the executives, the quality of the teaching on the postgraduate programme sometimes suffered in the early 1970s.

External circumstances also played a role. Candidates were reluctant to leave their jobs in a climate of recession and uncertainty, producing a temporary dip in the number of applications. Yet the global figures concealed interesting sub-developments. The British contingent, for instance, under the impetus of Britain's Common Market entry in 1973, shot from 10 per cent of the intake in 1972, to 19 per cent in 1975. Conversely, the German contingent, which no longer received grants from the DAAD,[63] slumped from 18 per cent to 6 per cent over a similar period. Insead's diversified intake gave the school a certain resistance to economic cycles.

The drop in applications once again raised the issue of language requirements. As Dean Berry pointed out: "The current demands limit the number of candidates, some of whom then feel rather disappointed that their efforts to improve their German were in vain as it is not used, or very little."[64] As always this raised heated debates. Trilingualism was regarded by the older alumni as being at the very heart of the school's distinctiveness and indeed its success. On the other hand, it constrained Insead's appeal in many countries, notably among potential Latin European, South American or Asian students. In 1973, the decision was taken to relax the German entry requirement, demanding rather that students achieve some degree of proficiency by the end of the course.

SEEN AND HEARD

Within a few months of Cailliau's appointment it became clear that he and Berry could not agree on their respective roles, based on the dominant position of the director-general. Berry felt capable of managing the school alone, but that was not on the agenda either with Cailliau or with the board. In early 1975, after long discussions together, Berry decided that he would not ask for his contract to be renewed when it expired in July 1976.

When Dean Berry announced his decision, at a faculty meeting in March 1975,[65] faculty feelings were mixed. He had clearly made some managerial blunders and continued to have difficulty dealing with the French element, both inside and outside the school. On the other hand, he was widely credited with having changed the professional standing of the school, having introduced some much needed systems; and he remained popular with the

---

[62] Minutes of the Board Meeting, 2/12/74.
[63] *Deutscher Akademischer Austausch Dienst.*
[64] Minutes of the Executive Committee, 14/2/72.
[65] Minutes of the Faculty Meeting, 6/3/75.

younger faculty and the participants who referred to him as 'Dean Dean'. He was more approachable than his predecessors; he had ushered in a more informal style and a first-name culture. Whatever their feelings, the faculty agreed on one thing: they intended to have a say in the choice of Berry's successor.

So it was that at the meeting of the executive committee, six weeks later, a delegation of five faculty, elected by their peers, requested an audience. Their demands actually went beyond the issue of the deanship. They also wanted to be more involved in determining the school's strategy; and they wanted full representation on both the board and the executive committee.

In the discussion that ensued, it emerged that the faculty had heard that the deanship had already been offered to someone by a member of the executive committee.[66] The rumour turned out to be unfounded, but its existence said a lot about the suspicion with which the faculty viewed the executive committee. Quickly, Loudon agreed that the faculty should indeed be involved in the dean search, but not necessarily in the final decision. As for faculty representation, these matters would have to be discussed at a full board meeting.

Claude Janssen exposed the issue to fellow board members at the meeting in June 1975. Taking a historical perspective, he explained that the school had initially been run by external people because there was no alternative. But now with a substantial faculty body, that solution no longer seemed appropriate. He established the principle that the "professors should play a more important role in the running of the school"[67] but did not want to push harder for fear of triggering resistance.

The matter was debated at the following board meeting in January 1976. As expected, there was a certain resistance from some board members, perhaps accustomed to more hierarchical structures, to giving the faculty too much say. Two members argued that the faculty might be consulted but should not have voting rights. In other words, they could be represented on the executive committee but not on the board. Dean Berry argued that this 'half-measure' risked causing more problems than it solved. Another board member disapproved of differentiated rights and considered that full faculty representation constituted "a modest step forward and no particular risk."[68] Pierre Cailliau actually went one step further, asking that the administrative side of the school be represented on the board too.

After much deliberation, John Loudon announced that there would be two members of the faculty on the executive committee; and three members of the faculty, plus a representative of the administration, on the board.[69]

[66] Minutes of the Executive Committee, 21/4/75.
[67] Minutes of the Board Meeting, 16/6/75.
[68] Minutes of the Board Meeting, 26/1/76.
[69] Minutes of the Board Meeting, 26/1/76.

It was an important victory for the future of the school. People can commit more easily to a strategy they feel they can influence.

MAKING IT HAPPEN

The fact that Berry's objective was well circumscribed at the outset did not make it easy to achieve. As it turned out, the school was far from ready for the arrival of a professional dean, nor for the professional faculty he brought in his wake, and certainly not to receive a 'matching grant'. The promise of funding from the Ford Foundation egged on the school to grow beyond its means, with the operating budget ballooning from 7.5m Francs in 1970 to 25m Francs in 1974. This merely exposed the lack of effective systems and planning, as well as the weakness of the fundraising structure and culture. It intensified pressure on the director general to find money and strained relations with the dean.

'Growing the school' turned out to be a unexpectedly painful process. To start with, it had meant sidelining certain people – both on the faculty and on the administrative side – who were often doing a good job, but whose profiles or activities were not compatible with the strategic orientation of the school. It had meant recruiting young professors with new profiles and managing their introduction so that the older members were not marginalised or made to feel less valued. From Berry's arrival to his departure, the permanent faculty nearly trebled in size. The surprise is not that this caused tensions, but that Berry was able to contain them.

Berry facilitated the rapid integration of the incoming faculty through careful selection and development. He provided a new repertoire of opportunities for the newcomers to accelerate their learning by supporting the development of elective courses and the creation of company-specific programmes. Allied to the Cedep experience, this presented rich exposure to diverse teaching situations. Cedep also offered a level of access to research sites which was unprecedented in the highly secretive European business context. All this helped the young faculty to learn, to contribute and to interact productively with the previous generation.

Very quickly, the growing faculty began to assert itself – as evidenced by the separate 'revolts' over evaluation decisions and over board representation – leading to changes in the governance structures. Within the school, the faculty became the dominant force. Previously, when the teaching load had been mainly discharged by visiting professors, the administrators had provided the continuity and had basically run the school. Under Berry, faculty members, like Rameau and Sauvage, had even spilled over into administrative positions. This shift in the balance of power created tensions which again had to be managed – not just internally, but by the board. The faculty's demands for more say in the running of the school, the strains between the dean and director-general became boardroom issues. The first half of the 1970s was perhaps the period when John Loudon was the most involved with the school, but surely not for the reasons he would have wished.

Berry's abiding legacy was to assemble a faculty with real credibility as a professional group. Their profiles pointed the way to the future success of the school and their number placed the school in a pre-eminent position in Europe compared to its rivals. The school had broken into what promised to be an ascending spiral of academic respectability.

This accomplishment took an enormous toll on Berry. Already in early 1974, he had written to a close American colleague: "The strategic plan we launched, on top of the budgeting exercise, and the Ford Foundation narrative report, damn near killed me and about four other people in the organisation."[70]

In February 1976, nearing the end of his deanship, Berry again confided that it had been no sinecure: "I am finishing up a five year contract with Insead ... These years have been frustrating, stretching, developmental, and exciting. At the moment, my predominant motivation is that I could use a spell of calm."[71] Berry accepted the offer of a one year visiting Professorship from Dean Fouraker at *Harvard Business School*: "The duty requirements are very low and I think this provides just what I need at this stage."[72]

Writing to alumni, Berry once compared himself to Don Quixote, saying: "If he had possessed more self-knowledge and foresight, he would not have had any adventures."[73] Insead clearly had more problems than Berry bargained for at the outset. Five years of effort stretched the limits of even Berry's adventurous spirit.

---

[70] Letter from Dean Berry to H. W. Boyd, professor at University of Arkansas, 8/2/74.
[71] Letter from Dean Berry to Robert MacDonald, 4/2/76.
[72] Letter from Dean Berry to Jonathan More, Harvard University, 18/3/76.
[73] Communication to alumni, *Salamander Letter*, 15/12/70.

CHAPTER 6

Keeping the show on the road

"It was the best of times, it was the worst of times, it was the age of wisdom, it was the age of foolishness, it was the epoch of belief, it was the epoch of incredulity, it was the spring of hope, it was the winter of despair." Charles Dickens, *A Tale of Two Cities.*[1]

LOOKING FOR THE DODO

In June 1975, the board was informed that Dean Berry did not wish to renew his mandate after August 1976. After a brief tribute to Berry's accomplishments, the discussion quickly moved on to the profile of his successor. The issue of nationality was uppermost in the minds of many board members. The general view was that the new dean should have an international or, more specifically, a European dimension, but should not be French; and should be capable of speaking two or three languages and be at ease anywhere in Europe.

These requirements were supplemented by a rather more demanding list of desirable qualities from the faculty side. A five-strong faculty team[2] was assembled to come up with two candidates from which the board would make its choice. An important early assertion, however, was that: "The recommendation of candidates to the Board should come from the faculty and not the [dean search] committee."[3] The faculty were concerned to present a united front.

The selection criteria published by the dean search committee in September 1975 looked draconian: they described someone of '*substantial*

[1] Cited by Uwe Kitzinger in his welcome speech to the incoming MBAs, 9/9/78.
[2] The dean search committee was composed of Robin Hogarth, Claude Michaud, Jim Stevens, Heinz Thanheiser and Kenneth Walker.
[3] Memo from Jim Lyons and Deigan Morris to all faculty, 18/6/75.

stature' capable of relating "meaningfully to academia, business and the public service" and whose very name would attract 'faculty of the highest quality'. The ideal candidate would combine academic reputation, having completed "*substantial* research and writing", and business or public service credentials, having held positions of "*substantial* responsibility in ... multinational business firms ... or international institutions".

Such exigencies clearly ruled out internal candidates. The perception was that the school needed someone who was anchored in the outside world and who would have sufficient authority to be credible, *vis-à-vis* the board, as a *partner* for Cailliau. An internal candidate would not be given sufficient elbow room and would always be perceived as a subordinate. Behind these hefty requirements also lay a vague notion that the ideal candidate would have the potential, at least, to assume the joint roles of dean and director-general, should circumstances evolve in that direction. It was the Insead version of the holy grail: the quest for the so-called 'maxi-dean'.[4]

The search committee embarked on an exhaustive trawl, contacting 56 people asking them to nominate likely candidates. Altogether 90 names emerged, the fruit of faculty and outsider suggestions, an advertisement in the *Economist* (13/9/75) and an article in the 'Jobs column' of the *Financial Times*. The article drew particular attention to the school's mission, previously defined by Berry as providing "high quality business education that is international in scope, European in content, and managerial in emphasis."[5]

From this preliminary harvest, 20 people were formally approached and nine came along, each for two days, to meet the faculty and management of the school and to present their views on 'The prospects of business education in Europe'.[6]

In December 1975, the board was told that the shortlist was down to four serious candidates.[7] This prompted a board discussion of the future dean's job responsibilities and possible changes to the structure. As John Loudon saw it: "Changes in the structure will depend on the attributes of the new dean." Claude Janssen went further, considering that: "To the extent that the academic dean also possesses the necessary administrative qualities, the posts of director general and dean could even end up being merged."[8] Alexander King considered this an unlikely possibility: "The task of managing the school is too heavy for one person to assume. It must inevitably be entrusted to two 'senior people', whatever their titles and the distribution of their responsibilities."[9]

[4] All this for an estimated $50,000 a year according to Michael Dixon in the *Financial Times*, 22/9/75.
[5] Dean Berry's definition of the mission in the Insead Four Year Plan: 1974-1977.
[6] Minutes of the Board Meeting, 8/12/75.
[7] Minutes of the Board Meeting, 8/12/75.
[8] Minutes of the Board Meeting, 8/12/75.
[9] Minutes of the Board Meeting, 8/12/75.

Other board members, some accustomed to more traditional corporate structures, had profound misgivings, especially concerning the principle of fitting the job to the person. Emile Arrighi de Casanova, representing the Paris Chamber of Commerce and Industry, felt that the 'logical approach' would be: "First, to define the powers of the director general and the dean, and then to recruit the latter in function of the responsibilities to be exercised and not the reverse."[10] The discussion revealed various biases and blind spots, sometimes rooted in cultural models, as to what constituted a 'proper structure' and a 'proper role' for a dean. But the multiplicity of backgrounds and experiences also ensured that the debate yielded more options and insights than might have come from a 'mono-cultural' board.

The conclusion was that the future dean should be given "wider responsibilities, to the extent that the candidate was able and willing to accept these"[11]. Inevitably, this left some scope for misunderstanding about the responsibilities on offer to the incoming dean. Those shortlisted were informed by Cailliau that the power structure was under review, and that the future responsibilities of the dean might be enlarged.[12] One of the candidates, writing to John Loudon, expressed his reservations: "While a certain amount of domestic friction is fine, I frankly could not afford to waste much intellectual or emotional powder on infighting with the director-general. Motivating faculty, strategic and operational planning, assisting in the recruitment of students and funds, are functional activities adding up to a demanding task. My experience indicates to me that the head of an advanced educational institution must also be in charge of its budget ... I could not live with the idea that [the director-general] would have the power to accept or reject [my plans], or to prevent their execution once approved."[13] Another candidate observed that if the dean had the academic leadership and shared financial responsibility then the dean should be the senior person.[14] And a third commented that his ability to co-operate with the director-general "certainly depends on the nature of our respective roles".[15] Even outsiders could see that demarcation disputes between director-general and dean threatened to remain a source of tension and a drain on their energy.

On the other hand, the school clearly held many attractions. The first of these was what Berry liked to call his 'bastard staff',[16] meaning professors with interest in more than one field of academic specialisation. As one candidate wrote: "Insead with a young and talented faculty, a reputation for

---

[10] Minutes of the Board Meeting, 8/12/75.
[11] Minutes of the Board Meeting, 8/12/75.
[12] Minutes of the Board Meeting, 8/12/75.
[13] Letter from Hans Thorelli to John Loudon, 17/12/75.
[14] Notes from meeting with Michael Shanks, 23/1/76.
[15] Letter from Richard Meyer, Professor at Harvard, to Claude Janssen, 19/1/76.
[16] *Financial Times*, 26/7/76.

practicality and innovation, important connections across a continent, and most importantly, freedom from the bureaucratic meshes of the old traditions (e.g. universities, government departments) is uniquely equipped to become a centre of thought and influence."[17]

Later, addressing the incoming students, Pierre Cailliau observed: "Probably the finest testimony to our standing is that when Insead sought a new dean, it was capable of drawing applications from nine professors with first-class international academic reputations and all the requisite qualities."[18] The richness of applicants confirmed Insead's market recognition and its perceived dynamism. The school had never found it easy to fill its top positions. This time round, no one had any trouble seeing its potential. They were queuing up.

THE CAPED CRUSADER

Encouraged to apply by Guy de Carmoy, Uwe Kitzinger reconciled many of the diverse qualities expressed by the search committee. He was a scholar from an Oxford research college, who had published extensively and had even launched the *Journal of Common Market Studies*. He was a militant European, having long campaigned for the cause of European unity. Back in 1951, he had been the first British economist in the Council of Europe in Strasbourg. He spoke five languages and had taught in French, German and British universities; and most recently he had worked in Brussels as adviser to the vice-president of the EEC Commission in charge of external relations, Sir Christopher Soames. He systematically used green ink – the colour of Europe – to sign documents, including his letter of introduction to Insead.

In terms of business experience, he had served for 12 years as investment bursar responsible for the Nuffield College endowment – "a number of million pounds" as he put it nonchalantly[19] – which kept him in daily contact with brokers and financial institutions in London and New York. And he had acted as advisor to a small number of large companies. Apart from being unfamiliar with the specifics of a business school, his credentials looked hugely impressive. When he came to meet the faculty in mid-November 1975, he made even more of an impact, first in his one-to-one encounters and then in front of the assembled faculty.

Sweeping into the main Insead meeting room with his ermine-trimmed academic robes, fair locks, and Moshe Dayan eye-patch, Kitzinger cut a striking figure. A former president of the Oxford Union, he was a natural showman and an accomplished speaker. Just before coming to Insead, he had been writing speeches for the vice-president of the European commission,

---

[17] Charles Handy, "Insead – Beyond the present tradition", Confidential note, December 1975.
[18] Pierre Cailliau speech at the Opening Ceremony of the MBA Programme, 11/9/76.
[19] In Uwe Kitzinger's letter of introduction to Kenneth Walker, 21/10/75.

delivering many of those speeches himself when Sir Christopher Soames was unavailable. He knew how to address an audience.

Gesturing expansively, peppering his speech with imagery, quotations and allusions to the classics, he explained in 15 minutes what he could bring to Insead. His vision was both exalting and original, talking of Europe and the role that Insead could play in it. Those present were spellbound – there was no one at the school remotely like him – and they emerged from the presentation convinced that they had found their future dean. In many ways, he was a throwback to Insead's inaugural years, when the school was a natural forum for European pioneers. He embodied so much of what the school aspired to: a desire to rekindle its European mission, to play on a larger stage, to find support within the European community,[20] and to acquire university values, if not university status. The school was also looking for external visibility, particularly in Britain and Germany, countries in which Kitzinger was well-connected. But the overriding argument, from the faculty's viewpoint, was that Kitzinger seemed capable of generating the kind of organisational excitement from which all else would flow.

Three weeks later, the faculty were asked to vote for one of the three remaining candidates. Longstanding faculty members cannot recall any faculty decision, before or since, being taken so easily. The occasion made a lasting impression on Claude Rameau: "For once, nearly all the faculty were present. Normally, it was virtually impossible to get them to agree on anything. Uwe received around 95 per cent of the votes. The other two candidates got nothing. So it was quasi-unanimous."

The rigorous efforts of the dean search committee, together with the massive backing of the faculty for Kitzinger – 'accidentally' leaked to the board by Heinz Thanheiser – made it difficult for the board to back another candidate. Several board members had reservations but, ultimately, they could not overrule the faculty's choice without provoking a new crisis. It was a piece of brinkmanship, a way for the faculty to reassert its growing strength. In some ways, this was the faculty's retaliation for having a new director-general imposed on them by the board, without consultation or prior warning, two years earlier. In the board meeting of January 1976, Pierre Cailliau was asked to make a formal offer to Kitzinger.

GREAT EXPECTATIONS

Kitzinger was not lacking in courage. To take up the deanship, he had to give up his life-tenured position as an Oxford don. Moreover, Insead's financial situation was widely reported to be shaky after the last instalment of the Ford Foundation grant which had come to its term in August 1975. 'Hard times

---

[20] There was also a vague hope, expressed in the Board Meeting of December 1975, that the EEC might take over where the Ford Foundation had left off. Kitzinger also opened up that possibility.

at Fontainebleau' headlined the *Financial Times* prior to Kitzinger's arrival. The article went on to explain that Kitzinger was joining a school "facing unprecedented financial difficulties" and quoting Dean Berry predicting that: "When Uwe arrives, there'll be no honeymoon period for him, I fear."[21]

Kitzinger was also coming to an institution whose academic reputation was still to be established. As he recalls: "When I was recruited, I asked people around me what they knew of the place, and they said, good teaching but no research. Not an academic institution." This was perhaps unfair in that Berry had clearly set it on course to become one, but outside perceptions take time to catch up. As Berry himself had once remarked: "Our difficulty is that confidence in educational institutions suffer an enormous time lag between past customer beliefs and current reality; one is always emerging out of an image of the past."[22]

In spite of these challenges, Kitzinger remembers being attracted, "First by the European aspect, but also it seemed to be a school that was ripe for real development. It had a lot of potential and a rather bright faculty." He could see opportunities to turn the school into a much more outward looking institution, with greater involvement in European contemporary problems of public as well as private management. As Kitzinger explained to the *Financial Times*, prior to taking office: "Bodies such as the EEC are having great influence over managers' options. The public sector is taking on far more importance in economic matters. In sum, management is now much more concerned with public as well as a private sector activity."[23] Given such a context, it seemed indeed that "the choice of an academically eminent political scientist with high-level experience as a European civil servant as Insead's next dean could well prove a very practical aid to the school's future development."[24]

Numerous outsiders wrote to Pierre Cailliau to applaud what they considered a particularly appropriate yet imaginative appointment for the school.[25] Kitzinger was welcomed as a reinforcement of Insead's European vocation – by his personality, his career and his publications.

The students too, were enthusiastic. Like the faculty before them, they were seduced by Kitzinger's showmanship and powers of oratory, as epitomised by his opening address to the intake of September 1976. Switching fluently between three languages, Kitzinger revealed his ambitious plans for the school: "Insead is not simply a business school, transmitting to

[21] *Financial Times*, 26/7/76.
[22] Minutes of the Board Meeting, 18/6/73.
[23] *Financial Times*, 16/2/76.
[24] *Financial Times*, 16/2/76.
[25] See, in particular, letters of congratulations to Pierre Cailliau from Philip Nind, Director of the Foundation for Management Education (17/2/76), George Lombard, Associate Dean at HBS (20/2/76), James Howell, professor at Stanford University (23/2/76) and H.S. Langstaff, Director of Development at McKinsey (24/2/76).

tomorrow's managers yesterday's tired intellectual capital. Insead is a young and vibrant Institute steeped and involved in the international realities of the day ... Insead is a resource to help modern management grasp its strategic options: it is a crucible of synergy between problem solving, teaching and research."[26]

He went on to tell the incoming students that they would emerge "enriched as human beings by this experiment in multinational living; but above all not as mercenaries simply out to sell yourselves to the highest bidder, but as missionaries of questing open-mindedness and innovation, who see the job of management as the task of strategic choice."[27] Kitzinger had no problem in evoking uplifting visions or spreading the word about Insead. As he recalls: "The obvious niche for Insead was the transcultural idea. That linked up with my mission of uniting Europe. It made a philosophical whole which I could carry with full conviction wherever I went to market the place. It made a story and I rejoiced in telling it."

PLAYING CATCH UP

As mentioned earlier, Insead was in a precarious financial situation when Berry left. The school had experienced two deficits in a row and was finding it difficult to make ends meet. As though to drive home the point, a group of executives on a short course had, sarcastically, organised a whip-round for the purchase of an overhead slide projector. This put considerable pressure on Pierre Cailliau who was trying to guide the development of the school while adjusting to the priorities of a new dean; but who also needed to boost fund-raising while exercising more rigorous cost control.

While the manner of Pierre Cailliau's appointment as director-general had not gone down well with the faculty, Loudon had made a sound choice in Cailliau. He had considerable organisational experience, as well as patience. He had quickly developed a subtle understanding of the school and a strong sense of commitment to it. These had helped to win round members of the faculty who had initially been hostile to him. He had also instilled a more participative form of decision-making at the top by establishing a senior management committee comprising himself, the dean, the associate deans, and the directors of finance/administration and development. It was a first step towards establishing a better balance between the academic and administrative sides of the school.

Under Dean Berry the size and quality of the faculty had risen dramatically, but the administrative side had not kept pace. It now found itself overstretched and unable to provide the level of support needed. At Insead, the attitude had always been one of '*l'intendance suivra*'. Cailliau

[26] Dean's inaugural address to the 18th MBA Programme, 11/9/76.
[27] Dean's inaugural address to the 18th MBA Programme, 11/9/76.

realised that the school could no longer rely exclusively on home-grown talent – such as Odile Jacquin, Odette Jeanguenin, Raymonde Lefrançois or Nicole Orlhac – to run the school and support the faculty. In anticipation of future needs, the school would need to recruit professionals with experience in larger concerns who, though overqualified for the current needs of the school, would help it to assume new dimensions. Taking the unprecedented measure of calling on a headhunter, Cailliau quickly hired Patrice Triaureau as administrative and finance director, then Joanna Foster to look after external and internal communication.

Foster's appointment merely underlined Insead's *ad hoc* development. The school had started out by taking press relations very seriously but, with rapid growth, it had tended to 'slip through the cracks'. For the first time, there would be someone responsible for developing Insead's communication which until then had amounted to little more than responding to press enquiries and producing an amateurish newsletter. Her initial task was to establish from scratch an accurate mailing list of the key journalists in the press, radio and television networks for each of the main countries. The announcement of Uwe Kitzinger's appointment provided the first opportunity for putting that mail list to use. Press releases were sent in German, French and English to 310 papers in 18 countries. The occasion was also used to "put Insead onto the journalistic map"[28] by sending Insead leaflets and programme brochures with the press release.

Of course, the geographic spread of Insead's target audience made it all the more difficult to nurture a core of well-informed journalists who understood what the school was about. It also made it difficult to find a press cuttings service capable of sifting through articles in multiple languages – and subscribing to several services was out of the question given the school's thin resources. Instead the school was forced to rely on the national alumni associations to pick up articles appearing in their countries.

Triaureau, for his part, started investigating where the school could save money and very quickly identified a problem with the existing student residences which the school still leased from the American Art School. These were in a state of some disrepair and needed regular maintenance. They also employed live-in caretakers. In January 1977, Triaureau published a document describing the existing residential situation and the alternatives to it.[29] He showed that the school was subsidising this accommodation to the tune of Frs500,000 a year and commented that it was "absurd to make a deficit on an activity which is incidental to the school's primary mission".[30] He proposed that the school build residences and a restaurant on its grounds and turn it into a real campus. One of Triaureau's strengths was his ability to

[28] Joanna Foster, Resume of Press Activities, Report for the Executive Committee, 10/5/76.
[29] Patrice Triaureau, Insead Residences, Report for the Executive Committee, 14/3/77.
[30] Patrice Triaureau, Insead Residences, Report for the Executive Committee, 14/3/77.

put together a convincing and rigorous proposal. The board had little trouble in seeing the merits of an initiative capable of generating income rather than swallowing it. In October 1977, Olivier Giscard d'Estaing, who had worked closely with the original architect, proposed a small committee to study the various building projects.

Cailliau's concern with beefing up the administrative quality of Insead extended to the faculty. He was keen that professors who invested effort in the institutional development of the school should be recognised: "Several professors have turned down the position of associate dean for the MBA programme; the last one is put off by the advice of his colleagues ... How can we build and develop an institution in these circumstances? Isn't it about time we gave some positive signals to the faculty? Should we not reward, with promotion or even tenure, those who assume sustained responsibility for the running of the school?"[31]

On the fund-raising front, Pierre Cailliau and Jacqueline Tourlier-Pope continued to visit firms and foundations, but they also set up an infrastructure which might do some of the work for them. Through 1976, they worked intensively to establish national development committees. Their chief role would be to provide support for fund-raising, but they could equally get involved in promoting the school or indeed looking for professors.[32] By mid 1977, five committees were in place: in Germany, France, Britain, the Netherlands and the US These were high profile affairs, comprising senior alumni and well connected business figures such as Philip Caldwell (CEO of Ford) on the US committee, Ambroise Roux and Jacques Maisonrouge (respectively heads of Compagnie Générale d'Electricité and IBM Europe) in France and the British banker David Montagu. The reason Insead could attract such respected figures was largely due to John Loudon whose reputation opened many doors.[33] It should be added that these figures were not just status lenders; they actually did work on behalf of Insead. Caldwell, for example, took the time to accompany Cailliau on his extensive trips to the US in order to introduce him to the right people. It was a major effort.

Yet it was clear that fund-raising would never yield the margin necessary to invest significantly in research. So Claude Rameau was encouraged to develop the volume of executive programmes. New programmes were launched such as the Young Managers' Programme and a French version of the successful International Executive Programme, given the unfortunate acronym PIGG. Mainly thanks to this income, Insead raised its self-financing capacity from 62 per cent in 1976 to 75 per cent in 1980. These

---

[31] Memo from Pierre Cailliau to Uwe Kitzinger, 7/12/78.
[32] From document, "Proposal for Modifications to the Structures of Insead", 2/12/74.
[33] Within weeks of Cailliau's appointment, Loudon organised a small function, attended by Henry Ford, David Rockerfeller and a few others, so that Cailliau might introduce himself and the school.

efforts, plus the intensified fund-raising drive, assumed all the more importance in view of Kitzinger's ambitious plans for the school.

THE FONT OF COMPETITIVE ADVANTAGE

From the outset, Kitzinger was convinced that sustainable success would depend on the school's capacity to generate new knowledge. As he commented in his report to the board one-year into the job: "By 1976, the bulk of [the faculty] had become very good teachers. But they needed their intellectual batteries recharging on the substance of what they should teach. The institution had become known for good teaching but a dearth of research – a trend which could not but, in the long run, affect its supply of good academic staff and of good programme participants."[34] This is an important insight, in that research, for a business school, is both an end and a means. Research provides a direct competitive advantage in supplying leading-edge content for the faculty to dispense. It also works indirectly as a way of attracting outstanding people and maintaining the brand.

Before even taking up his post, Kitzinger insisted that the board pass a resolution, pledging its commitment to research. The board expressed "its conviction that the research budget for the academic year 1976–77 represents a minimum investment which could not be reduced without endangering the future of the Institute, and its willingness substantially to increase that part of the budget for 1977–78 and then to pursue this effort in the years to come."[35] In the same board meeting, board members were informed of the 10 per cent cut in salary accepted by staff as a 'voluntary and temporary measure' over nine months to contribute to the research funds.[36] This shows to what extent resources for research were short, but also the possibility of appealing to 'corporate patriotism', characteristics of a still-emerging organisation.

Kitzinger recalls that several members of the board were not entirely receptive to the notion of research, for two reasons: first it took professors away from teaching which was the school's bread and butter activity; and secondly, because it gave the professors an independent value in the market place. To help lower their threshold of resistance to the idea of research, he carefully relabelled it 'academic investment' which had more resonance in their business minds. The term cropped up a lot in his addresses to the board.

Also before arriving, Kitzinger tried to find a high profile academic able to take charge of the school's research and development activities. For several months the school was in negotiation with a German professor, who had been a candidate for the deanship, but it did not work out, leaving Kitzinger to cumulate responsibilities for research with his role as dean.

[34] Annual Academic Report, 1976–77.
[35] Board resolution, 14/6/76.
[36] Thank you letter from Pierre Cailliau to staff, 9/7/76.

A year later Kitzinger managed to lure Dick Meyer, a Harvard professor, to the school to head up the research activities. By consolidating the two associate deanships, for the MBA programme and for executive education, under one person, Kitzinger freed up the funds to create an associate deanship for research. This minor restructuring was driven by financial necessity. But it also made symbolic sense. Formally, at least, this left teaching and research activities on an equal footing, with both associate deans reporting to Kitzinger. In reality, the associate deans were far from equivalent since Dick Meyer was in charge of a still miniscule research activity, while Claude Rameau was left with responsibility for the full range of teaching activities – MBA, EDP and MDU. But it sent a signal, serving to "reflect and reinforce our new balance of priorities".[37]

Another landmark recruit was the appointment of the eminent economist Edith Penrose, widely respected as the author of the standard work on *The Growth of the Firm* (1959). She was perhaps the school's first 'world class' hiring in research. The likes of Meyer and Penrose were very different from the traditional profiles of Insead professors, hired straight out of doctoral programmes. The average age of the faculty was under 37 at the time; there were only five permanent faculty over 40; and the youngest was 26. These senior appointments increased the school's institutional respectability.

Kitzinger took other measures to try to encourage research. A research committee was established in October 1976 and some research and development projects were approved for the allocation of resources. The teaching loads were reduced. Professors were granted sabbaticals. By October 1977, Pierre Cailliau was able to report to the Executive Committee that the school had never before devoted so much time to the development of professors, with four of them away on sabbatical.[38] But more than anything, Kitzinger beat the drum for research in his speeches and in his regular contacts with the press. As reported in the *International Herald Tribune* in 1979, Kitzinger was grateful for the 'inherited stock-in-trade' of US management practice, but stressed that the school could no longer "live off imported capital". He went on: "We cannot go on teaching what we ourselves were taught: what worked in Milwaukee under Eisenhower in the days of Western economic dominance, liberal economies, abundant energy, cheap materials, shortages of labor ... , an apparently infinite environment, perpetual prosperity and exponential growth .... Europe is running into stiff international competition, industries are wilting, and people are out of work; parts of the environment are choking on the by-products of our technology... So we have to question the old assumptions and get down to new research and reflection, we have to do our own thinking and teach our own thing."[39]

[37] Academic Report, 1976-77.
[38] Minutes of Executive Committee, 17/10/77.
[39] *International Herald Tribune*, 20/11/79.

Berry had held a similar line before him, but not with the same flourish.

In 1977, Cailliau announced that the school would be launching its first 'development campaign', the idea being to find funds in order to create five endowed chairs.[40] At the time, the private endowment of chairs was pretty much unheard of in continental Europe, so the school was breaking new ground.

All these changes and initiatives were the upside of Kitzinger's research drive; but there was also a downside.

GROWING PAINS

Kitzinger's change of thrust inevitably generated some internal tensions. The recruitment process, for professors due to start in September 1977, offered the earliest chance to "signal and facilitate the shift in the balance of the institution".[41] The tone was set with the first recruitments which were clearly oriented towards research. The example of Edith Penrose was perhaps the starkest. Eminent though she was, her overtly academic profile was unlikely to appeal to students or executives.

Then came the renewal and promotion process. With 13 out of a total of 38 career contracts up for renewal at the end of Kitzinger's first year this provided ample opportunity to reinforce the message. But Kitzinger also had to consider the likely "effects on the morale of the institute as a whole".[42] He had scrupulously avoided 'fraternising' with the faculty so as not to lay himself open to accusations of favouritism. Four career contracts were not renewed and two were renewed after split votes from the committee. Also three out eight assistant professors applying for promotion were turned down.

This was not a one-off. There being no tenure at the time, even the longest professorial contracts were renewable every five years. Arithmetically, just about every professor would at some time come up before the evaluation committee in the course of Kitzinger's term in office, assuming he completed his mandate. The pruning process engaged at the end of Berry's reign was about to enter into full swing. There were of course some winners. The dynamic marketing department saw four of its professors promoted on the same day. Again this was a signal. Kitzinger had no particular passion for marketing but it was an indication that equity, not equality, would drive the promotion process. The evaluation guidelines specified a need to be very good in at least two of the three categories. So, for those with little interest in

---

[40] Previous 'chairs' had involved individual companies directly paying the salary of a particular professor. The new campaign aimed to create a permanent capital base whereby the professor would be paid from the interest.

[41] Annual Academic Report, 1976–77.

[42] Annual Academic Report, 1976–77.

research and no particular urge to take on administrative duties, the writing was on the wall – however good their teaching.

Of course, this produced clashes, particularly between people who were at polar extremes on the teaching versus research continuum such as Dominique Héau and Spyros Makridakis who virtually came to blows over one case in 1977. The case which brought these tensions to a head concerned a French-speaking professor who taught regularly at Cedep and who was widely acknowledged at Cedep as being "an outstanding teacher".[43]

Inevitably, this decision had serious institutional repercussions on the relations with Cedep. For some at Cedep, this incident was the final proof that Insead was becoming an ivory tower institution. When Cedep was launched, it had been very much complementary to Insead – a forum where Insead's faculty could experiment and discern executive realities. Both had been very much teaching-centred institutions, even if their audiences differed. But the shift towards research had changed all that. Their missions had drifted apart, reducing the possibilities of close partnership between them.[44] They were two separate legal entities, with a common faculty, but no real possibility of arbitration.[45] The arrangement was tending towards one of customer and supplier.

Nevertheless, the prospect of Insead becoming an ivory tower institution was quite ludicrous. To start with, it could not afford to do so. It had to stay close to business to generate income. And for all the fuss about research, the research budget represented barely more than 6 per cent of the operating budget. Measured another way, in terms of faculty activity, research represented around 10 per cent of their time. This did not compare particularly favourably with the commitment to research of the leading business schools: "At Stanford 33 per cent of faculty time is devoted to research, at Harvard 40 per cent and at LBS at least 50 per cent."[46] As Kitzinger once pointed out: "Ours is progress from a derisory base."[47]

Ironically, there was another force preventing the school from going overboard on research: the evaluation guidelines. In reality, the evaluation guidelines were sufficiently vague to allow a variety of profiles to co-exist, provided they did 'enough' in more than one category. There was no 'up or

---

[43] See letter from Pierre Cailliau to Claude Janssen, 5/10/78.

[44] There had actually been an early warning, barely one year into the Cedep programme, of this likely divergence of interests. For the annual meeting of the Cedep company heads, Henri-Claude de Bettignies, in his customary style, wrote a provocative newsletter to stimulate their thinking. The content provoked an allergic reaction from the company heads who had arrived in a spirit of celebration. Copies of the article were gathered up and burned. For de Bettignies this was an infringement of academic freedom and he gave up his office, based in Cedep. The incident in itself was merely a storm in a tea-cup. But it showed a difference in perspective between Insead and Cedep, a symbolic assertion of Insead's emerging academic stance.

[45] Minutes of the Executive Committee, 23/10/79.

[46] Figures cited by Kitzinger to the Executive Committee, 14/3/77.

[47] Summary Academic Report, 1976–77.

out' policy as applied in many US schools, so professors could invest for the long term and had a chance to redistribute their efforts if the evaluation committee found them wanting. It also helped that research was considered broadly, not just as published output but also including pedagogical innovation. Notwithstanding some dramatic terminations, the school managed to retain a highly diversified faculty. For the same reasons, Kitzinger's vision of Insead "becoming *a whole management institute* rather than merely a *business school*",[48] remained a distant project.

APPEARING ON NEW RADAR SCREENS

Kitzinger's ambition for the school was that it should be involved in problems of public as well as private management and that it should be capable of providing policy advice to European institutions. To do this, the school had to reach out to new audiences. While Insead was clearly 'on the map' as a leading European business school, it remained an unknown quantity among numerous constituencies, both occupational and geographical.

Kitzinger wasted little time in plugging the school into his extensive network. Within weeks of starting, he was attending a high-powered fund-raising dinner for the school in London. The guest speakers were Roy Jenkins, on the verge of assuming the presidency of the Commission in Brussels, and Edward Heath, the prime minister responsible for the entry of Britain into the Common Market. Throughout Kitzinger's deanship, Heath and Jenkins would continue to support Insead on public occasions, featuring as guest speakers at various opening and graduating ceremonies, as well as the celebrations for the 20th anniversary of the school in 1979. Heath even sponsored an annual prize to be presented to the student writing the best paper on a European theme.

Other eminent Europeans invited to address the students in Kitzinger's first year included Aurelio Peccei (Club of Rome), Ernst Hans van der Beugel (chairman of the Institute of Strategic Studies) and Christopher Tugendhat (European commissioner). The guest speaker for the MBA opening ceremony in 1977 was another European commissioner, Etienne Davignon. Within such circles, the school had not had much visibility since the departure of Olivier Giscard d'Estaing.

Kitzinger himself travelled extensively to promote the school. He recalls: "I saw myself as a salesman for the idea. It needed somebody with enthusiasm to go out and talk to different audiences. I didn't have to put it on." In fact, he worked himself close to exhaustion. During one particularly intensive spell, Kitzinger was giving a speech in Munich and was suddenly aware of an

---

[48] Annual Academic Report, 1976–77.

embarrassed silence in the audience. He had momentarily fallen asleep in the middle of his own speech.

Kitzinger's attempt to reposition the school as a policy-oriented institution received an important boost with the arrival of Robert Bourassa, the recently unseated Quebec Premier. Bourassa wished to spend time away from politics to research into the financial and economic implications of European federalism. Kitzinger jumped at the chance to take him on as a visiting professor. Although it was only a one-year appointment, Bourassa's profile captured Kitzinger's hopes for the school: that it should become the kind of institution which might attract thinkers from various fields with an interest in European public affairs.[49]

That interest in public affairs was reflected in dispersed efforts to do more work with public sector organisations. For example, the management development unit did work for the French Ministry of Health, the Organization for Economic Co-operation and Development and the EC. The Brussels Commission even recognised the school by making an institutional contribution of 250,000 Belgian Francs, which had symbolic significance.

Edith Penrose, mentioned earlier, was another important capture, in that she gave the school new-found academic visibility, particularly in Britain. She was also the first female professor at Insead which was an important signal for budding faculty members. Her appointment happened to coincide with a wider societal movement in favour of equal opportunities for women. There had been International Women's Year in 1975 and two directives of the European Council calling for equal pay in 1975 and for equal opportunity in 1976.

Insead had never been particularly proactive in this domain. For example, on the student body, the proportion of female students had never exceeded 8 per cent – "a reflection not of our policies, but the cultures from which our candidates are drawn".[50] This was true, but it was not the whole truth. There was also inherent bias in the system. With the encouragement of Kitzinger, the chosen theme for the school's annual colloquium, in May 1977, was 'Women in Management'.

The colloquium attracted a good deal of public attention and prompted internal efforts to promote the MBA course to women. These efforts were reinforced by the recruitment of a former MBA, Claire Pike (Class of '69), as head of admissions. She started with some overdue 'cosmetic' changes, such as including photos of women in the brochure and changing the French application form which referred exclusively to '*le candidat*'. She solicited the

---

[49] In the same spirit, Bertrand de Jouvenel, a renowned political scientist – "able to illustrate his arguments with points from personal discussions with Churchill and Hitler" – was honoured as "Distinguished Visiting Professor" under Kitzinger.

[50] Summary Academic Report, 1976–77.

women alumni to get more involved with the screening of prospective students so that they might gain more of a sense that this might be a place for them; and scholarships were sought out to lower the financial barriers.

By June 1980, 20 scholarships had been found: six from the retailer Marks & Spencer and 14 from the German Marshall Fund. These were well publicised in the press – not just the business press, but also in magazines like *Cosmopolitan* (August 1979) giving Insead greater visibility with a 'new population'. In the space of two years, the number of women per promotion doubled. The 1980 intake counted 41 women (17 per cent). This put Insead more in line with the four leading US schools: Chicago, 17 per cent, Harvard, 25 per cent, Stanford 26 per cent and Columbia, 35 per cent.[51]

In terms of geographic visibility, the results were mixed. The school was having difficulty making any impact on the German market. With seven students in the 1979 intake, the German contingent was no bigger than the Lebanese or Israeli contingents. Progress in the French market was also slow. In 1979, an investigation of Insead's image among big French companies concluded that: "The Insead brand is fairly fuzzy, too fuzzy in fact for people to grasp clearly what they can expect from the school. Some don't know the school at all, though these constitute a small minority."[52]

On the other hand, the school was gaining ground in other regions, notably in Britain which was Kitzinger's home territory, but also in Brazil, parts of Eastern Europe and, of course, South-East Asia.

EASTERN PROMISE

The roots of Insead's Asian involvement dated back to 1972. Under the umbrella of the Management Development Unit, Henri-Claude de Bettignies had organised a number of seminars for Europeans with an interest in Asia, starting with a programme to help prepare European managers to work in Japan, soon followed by a programme for Japanese junior managers.[53] In developing these links with Asia, de Bettignies worked pretty much unsupported internally. The faculty had other concerns. The school was trying to constitute a professional faculty, Cedep and executive education were taking off, so Asia was really at the bottom of the list.

That movement towards Asian business received an unexpected boost, in July 1973, thanks to a two-week-long graduation trip to Japan. With a helping hand from de Bettignies, the students organising the trip managed to get the Japanese employers' association (*Keidanren*) to cover most of the costs of the trip. The students received their diplomas from the prime minister,

[51] *The Business Graduate*, Spring 1980.
[52] Letter from Philippe Rousseau, Independent Consultant, to Claude Rameau, 27/3/79.
[53] The two seminars were called "Management and Business Opportunities in Japan" and "Management and Business Opportunities in Europe".

Kakuei Tanaka,[54] and for many of the 15 or so professors who accompanied them, it was their first exposure to Japan. It proved a real eye-opener. They grasped to what extent Asia, with Japan at its head, was set to become an economic powerhouse.

At the faculty retreat the following year, de Bettignies floated the idea of setting up a centre devoted exclusively to Euro-Asian issues, and recalls 'having a tough time'. As long as the Euro-Asian activity had been part of the MDU, it had attracted little more than indifference. Now, with the idea of an independent centre, it became a much more intellectual and strategic issue as to the use of the school's limited resources, the academic legitimacy of such an activity and the signals such a departure might convey about the European vocation of the school.

A formal proposal was put before the executive committee by Henri-Claude de Bettignies and Claude Rameau in May 1976. It outlined the mission, organisation and legal structure of the proposed centre which would work bilaterally, undertaking research assignments, conducting seminars or advising European firms doing business in Asia and Asian firms operating in Europe.

In June 1976, the board gave de Bettignies the go-ahead to create a Euro-Asia centre, but demanding rigorous financial safeguards so as not to expose the school to further risks. He would need to find a 'club' of 40 founding companies, split equally between Europe and Asia, which were prepared to back the project financially, the aim being to attract about 250 members in the long run. Over two years later, Pierre Cailliau was publicly lamenting the delays in launching the Euro-Asia Centre "for want of support from a certain number of European companies".[55] A key deterrent, it transpired, was the likely overrepresentation of Japanese firms compared to the other Asian countries. At the time, European companies were highly sensitive to the threat represented by Japanese companies and the idea of open exchanges with a large number of Japanese companies seemed too much of a risk. There was a question of aborting the project, yet Euro-Asian activities continued to flourish, showing that the demand existed and was growing.

The project was modified to increase the proportion of firms from South-East Asia and, in its meeting of September 1978, the executive committee "took note of the decision to proceed with the establishment of a Euro-Asian Centre, although on more modest lines than those authorised by the Board on 14th June 1976".[56] The school itself would have to assume a larger responsibility for the management of the centre than was initially envisaged – in other words, this entity would be less independent than Cedep.

[54] Micheline Dehelly recalls staying up all night on the eve of the ceremony to roll the certificates into scrolls held with a small ribbon in order to conform with Japanese protocol.
[55] Pierre Cailliau, Opening Ceremony of the MBA Programme, 9/9/78.
[56] Annual Academic Report, 1977-78.

A year later, in November 1979, the school still only had eight European backers, plus about a dozen Asian concerns.[57] The European backers included Inchcape, Unilever, Barclays, BASF, Lafarge and Paribas – the Asian ones included Nippon Steel, Mitsubishi, and Malaysian Banking Corp.

In early 1980, after numerous setbacks, the centre finally saw day as an independent, non-profit organisation, with Washington Sycip, the well-connected head of the SGV Group in the Philippines, as its first chairman. Located in Fontainebleau with a liaison office in Asia, it was a tribute both to the perseverance of Henri-Claude de Bettignies and also to the strategic flexibility of Insead.

BUSY BUILDING

Patrice Triaureau turned out to be far more than a highly competent finance and administrative director. He was also a natural project manager. According to his calculations the school needed to construct its own restaurant and residences, not just because it made financial sense but also for capacity reasons. For perhaps the first time, the board started to have some faith in the school's financial forecasts.

The projected residences were not intended to accommodate all the students, but rather to relieve the shortage of available housing which was rapidly becoming the main bottleneck on the growth of the MBA programme. Adding a self-service restaurant would foster a more convivial atmosphere and save everyone having to march ten minutes down the road for their meals.

The go-ahead was given by the board in June 1978 and work started the following month. The first problem had been to find a successor to Bernard de La Tour d'Auvergne, the original architect, who had died prematurely. Among the three rival projects presented, the architecture committee settled on Guy Calderon's design.[58] Calderon's challenge would be to build with the same materials and in the same spirit as La Tour d'Auvergne, but with far more stringent cost controls. Calderon would find Triaureau an invaluable ally in the battle to hold subcontractors to their original estimates.

Calderon's design for the residences proposed several small buildings constituting a harmonious whole, but full of twists and free spaces, not linear or monotonous – one French journalist deemed it "a very Latin architecture, favouring contact and interaction, in contrast to the immensity of American architecture".[59] There was very deliberate choice to arrange the 99 bedrooms into apartments each consisting of three bedrooms, a shared living room and a bathroom. Corridor space was squeezed in order to maximise the space available for living rooms, for relaxation and group work.

[57] *Europe: Magazine of the European Community,* November 1979.
[58] See minutes of Executive Committee, 15/2/78.
[59] *Le Parisien Libéré,* 6/9/79.

The restaurant would have a terrace spilling over onto the semi-wooded lawns and no segregated area for faculty. Beneath the restaurant there would be a lounge area, bar and squash court to provide some balance to a campus that might otherwise seem overburdened with working facilities.

In the residences and the restaurant and bar area, the idea was to multiply the opportunities for interaction. Like La Tour d'Auvergne before him, Calderon was conscious of the need to design buildings which would reinforce the principles of cross-cultural exchange and group learning which had made the reputation of the Insead experience.

Thanks to Triaureau's relentless efforts, the buildings were completed in time for the 1979 intake of students. Triaureau was not an easy person to manage. He had vision and ambition for the school, but also for himself. His staff euphemistically referred to him as 'demanding'. He had frequent run-ins with the faculty, partly because he did not hesitate to stand up to them or to pass comment on academic policies. For example, he argued against the proliferation of elective courses on the grounds that they were uneconomical. It took all of Cailliau's personnel experience to preserve Triaureau as a creative force within the school.

But under Cailliau's skilful management, Triaureau pushed for priorities that gave the school a first-class campus. He was relentless in his attention to detail and demanded work be redone if it was not thorough. He finished all his building projects on time and under budget, virtually driving some of the subcontractors into bankruptcy in the process. He brought a systematic spirit to the school which had been lacking before. Triaureau was also the main champion behind the school's investment in IT infrastructure.

Under normal circumstances, the person behind the development of a school's physical plant and infrastructure should not rate much of a mention. But Insead's situation was different. Without an endowment cushion and with little margin for overruns, the school needed to get it right first time. 'Anyone' can manage a building project, but it takes talent, courage and discipline to do it without a safety net.

The new buildings confirmed the renewed financial self-confidence of the institution. As Cailliau put it at the inauguration of the new facilities: "The fact that the school commits itself to an investment of Frs14m is the best possible proof of our belief in the future."[60]

STRUCTURAL TENSIONS

Just over a year into the job, Kitzinger had drawn the attention of the board to the "clumsy, complex and costly structure of decision-making".[61] Including Cedep, there were three separate managers responsible to two

[60] Pierre Cailliau's speech at the opening ceremony of the MBA programme, 9/9/78.
[61] Minutes of Board Meeting, 12/12/77.

separate committees for the closely interlocked aspects of one tiny campus. And that was before the creation of the Euro-Asia Centre!

The crux of this "messy structure" was the relationship between dean and director-general. In Kitzinger's mind, the fact that he had been named by the board implied that he reported directly to the board, not to the director-general.[62] That was not Cailliau's understanding of the structure, and while the two men maintained a good relationship, there were some controversial issues.

For example, in one *Faculty Information* bulletin, in June 1978, Kitzinger had noted: "The Dean appointed [Jean-Claude Thoenig] Associate Dean for research and development ... and the Dean named Henri-Claude de Bettignies, Director of Insead's Euro-Asia activities."[63] Pierre Cailliau took exception to the wording since nominations to key posts required the official seal of the director-general: "Without being overly formal about it," wrote Cailliau, "important nominations should go out under the name of the director general, adding *on the dean's recommendation* where they concern academic posts."[64] It was but one manifestation of the lack of clarity concerning their respective responsibilities, an ambiguity that could result in time-consuming discussions, sometimes requiring arbitration from the chairman and vice-chairman.

More serious, for Kitzinger, was his lack of real control over resource allocation. In December 1978, he told Cailliau that for the first time in their relationship he was in serious disagreement with the level of research investment. From Cailliau's point of view it was more a problem of timing than of principle. Cailliau fully supported the drive towards research but felt that "it would be premature and dangerous to force the pace".[65] He added that the school was "already quaking from the lack of secretaries, analysts, programmers, equipment, instructional material, classroom and office space, marketing and public relations activity ... But I am fully prepared to consider the pros and cons of rival claims on resources as soon as we have the necessary information."[66]

Cailliau was also sceptical about Kitzinger's idea of hiring seasoned professors with strong research records for the recruitment needs. This constituted a break with Insead's established policy of targeting recruits, like Mike Brimm or Philippe Haspeslagh, still on doctoral programmes. In voicing this concern, Cailliau was not attempting to encroach on Kitzinger's academic turf; rather, he was trying to ensure that the recruitment policy remained in line with the school's resources and its range of activities. First,

[62] Letter from Pierre Cailliau to John Loudon, 30/1/79.
[63] *Faculty Information*, No. 91, 9/6/78.
[64] Memo from Pierre Cailliau to Uwe Kitzinger, 12/6/78.
[65] Memo from Pierre Cailliau to Uwe Kitzinger, 7/12/78.
[66] Memo from Pierre Cailliau to Uwe Kitzinger, 7/12/78.

established names would cost more to attract; and second, given the growing executive education needs, the school would soon run into difficulties if it recruited too many pure researchers. Moreover, Cailliau feared that instead of first class talents, the school might end up with 'middle aged' second or third rate professors.[67] Such debates were evidence of the on-going tensions generated by the 'one-over-one' structure.

Adding to these strains were the ambiguous relations with Cedep. As Pierre Cailliau summed it up: "How can the Director of Cedep be responsible for the quality of his programme when it is the Dean of Insead who decides on the recruitment, promotion and assignment of faculty? And how can the Dean decide on the assignment of faculty, the key to successful programmes, if he does not feel the same responsibility for the quality of the Cedep programme, as for those at Insead?"[68]

The tensions which several candidates to the deanship had noted back in 1975 remained unresolved; and goodwill could only achieve so much in overcoming them. Sensing that an insider might be better placed to resolve some of these differences and make the right trade-offs for the school, Cailliau shrewdly started to push Claude Rameau as his potential successor.[69] Rameau's background and career at Insead meant that he had both the trust of the board and that of the faculty. Cailliau was only too aware of the difficulties for an outsider to gain legitimacy with the faculty.

After discussing this 'succession plan' with Kitzinger, Cailliau wrote to Loudon indicating that both Kitzinger and Rameau seemed prepared to make a go of it: "Bicephalism has some serious drawbacks," wrote Cailliau in December 1978. "On the other hand, at this stage we prefer to opt for a solution of continuity than to risk a disruptive break."[70] This arrangement would also avoid having to lift the lid on what Cailliau described as "the Pandora's box of Insead's structure".[71]

In March 1979, as part of grooming Rameau to succeed him, Cailliau informed the executive committee that he planned to give Rameau responsibility for Public Relations, as well as for continuing education and MDU. At the same time, Rameau would relinquish responsibility for the MBA programme, which would once again become an associate deanship position, and would be entrusted to Gareth Dyas. He also proposed that Rameau be named deputy director-general, a nomination which was approved by the board in June 1979. The idea was that Rameau would become director-general from June 1980.

Kitzinger had still believed that he might one day become single dean.

---

[67] Memo from Pierre Cailliau to Uwe Kitzinger, 7/12/78.
[68] Memo from Pierre Cailliau, 6/8/77.
[69] Letter from Pierre Cailliau to John Loudon, 9/10/78.
[70] Letter from Pierre Cailliau to John Loudon, 11/12/78.
[71] Letter from Pierre Cailliau to John Loudon, 9/10/78.

These developments certainly killed off whatever hopes he retained of 'running the whole show'. When Kitzinger tendered his resignation to John Loudon on 25 September 1979, Loudon was half-prepared for the news. Just two months before, Kitzinger had written: "After our various conversations on the structural problems of the campus it will come as no particular surprise to you if I now write formally that I shall not seek any renewal of my Deanship and may indeed leave Insead in the autumn 1980."[72] In the event, Kitzinger who had been offered the Directorship of the Oxford Centre for Management Studies would be leaving with one year still to run on his contract.

A week after announcing his departure, Kitzinger met Loudon and told him: "Though we have achieved a great deal in the past few years, it has been less than we might have done. With the best will in the world even when there is broad agreement on goals, the present form of organisation is too complex."[73]

UNFULFILLED AMBITION

Under Kitzinger, Insead undoubtedly consolidated its research capability and orientation, through his recruiting policies, through his public addresses and through his systematic appeals to the board. In many ways, he was responsible for injecting more scholarly values into the school. Kitzinger attracted prominent figures from the world of public affairs to the school and encouraged greater involvement in public sector activities, notably organising seminars for civil servants from the European Commission. Kitzinger also helped increase visibility in Britain and with the press. Yet, for all his hard work and promotional efforts, the achievements fell some way short of the faculty's hopes when they had elected him. The outlay on research remained fairly paltry, there had been little progress in Germany and the school's links with European business had not appreciably changed.

As stressed by Kitzinger, the complex and ambiguous structure was partly to blame. Having been appointed largely because of his academic reputation and his public standing in Europe, Kitzinger found much of his time was spent discussing issues which could have been clear cut.

It is also likely that the faculty's initial expectations were excessive. They were looking for someone with all the qualities of Dean Berry, but with a bigger vision, better contacts, more charisma and without the American heritage. As Gilbert Sauvage had once commented, it was a search for "God almighty, bogeyman and shrink, all rolled into one".[74] No one could live up to those expectations for long.

[72] Letter from Uwe Kitzinger to John Loudon, 20/7/79.
[73] See letter from Uwe Kitzinger to John Loudon, 25/9/79.
[74] Memo from Gilbert Sauvage to Dean Search Committee, 2/9/75.

Beyond the issue of unwieldy structure or unrealistic expectations, another argument can be advanced to explain why Kitzinger's contribution was not what it might have been. With hindsight, it is possible to say that Kitzinger and the school were never quite in sync. And the warning signs were there from the start.

The key is Kitzinger's background. Coming from Nuffield, a renowned Oxford research college, it is hardly surprising that his vision for the school was that it should become a policy-oriented institution. European unity having been the 'guiding star' in his life, it was also understandable that Kitzinger should see Insead as a vehicle to promote that ideal. The specific model he carried around in his head, as expressed in an interview towards the end of his mandate, was that Insead would become "a sort of European Brookings Institute".[75] What Kitzinger stood for should have been fairly clear. As he understood his appointment, it showed that "the institute welcomes a change of direction".[76]

The notion of turning the school into a think-tank for European affairs had some appeal for the faculty, but they had grown too fond of their academic freedom to be confined to issues of relevance to the European cause. With its expanding links in South America and Asia, Insead had already 'outgrown' its strictly European phase. Kitzinger was expected to give the school better access to various European networks, rather than try to change the mission of the school. And in any case, the school simply did not have the resource base needed to become a policy unit. So there was a degree of wishful thinking on both sides.

Of course, Kitzinger's aspirations for the school shaped his activities and preoccupations. He was reported to be averaging four days a week away from Fontainebleau on promotional activities.[77] By his own admission, Kitzinger enjoyed the representational work but was never especially keen on the managerial duties: "I didn't like sitting on committees, deliberating about someone's promotion. That was not what I felt was the priority. What I did want to do was to go all over the world making speeches about the importance of Europeans finding their own style of management in a Europe which was coalescing – because for me this was part of a political mission."

Another characteristic of Kitzinger's background was his concern with public affairs, rather than business. He was accustomed to dealing with civil servants and politicians, but Insead's chief constituency was composed of business people. This was a pragmatic population for whom Europe was a market, more than an ideal. Kitzinger continued to cultivate economic-cum-political contacts on behalf of the school but somehow they remained separate worlds. He was unable to find a way of bridging the gap between

[75] Report From Europe/Chemical Bank, May 1980.
[76] *The Times*, 16/2/76.
[77] *Financial Times*, 26/4/79.

what he brought to the school and the reality of the school. So it never quite gelled.

Internally, there was a gap too, in terms of style. Kitzinger tried to introduce faculty coffee mornings on Tuesdays. These seemed more in keeping with the pace and interaction of Oxford common rooms than the bustle of a business school, and the ritual failed to catch on. Similarly, Kitzinger's habit of wearing academic robes was initially regarded as part of his colourful and donnish persona. But quickly it came to symbolise the distance between the dean and the young faculty. Kitzinger himself recalls: "People were astonished that I would wear a gown at faculty meetings. It was essential that I should make the point that this was an academic institution. I could not insist on other people wearing gowns. But it was a way of emphasising the academic values."

That psychological distance was not erased by Kitzinger himself. He was not like Dean Berry playing poker late into the night with the faculty. He kept himself apart. As he recalls, this was a conscious choice: "One of my first decisions was to have no outside social interaction with the faculty so as not to become hostage to any coterie, but it also meant that I had no coterie on my side. I felt it was morally the right thing to do since I was so uncertain about what went on in business schools and I had to find out." Looking back, Kitzinger concedes it may not have served him well.

Kitzinger also cultivated a certain eccentricity, perhaps best illustrated by the story of the secretary who walked in to his office to find him crouched beneath his desk trying to put his dodgy shoulder back into place, having dislocated it while putting on his academic gown. Ultimately, there was a similar dislocation between Kitzinger and the school. He failed to develop a sufficient following among the faculty to enact his vision.

GRASPING THE NETTLE

Ironically, the announcement of Kitzinger's resignation fuelled the debate about the school's management structure, the very issue which he had long regarded as his prime stumbling block. Even though he was leaving, Kitzinger continued to campaign for a simpler structure, arguing that: "This opportunity to explore the issue of structure in an objective and constructive fashion must not be allowed to slip by."[78] His calls carried all the more weight given that he no longer had a personal stake in the outcome.

The main problem lay in the division of responsibilities between dean and director-general. Kitzinger urged Loudon to consider making the next dean "responsible to the board not only for the academic activities, but also for finance and administration which cannot in practice be divorced from

---

[78] Letter from Uwe Kitzinger to Guy Landon, 16/10/79.

them".[79] In October 1979, Pierre Cailliau proposed to the executive committee that a task force be set up to study structural reforms, "not to criticise the past, but to shape the future".[80]

John Loudon and Claude Janssen did not take very much convincing. The bulk of their efforts through the early 1970s had been devoted to arbitrating intensively between Dennis and Berry. Cailliau's more conciliatory style meant that fewer problems required arbitration, but the underlying tensions remained both with Berry and with Kitzinger. There was a structural problem, underpinned by a cultural misunderstanding: the dean expected to be dean in the US sense of the term, while the director-general expected to be *directeur général* in the French sense of the term. Roger Godino, the former dean of faculty, who had a feel for both the academic and business dimensions, was asked to head the task force.

A new proposal was needed quite soon as it would be inappropriate to look for a successor to Kitzinger until the new structure had been determined. Cailliau self-effacingly added that "the study on the management structures should be carried through without reference to the people in charge."[81] The implication was that he would step aside should they decide to do away with the position of director-general.

Over the weeks that followed, the task force came up with a number of proposals ranging from a single dean to an eminent business figure seconded by two internal persons.[82] The board was resistant to the idea of a single dean. It also wanted to see Claude Rameau as part of the set-up. The problem was that the new dean needed to have a doctorate, which was not Rameau's case. A compromise solution emerged whereby Rameau would share responsibilities with Heinz Thanheiser, like "joint managing directors" as Loudon put it.[83] The fact that the French services company, Accor, happened to have a similar top management structure did not serve as inspiration, but it did help support the case – the argument being that if this could work even in a French company, then it could work anywhere.

This solution had the merit of spreading the heavy internal and external duties between two people. It also offered a mix of cultures, competencies, and circles of influence which could not be captured in a single person. In typical Insead fashion, however, the responsibilities would not be formally split. They would have to work it out between themselves and would be jointly responsible for all the decisions. Cailliau would stay on, to help usher in this new structure, which would not be officially approved until March 1982.

[79] Letter from Uwe Kitzinger to John Loudon, 20/67/79.
[80] Minutes of the Executive Committee, 23/10/79.
[81] Minutes of the Executive Committee, 23/10/79.
[82] Letter from Pierre Cailliau to Claude Janssen, 6/5/80. The idea of a single dean was rejected by the faculty which was more sensitive to the potential risks than the potential benefits of such a proposition.
[83] Minutes of the Executive Committee, 12/5/80.

It took a lot of effort from Rameau and Thanheiser to persuade the faculty to buy the idea of joint executive responsibility. There was widespread scepticism regarding the likelihood that it could function efficiently. On the other hand, the faculty understood that it might allow the school to do away with the position of director-general. They saw it as a structure which had little chance of lasting, but if it was a way of moving towards a single dean, then it was the price to pay.

CARRY ON REGARDLESS

Kitzinger had started out optimistically, telling journalists of his '12-year plan' to turn Insead into "an institution that teaches, does research into European society with an outward orientation, particularly toward the third world, and directly involves itself in the solution of European problems."[84] In the event Kitzinger's bold plan was thwarted by various factors, not all of them within his control.

Nevertheless, the school continued to make headway, especially on the operational front. Under Cailliau's guidance and capacity to channel energies, the school established a much more solid infrastructure. Together with Jacqueline Tourlier-Pope, he set up the first national development committees which raised the school's visibility considerably. The two of them also worked tirelessly to develop fundraising and to launch the first endowment chairs. Triaureau was encouraged to drive the development of the campus. And in terms of programmes, Rameau oversaw the proliferation of continuing education and de Bettignies spearheaded the expansion of Euro-Asian activities.

During a period when the school was searching for its path, Cailliau was a vital stabilising force. When he arrived, the school was financially, structurally and emotionally fragile. He brought organisational know-how, financial consolidation and a sense of calm and order to the school. As a journalist from the *International Herald Tribune* observed in November 1979: "Despite nagging problems – academic, financial and organizational in nature, plus lingering doubts regarding its usefulness, particularly in Germany – Insead continues to flourish."[85] It was a sign that, under Cailliau's discrete leadership, the school had become sufficiently robust to progress in spite of difficulties and distractions at the top.

By its capacity to reconfigure itself, the school again showed its organisational adaptability and pragmatism. The new structure was not seen as a finality but as a transitional stage to be re-examined when new circumstances demanded. But for the time being, it served its purpose and even reinforced the school's twin allegiances to academia and business.

[84] *The Financial Post*, 20/5/78.
[85] *International Herald Tribune*, 20/11/79.

PART 4

From prominence to impact

CHAPTER 7

Coming of age

"A boy climbs into the cellar of a great and ancient dwelling, irregular in its plan. The boy advances, lingers on the discovery of some treasure, glimpses an entrance, a dark passage, and imagines some alarming presence there, postpones the search to a later occasion, and he proceeds always in tiny steps, on the one hand fearing to go too far, on the other in anticipation of future discoveries." Umberto Eco, *The Island of the Day Before.*

SHUFFLING STRUCTURES

Insead had made a lot of progress through the 1970s. It had acquired an impressive faculty body, a highly regarded MBA programme, and had built an executive education platform capable of generating sufficient revenues to cover three-quarters of its operating budget. It had a reputation for excellence in teaching and real credibility within sections of the business community. But given the impending changes in top management structure, the burning question was whether two people drawn from the faculty ranks would not squander this hard-earned reputation in their pursuit of academic respectability. There was a lot of pressure on Thanheiser and Rameau to show they could be trusted not to alienate the business community. Some on the board still suspected that not replacing Cailliau would be like letting the lunatics run the asylum.

Thanheiser and Rameau, who had given up teaching, were respectively seen as the faculty candidate and the board candidate. Neither was fully acceptable to all stakeholders, so they were forced to work together. This was helped by the fact that they knew each other well, as long-standing faculty members and former Insead students. But it was not helped by the fact that they were working in a structure which was undefined and which no one expected to last. Even as they tried to make a go of it, there was widespread speculation as to what structure should supersede it. The structure's only merit, for the faculty, was that it would help reduce the influence of the board on the school since the board would no longer be able to impose a director-general.

The suspicion of the board and the impatience of the faculty did not make for a comfortable working situation. Fortunately, Cailliau was committed to making it work. He argued for it with the board and carefully managed the transition period. Having seen the frustrations engendered by the previous structure, he realised that someone from the business world would never have full legitimacy with the faculty. He progressively withdrew from day-to-day operations, handing them over to the new duo, and devoting himself increasingly to fund-raising activities. This reflected both his capacity to take a long-term view for the school and his participative style of management. His quiet determination and pragmatism helped bring the dual deanship to life.

For symbolic reasons, Thanheiser and Rameau swapped offices when Cailliau stepped down in July 1982. Thanheiser took over the director-general's office. Rameau, newly promoted from deputy director-general to co-dean, moved into what had traditionally been the dean's office. The intention was to dispel the notion that whatever their titles, this was effectively the same old 'one-over-one' structure of dean and director-general. Under the new system, the responsibility for raising money and spending it was shared. This was fine in theory, but it could take a lot of behind the scenes negotiation to reach agreement.

These internal governance changes coincided with changes in the supervisory structures. Through the 1970s, Insead's board had been one of the school's leading growth areas. Thanks in large part to Loudon's notoriety, the board had attracted or retained numerous influential figures, including Carl Hahn, Philip Caldwell, Paul Delouvrier, Ambroise Roux, Jacques Maisonrouge, Louis Franck, Lars-Erik Thunholm, David Montagu and Edmond de Rothschild. This was of great help in terms of visibility but had enfeebled the board's decision-making capacity. As Warren Cannon recalls: "Many of the board members were not really emotionally involved." Over time, the close-knit executive committee had become the real decision-making forum, the unwieldy board merely ratifying those decisions. From an internal perspective, the existence of several bodies was also unsatisfactory, as pointed out by Pierre Cailliau: "A certain frustration stems from the need to present initiatives successively to the executive committee, then the board, and sometimes the general assembly."[1] With John Loudon, now 75, planning to step down as chairman, and Claude Janssen nominated as his successor, it

[1] Letter from Pierre Cailliau to Claude Janssen, 13/11/80.

seemed the right moment to reduce the size of the board and to restore it to its proper role.

Loudon's statesman-like qualities had brought connections, reputation and visibility to the school. But his influence had also introduced more subtle changes. He established a new role for the chairman of Insead – much more hands-off, yet proactive and ambitious for the school. In terms of style, he shared with Doriot a talent for listening, for asking thought-provoking questions, and for raising the expectations of others. Like Doriot, he had a huge influence on Janssen who, for over a decade, had seen him operate at close quarters. Having been involved from the outset, Janssen was in many ways more 'plugged in' to the school than Loudon, and could afford to pursue a 'hands-off' policy, safe in the knowledge that he would never lose touch with what was going on inside.

Janssen's first challenge was a tricky one. A decision had been made to slash the board from 50 to 24 members, with a strong recommendation "not to exceed twenty members".[2] But how could this be done without losing the goodwill of those effectively 'dropped' from the board? Careful communication of the anticipated role of board members, together with the obligation to attend board meetings three or four times a year, resulted in numerous voluntary withdrawals. In order not to lose these people altogether, another body, called the International Council, was created. Convening just once a year, "composed of eminent personalities", and headed by John Loudon, this advisory body would have all the prestige of the Insead board, with none of the obligations.

Shrewdly, no upper limit was set on the membership of this new body which gave the school a good excuse to go out in search of fresh blood, and to improve its uneven visibility, especially in Scandinavia, Latin America and Asia.[3]

RISIBLE ASSETS

Although Thanheiser and Rameau were now free to run the show, the medium-term outlook for the school, as summarised in their first three-year plan, looked none too bright.[4] The business community was still recovering from the economic downturn of the late 1970s. Finding new sources of public and private subsidies had proved difficult – and income from on-going pledges had been eroded by inflation. Contributions from Cedep had also dropped off quickly, as more visiting instructors were used and

---

[2] Minutes of the Board Meeting, 7/12/81.
[3] Summary Report of the first meeting of the International Council of Insead, 10/10/83.
[4] The three year planning horizon was considered "short enough to project activities and fund flows with reasonable confidence and long enough to break away from the year-to-year incrementalism of budgeting". (Memo from Heinz Thanheiser to faculty, 9/9/80.)

programmes were cut back. Nor was there much prospect of additional income from the MBA programme, since applications and enrolments had been virtually static for a decade. The three-year plan tentatively estimated a growth in class size of six students per year.

The only bright spot was executive education where the school had established a solid reputation: "The international orientation of our programmes combined with a reputation for quality, place us in a market segment where demand is growing and not very price sensitive."[5] Yet optimistic forecasts of 50 per cent growth in this area demanded significant investments "in new programmes and materials, and infrastructure improvements in accommodation on campus, promotion and support facilities and staff." Without these investments, "we are exposing our reputation to more and more risk every year".[6] The warning signs were already there: "The pain is felt, so far, by the staff of the institute, and not yet by our clients."[7] But it was only a matter of time.

The problem was that such investments required money. The down payment on the restaurant and residences had already reduced the school's liquidity to a minimum. And the absence of capital and reserves deprived the school of borrowing capacity. The school was ill-equipped to deal with the routine cash-flow fluctuations which plague any growing organisation.

Indeed it was this shortage of funds which explains what many regard as Insead's greatest missed opportunity. At the start of the 1980s, Cedep ran into serious financial difficulties and Insead was offered the possibility of taking control of the whole operation. The board and deans were initially receptive to the idea, but looking into the deficits they started having doubts. They feared that Cedep might continue to make losses and drag Insead down with it. Of course, it was a tremendous opportunity to expand physically and it would offer access to a supplementary network of companies, but now the school also had 'something to lose' and was reluctant to wager it. Perceptions of risk and opportunity depend on where one stands. With hindsight, it is clear that this was just a blip in Cedep's fortunes. At the time, it was less obvious. Yet, for Insead which had built its strategy on opportunism, it was a rare case of institutional faintheartedness.

Lacking the confidence that it could quickly turn the situation around, Insead came back with a counterproposal – and this is where it made a mistake. It asked for guarantees from the Cedep companies. To put it mildly, this was not well received. If the Cedep companies were to provide guarantees, then why would they need Insead's help? The offer was indignantly withdrawn and relations between the parties would take a long time to recover from this gaffe.

---

[5] *Insead: Medium-Term Outlook*, Heinz Thanheiser and Claude Rameau, 28/4/81.
[6] *Insead: Medium-Term Outlook*, Heinz Thanheiser and Claude Rameau, 28/4/81.
[7] *Insead: Medium-Term Outlook*, Heinz Thanheiser and Claude Rameau, 28/4/81.

Besides the perennial lack of funds, an additional bottleneck to growth was also emerging. Faculty recruitment had become increasingly problematic in the late 1970s. By 1980, Insead was having difficulty even filling its recently created chairs. There was an easy explanation. Without offering tenure, Insead could not lure experienced candidates who already had tenure in their own institutions. This, together with the fact that Insead's own maturing faculty were now being offered that status elsewhere, precipitated the introduction of tenure in June 1981. The first beneficiaries were: Henri-Claude de Bettignies, André Laurent, Spyros Makridakis, Claude Michaud, Claude Rameau and Lee Remmers.

Tenure perhaps helped retain some faculty members the school could ill-afford to lose, but it did not apply to young newcomers. So, even with tenure in place, recruitment problems continued to plague the school. Again, there was a fairly straightforward explanation: "Insead's compensation package is relatively low and research support is not yet so good, while performance pressure is uncomfortably high."[8] Recruitment could barely keep pace with turnover and, by 1981, the school had 34 full-time professors – two less than five years earlier.[9]

It did not help that there was also a severe shortage of doctoral students graduating from the US schools which persisted throughout the early 1980s. "A survey of the American Assembly of Collegiate Schools of Business member schools indicated 3,145 unfilled faculty positions in 1985–86 versus 876 doctorates granted."[10]

Notwithstanding these difficult conditions, the school still managed to entice some high quality recruits, including Antonio Borges, Yves Doz, Arnoud De Meyer and Philippe Naert. Asked why he had traded his job at Harvard for the same position at Insead, Doz once explained: "Insead was more willing to give me entrepreneurial freedom. They let me set things up pretty much as I wanted."[11] But there were not so many academics prepared to accept the material sacrifices.

To complete a fairly bleak picture, Insead also suffered from a certain stagnation in terms of visibility: "Our active clients are satisfied with our programmes but we promote and explain our services to too few *new* companies, even in France."[12] As asserted by John Loudon, in early 1983: "Neither enough time nor money was ever devoted to external relations, to publicise our philosophy and attract participants as well as professors. This issue is a top priority."[13] Soon after, Jean-Pierre Salzmann was recruited to look after external relations on a full time basis.[14]

[8] *Insead: Medium-Term Outlook*, Heinz Thanheiser and Claude Rameau, 28/4/81.
[9] *Insead: Medium-Term Outlook*, Heinz Thanheiser and Claude Rameau, 28/4/81.
[10] *Reflections on Insead's Strategy*, unsigned document, June 1986.
[11] *Town & Country*, April 1985.
[12] *Insead: Medium-Term Outlook*, Heinz Thanheiser and Claude Rameau, 28/4/81.
[13] Minutes of the Board Meeting, 21/3/83.
[14] Minutes of the Board Meeting, 24/6/83.

TENDING THE FLAGSHIP

Pierre Cailliau was not entirely convinced by the proposed strategy, and wrote: "Our current plan is oriented exclusively towards growth in executive education. It is a debatable option which could, in a few years, prove unhealthy. Insead's management might be forced to increase the size of the MBA or even create a doctoral programme as a counterweight."[15]

At the time, neither of these options seemed likely: the doctoral programme for cost reasons, the MBA programme for demand reasons. As noted in a 1979 report by the MBA task force: "Our current market has little natural growth in it. In particular, projections from US MBA market experience are nearly irrelevant given the totally different nature and structure of education on the two continents."[16] To give an idea of the difference in scale, the US was turning out around 48,000 MBAs a year in 1978, while Europe barely produced a measly 1,500.[17]

Whatever the growth trend, Insead's current MBA offering was in need of an overhaul. The course content had to be made more attractive to potential students, and the programme itself needed to be re-organised to accommodate changes in the size of intake, whether up or down. These twin objectives were neatly reconciled by the notion of 'dual entry', proposed by the task force, and pushed by Gareth Dyas as head of the MBA programme.[18]

Dual entry would mean that instead of receiving four sections in early September, two sections would be admitted then and the other two in January of the following year. For prospective students this had a number of advantages. First, it gave them more choice about what time of year to attend. Secondly, it meant that elective courses would be available all year round, not just from March to June, thus opening up the possibility of exemptions from certain core courses. This would enable students to pack more learning into their year of study.[19] It would also help professors on core courses who had previously struggled to teach the basics to the uninitiated, while at the same time trying to maintain the interest of those who had already covered the subject extensively as undergraduates.

In terms of the future size and structural flexibility of the programme, this option also made sense. It would allow the programme to "adjust better to demands for change, either from the faculty or from the market place."[20] It

---

[15] Letter from Pierre Cailliau to Claude Janssen, 17/2/82.
[16] *MBA Task Force*, Draft Report, Reinhard Angelmar, Gareth Dyas, Herwig Langohr, 20/6/79.
[17] *MBA Task Force*, Draft Report, Reinhard Angelmar, Gareth Dyas, Herwig Langohr, 20/6/79.
[18] It was not the first time dual entry had been envisaged – Bob Boland, a longstanding visiting professor, had proposed a similar system nearly a decade earlier – but it was the first time the evidence had been marshalled and the arguments fully articulated to support it. The task force, headed by Gareth Dyas, made a strong recommendation to move to such a system.
[19] Letter from Pierre Cailliau to Claude Janssen, 17/2/82.
[20] MBA Task Force, Draft Report, Reinhard Angelmar, Gareth Dyas, Herwig Langohr, 20/6/79.

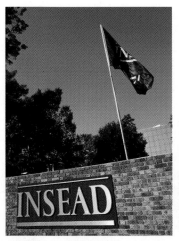

New Insead logo

Claude Janssen, Chairman of the Board, 1982 –

J. Marcou, O. Giscard d'Estaing, C. Janssen;

R. Godino, C. Janssen

Claude Janssen opening the September 1982 MBA class

1984 European Summit in Fontainebleau: Margaret Thatcher, British Prime Minister, prepares to meet the press

1984 European Summit: François Mitterrand, President of France, presents the new European passport in the main amphitheatre

Heinz Thanheiser and Claude Rameau, Co-Deans, 1982–1986

Gabriel Hawawini, Finance Professor

Paul Evans, Organisational Behaviour Professor

W. Chan Kim, Strategy Professor

Yves Doz, Strategy Professor

Arnoud De Meyer, Operations
Management Professor

Reinhard Angelmar, Marketing
Professor

Karel Cool and Ingemar Dierickx,
Strategy Professors

Henri-Claude de Bettignies,
Organisational Behaviour
Professor

*Claude Rameau and Philippe
Naert, Co-Deans, 1986–1990*

*Meeting of the Presidents of the INSEAD Alumni Association and of the
Alumni Fund in 1989: C. Rameau, J.-M. d'Arjuzon, founder of the
Association, R. Wippermann, J. Friisberg, M. Butt, C. Janssen, M. Gauthier,
founder of the Fund and J. Cutts*

*Mike Brimm, Organisational Behaviour Professor, accepting the "Best Teacher
of the Year" award from Per Kaufmann during the 1987 graduation ceremony,
the Guest of Honour being Pier Carlo Falotti, Chairman of Digital Equipment
Corporation International*

Antonio Borges, Associate Dean for the MBA programme introducing speakers for a "Business and the Media seminar" and featuring on the cover of Fortune

Born in Portugal, educated in the U.S., Antonio Borges, 38, now heads the MBA program at Insead in France.

Salvatore Teresi, Director of
Cedep, on the day of his
retirement in 1991

Claude Rameau and Ludo Van der
Heyden, Co-Deans, 1990–1993

Inauguration of the International
Information Centre and of the Georges
and Edna Doriot Library in September
1990; G. Caldéron, Architect,
P. Triaureau, Finance and
Administration Director

Lindsay Owen-Jones (MBA
1969), Chairman of
L'Oréal, during the opening
ceremony of the programme
on the same day

In January 1990, Gerard Van Schaik, Chairman of Heineken and President of the Netherlands Council hands over the cheque to Claude Janssen for the creation of the Alfred H. Heineken Chair in Marketing

Past and present Insead leaders pay homage to the departing Claude Rameau in 1995: D. Berry, H. Thanheiser, P. Naert, C. Rameau, R. Godino, U. Kitzinger, L. Van der Heyden and A. Borges, with M. Dehelly

Ludo Van der Heyden and Antonio Borges, Co-Deans, 1993–1995

Faculty win the 1994 European Case Clearing House Awards : R. Angelmar, K. Cool, J. Gray (ECCH), S. Schneider, L. Gabel, C. Pinson, Y. Doz and S. Goshal

PhDs with the Deans after graduation in 1995: A. Borges, F. Lajeri, L. Almeida Costa, J. Amaro de Matos, G. Szulanski, B. Leleux, L.T. Nielsen and L. Van der Heyden

 *Logo of the Insead campaign*

David Simon (MBA '66), Chairman of BP, John Loudon and Tuulikki Janssen, Jean-Pierre Berghmans (MBA '74), Chairman of the Lhoist Group during the launch ceremony of the Insead development campaign in September 1995

Antonio Borges, Dean,
1995–2000

David Scholey, Chairman of the International Council, Marie-Sophie L'Hélias
Delattre (MBA '92), President of Franklin Global Investor Services, Jürgen
Schrempp, Chairman of Daimler-Benz, during the 1997 March meeting of the
Council

Members of the Insead Alumni Fund Board of Trustees in 1998 : J. Boyer,
MBA '86, Chairman, B. Goldring, MBA '82, F. Burgel, MBA '73, L. Freling,
MBA '63, J. Walton, L. Consiglio, MBA '82, R. Chamberlain, MBA '70,
G. Hawawini, J. de Valk, MBA '81, E. Willam, MBA '78, J. Cutts, MBA '76

1998 Meeting of the Circle of Patrons: C. Rameau, B. Larcombe, CEO of 3i, M. Kets de Vries, the Raoul de Vitry d'Avaucourt Professor in Human Resource Management, J. Clarkeson, Chairman of The Boston Consulting Group

Ann and John Clarkeson during the naming ceremony of the BCG amphitheatre

1959–1999

Students at the Palace in 1961, and on campus in 1998

MBA class at the Collège des Carmes in Avon in 1963, executive course with J.-C. Larréché, The Alfred H. Heineken Professor of Marketing on campus in 1998

1959–1999

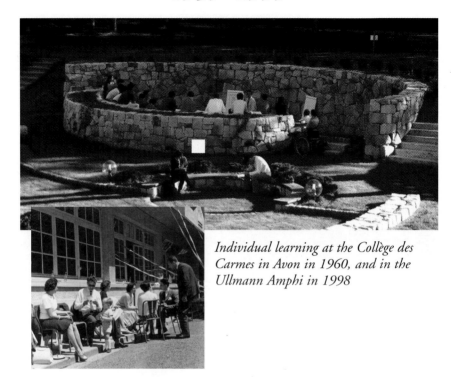

Individual learning at the Collège des Carmes in Avon in 1960, and in the Ullmann Amphi in 1998

Group work on campus in 1988 and in 1970

Library on campus in 1998 and at the Collège des Carmes 1961

Restaurant at the Collège des Carmes in 1962, at the Hôtel de France et d'Angleterre in 1968 and on the campus in 1999

1959–1999

Entrance of Insead at the Palace, with its temporary notice in September 1959

3-D rendering of Insead architectural plans for the campus in Asia

Entrance of the Fontainebleau campus in 1999

even opened up the possibility of offering a sandwich-type course.[21] Such flexibility would be welcome if there was a sudden drop in MBA demand. The 'dual entry' proposal was approved by the board in June 1982,[22] and launched in January 1983. Annual enrolments immediately topped the 300 threshold for the first time.

The new system affected staff, faculty and students in different ways. For the staff, accustomed to dealing with one massive admissions peak and one massive placement process, it helped to spread the load. The annual panic gave way to a more continuous rhythm and more specialised jobs. Similarly, it removed some of the burden for helping the students to set up the partners' programme or to organise events like the annual cabaret or the summer ball. But there was a price to pay. Because of the overlap between intakes, the student body suddenly acquired 'memory' – and as Jacqueline Tourlier-Pope puts it: "That meant there were no secrets anymore."

Until then, whatever mistakes had been made by faculty or administration in their handling of students were conveniently forgotten once the class graduated. Proposed changes and student complaints about aspects of the course or the running of the school could be dismissed by claiming there was a task force investigating the issue. With dual entry, the students were able to retort: "That's what you said last year, and the year before." This created a new pressure to improve standards, especially in teaching. Previously, an elective with a sexy title might survive indefinitely even with weak content. Now, less successful electives quickly developed reputations that became hard to overcome. Professors were forced to work harder on their teaching skills too because, if they flopped, they would not be starting with a clean slate for the following intake.

Of course, dual entry also had a social and psychological impact on the student body. It made it easier for incoming students to adapt and integrate themselves to life on campus. Until then, the only real 'glue' between successive intakes had been Joyce Allport who, from 1970 onwards, had welcomed, mothered and counselled students from her post at the round desk at the centre of the main amphitheatres, known as the 'camembert'. With the introduction of dual entry, the socialisation process was accelerated. Newcomers were able to draw on the experience of their peers, particularly vital now that students were managing their own paths through the learning system. The atmosphere became less volatile as the preoccupations of one class – workloads, exams, expulsions, job search – were offset by those of the other class. Dual entry gave perspective.

This argument did not feature in any of the official proposals concerning dual entry, but it had been very much at the forefront of Dyas' mind. While a student at Insead, in the mid 1960s, he had seen at first hand how collective

[21] Pierre Cailliau's speech at the Graduation Ceremony, 23/6/82.
[22] Minutes of the Board Meeting, 24/6/82.

hysteria could take hold of the student body in pressure situations. On taking charge of the MBA programme, he was only too aware of the risks. As he recalls: "For me, it was the apprehension of dealing with a potential student riot all the time. We'd had one in 1964, when there were only 130 of us, and it was barely controllable. If we had one with over twice that number, we'd be in trouble ... I'd seen at Harvard that even with limited contact between graduating classes, there seemed to be less sense of isolation and more stability."

THE LIFT FROM THE SUMMIT

In early 1984, Claude Rameau received an unusual request, via the regional prefect, from the President of France. Fontainebleau palace had been proposed as the venue for the next European summit, but only if Insead was prepared to house the vast press corps which would report on the event. It would essentially mean cancelling all programmes for three days in June. Rameau was given 24 hours to think about it. The answer was yes, provided that the European chiefs of state paid a visit to the school at some stage, otherwise it was merely an inconvenience. They agreed and the press conference, presided over by François Mitterrand, was conducted in Insead's main amphitheatre. Symbolically, Mitterrand chose this occasion to present the first European passport, with its maroon cover, to the audience.

This whole event may appear to be of tenuous significance to the strategic development of the school, even if some insiders saw it as a fitting tribute to the school's original mission. In truth, the choice of Insead probably said more about the school's facilities than its European credentials. It also said a lot for the school's ability to react quickly and pull off the whole thing. It demonstrated the school's alertness to unexpected opportunities and willingness to respond. It also confirmed Triaureau's capacity to orchestrate complex events and the staff's capacity to host people from multiple nationalities. It was on a larger scale from what they were used to, but it was the same game. As recalled by Gareth Dyas, the event had a very positive effect on employee morale: "It was an adventure. But also, staff who had perhaps thought of themselves as 'provincial amateurs' suddenly realised that they were highly competent professionals. The government officials went away very impressed."

Whatever the immediate payoff in terms of visibility or internal morale, this event also holds a much deeper contextual significance. The purpose of the summit was to agree on the calendar for creating a Single European Market. It was during this summit that the date of 1992 was finalised – indeed the official announcement of the accord was made in the school.[23]

---

[23] People tend to remember the Maastricht summit which was the follow-up to the Fontainebleau summit. The Fontainebleau agreement concerned the calendar for European integration, whereas the Maastricht agreement concerned preparations for further integration post-1992.

The state of Europe in the late 1970s and early 1980s was not particularly healthy. Economically, the context was one of unemployment and stagflation, with European currencies struggling against the dollar. Politically, Europe seemed unsure of itself. In France, the Socialists had recently come to power and nationalisation was the order of the day. In Germany it was the Christian Democrats, under a still unconvincing Helmut Kohl. And in Britain it was the Tories, with Margaret Thatcher engaged in a war of attrition with the unions, especially the coal miners. The prospect of finding some kind of common ground between these parties seemed slim. Euro-pessimism was all the rage.

Against that backdrop, Insead remained a slightly marginal institution, fighting an uphill battle to communicate its message, but having difficulty in reaching out beyond its existing following. The school's inconsistent visibility was inadvertently captured by the *Wall Street Journal*'s 1984 headline: "Europe's answer to Harvard Business School becomes a Mecca for Multinational Recruiters".[24] On the one hand, this trumpeted Insead's premier reputation with multinational corporations, prompting the journalist to comment: "The school's alumni directory has become such hot property for headhunters that Insead officials keep their copies under lock and key."[25] On the other hand, the fact that Insead was still being referred to as 'Europe's Harvard' showed that, for a US readership, the name Insead was far from meaningful in its own right.

The Fontainebleau summit, with its 1992 focal point, marked a sweeping renewal of interest in Europe. For Insead, it was a godsend. Suddenly, in the mid-1980s Europe started to become hot news. There were the first mutterings of cross border activity – launched in earnest, in 1986, by France's CGE and ITT in telecommunications, and Volkswagen and Seat in autos. The fact that '1992' eventually turned out to be a damp squib is unimportant. The sense of anticipation and anxiety which surrounded the run-up to the date is what mattered. As in the early 1960s, Insead once again became the focus of attention for anyone with an interest in Europe. The marketing of executive programmes became easier; so did the recruitment of professors and the placing of students. The school's message gained new resonance. As in the early years, the play of contingency may not have been decisive, but it was certainly beneficial.

---

[24] *The Wall Street Journal*, 30/10/84.
[25] *The Wall Street Journal*, 30/10/84. It is worth adding that the alumni directory was the initiative of an alumnus, Alan Philipp (Class of '67), who launched it and made a business on the basis of it, at the end of the 1960s.

TAKING LIBERTIES

Launching overlapping classes and taking on the Summit arrangements were both manifestations of the school's growing self-assurance under the dual deanship. But there were others. For example, the school boasted a highly successful joint venture with Stanford, the Advanced Management Programme (AMP), dating back to 1968. The AMP represented an important share of executive education revenues and played a critical role for the visibility of the school. But by 1980, many considered that the collaboration had run its course. Insead professors had developed their executive teaching competencies quicker than expected, thanks largely to their experience at Cedep, and no longer needed Stanford professors to 'hold their hand'.

As Claude Rameau put it to the board: "Today, the joint programme has more drawbacks than benefits. Far from enhancing Insead's reputation, it tarnishes it in that it suggests that Insead is not yet mature enough to conduct this programme alone."[26] The decision to terminate this agreement, as from 1982, underlined Insead's desire for independence.[27] Henceforth, the school would take full responsibility for its most prestigious programme. It would also pocket the full margin from the programme.

That self-confidence was also evident in the classroom, where professors were increasingly abandoning traditional case material in favour of their own approaches. In particular, the school was playing a pioneering role in the design of business simulations and computer aided learning tools. For example, Spyros Makridakis had found a ingenious way of introducing novices to statistics, by creating a software package baptised 'Interactive Statistical Program'. Students were presented with salary data for students from previous years, and asked to relate them to factors such as type of job, geographic location and sex of the incumbent. Students found the approach academically and professionally stimulating.

Some of these developments were so successful that teaching material was actually starting to flow back the other way across the Atlantic. By 1984, the *International Herald Tribune* was trumpeting the success of Jean-Claude Larréché's *Markstrat* simulation invented in the late 1970s but recently redesigned "for microcomputer use".[28] The visibility of this training tool was enhanced by launching an international *Markstrat* competition in conjunction with the *Economist* (22/12/84). Another simulation exercise,

---

[26] Minutes of Executive Committee, 24/3/80.

[27] The unpleasant task of informing the Dean of Stanford fell to Pierre Cailliau. It was particularly delicate in that the Dean of Stanford had helped organise fundraising dinners for Insead and was a member of Insead's US council.

[28] *International Herald Tribune*, 14/11/84. In second generation simulations, there was no set formula for winning. Decisions submitted to the model – the set of algorithms which translates decisions into results – would produce different results depending on the parallel decisions of the other teams.

Industrat, the brainchild of David Weinstein, achieved similar popularity and became a standard teaching tool in US and European business schools alike. These were significant pedagogical coups in that they helped to spread Insead's reputation in both the business and the academic communities.

Another measure of the school's growing self-assurance was its venturesome development campaigns. By 1984, the first development campaign had resulted in the endowment of three chairs – the John Loudon Chair of International Management, the Raoul de Vitry Chair of Human Resource Management and the Chair in International Finance. For its part, the International Alumni Fund funded a Fellowship in Entrepreneurship and Innovation. Encouraged by these results, Heinz Thanheiser decided that the time had come to approach companies for targeted research funds. The existing situation whereby research income was generated by increasing executive teaching seemed somewhat self-defeating in that it consumed faculty time.

After extensive consultation with the various international boards and committees, four priority research areas were defined. These areas would serve as umbrellas for portfolios of related research projects. Some were designed to build on existing strengths like 'International Financial Services'. Others were intended to put Insead 'on the map' in a particular area, as in the case of 'Management of Technology and Innovation'. The fund-raising programme, dubbed 'Partners for the Future' was officially launched in 1985. It was new in that the faculty were drawn into the fund-raising mechanism. The consultation process and the title of the programme, highlighted the school's determination to reconcile academic and business preoccupations, to invest in research which was both innovative and relevant. It also proved to rather sceptical board members that the school was now capable of attracting pledges without promising anything specific in return.

In a more general sense, the early 1980s saw the board progressively gain confidence in the judgement of the two deans. It was that confidence which persuaded the board to approve the deans' proposal for a massive salary increase for faculty over three years, starting in 1985. This salary rise was driven by sustained faculty complaints, but actually exceeded even their hopes. Needless to say, it also caused resentment from the administrative side, but it somehow symbolised the deans' new found latitude and their readiness to use it.

MONUMENTS TO THE FUTURE

Throughout the early 1980s, building work proceeded on a fairly continuous basis with the addition of new office space, residences and classrooms and the renovation of the main amphitheatres. The architect, Guy Calderon, became a quasi-permanent fixture on campus. But two building projects stood out as special challenges and symbolic developments.

The first concerned the Euro-Asia Centre which, by 1983, was taking up too much space within the school. Since the centre was already an established entity, the decision to give it a physical home could be regarded as the next logical step. True, but there were other options. Given that the Euro-Asia Centre was legally separate from Insead, the building could have been erected elsewhere, off-campus. Indeed, it could, quite appropriately, have been located in Asia. The school's decision to maintain the Euro-Asia Centre on its crowded campus was therefore significant. It was a symbolic assertion of the school's mission. It confirmed the school's shifting identity from a European school with an international outlook to that of an international school with a European emphasis.[29]

From a strategic standpoint, keeping the Euro-Asia Centre on campus would maintain access to the 100-strong network of partner firms which de Bettignies had assembled around the centre. Moreover, it would allow professors who were not already Asia specialists to acquire an understanding of Asian business. It subsequently enabled the likes of Gabriel Hawawini, Arnoud de Meyer and Christian Pinson to hone their Asian competencies.

In order to give Guy Calderon a better feel for the kind of building he had in mind, Henri-Claude de Bettignies took him and Patrice Triaureau to visit Japan and Taiwan. "I wanted them to see the oak parquets, the columns, the water channels, the gardens and so on. We went along the Taipei River for three weeks." The challenge for Calderon would be to give the building an explicit Asian dimension which was neither a caricature nor at odds with the existing architecture.

Outwardly, the final result was perfectly in keeping with the rest of the campus. But the interior held many surprises. There were four small gardens, only clearly visible from inside, which had been landscaped by Japanese gardeners. The interior decoration comprised wooden floors and a long ornamental pond, with small bridges leading into the work areas. The whole ambience was peaceful and reflective. As with previous building projects, Triaureau was intimately involved in its timely completion and inauguration in November 1985. The building gave extra visibility to the Euro-Asia Centre and its design was widely admired.[30]

However, there was another construction project which was even dearer to Triaureau. One month prior to the inauguration of the Euro-Asia Centre, Triaureau unveiled his grand design for an International Information Centre (IIC). The 50-page document, complete with architect's plans, proposed a fully integrated information centre which would centralise the school's library, information technology, telecommunication and printing facilities. The idea was that anyone needing information could locate it, access it, save

[29] Minutes of the Chairman's Meeting, 9/6/86.
[30] A doctoral student, unrelated to Insead, later completed a thesis on the conception and design of the Euro-Asia Centre.

it, manipulate it and share it as efficiently as possible. This was meant to be the heart of the learning community, the answer to the research, teaching, administrative and marketing needs.

While board members were comforted by Triaureau's track record of estimating costs and managing projects, they were understandably hesitant about a massive investment which would not help generate any revenues. Nor were the faculty convinced of the need to integrate those disparate activities. All they cared about was a well stocked and well run library, and powerful computing capabilities for research. These conceptual tensions were overlaid with faculty suspicions that Triaureau wanted to push his way into the top management set-up.

PASSING THE BATON

The period of Thanheiser and Rameau as dual deans was not really one of dramatic coups or strategic re-orientations. They helped prepare the school for a new growth trajectory by building up a complex organisation of people with matrix responsibilities for particular regions, particular industrial sectors or types of companies, and particular programmes. But in many ways their biggest achievement was actually the least visible one. They managed to find a *modus operandi* which confounded predictions that the management structure would never work. As Thanheiser recalls: "Deciding who would do what, splitting the roles was an evolving process, very organic. We learned as we went." Like bumblebees in flight, the wonder was not that they did it well, but that they managed it at all. Their trial and error apprenticeship established the dual deanship as a viable arrangement.

At the same time, by presenting a united front to the board and exercising sufficient control over the "unruly adolescents", as Thanheiser called them, they confirmed that the school was now mature enough to dispense with direct supervision from business people. Certainly for Claude Janssen, this was the least troublesome period he had known in his long association with the school,[31] and he argued strongly in favour of repeating the experiment, telling board members: "Of course, the value of such a structure is entirely dependent upon the quality of the incumbents. The complementarity of the two current deans has been instrumental to the progress of Insead over the last four years."[32] With Rameau's mandate due to run for two more years, it remained to find a suitable replacement for Thanheiser.

This proved more difficult than anticipated. The dean search committee identified several suitable internal possibilities, but there were no takers. To outsiders, the dean's job might appear to be the pinnacle of an academic career. But insiders saw it differently, having seen the high price paid by

[31] Minutes of the Board Meeting, 22/6/84.
[32] Minutes of the Board Meeting, 25/3/85.

Thanheiser for the privilege. First of all, there was the career damage incurred by losing touch with research developments in the field. The incumbent also faced a significant financial loss in that lucrative consulting work would have to be turned down for five years. Then, there was the job itself to consider: trying to handle temperamental faculty, truculent students and inquisitive alumni, accommodating the interests of diverse stakeholders, with lengthy spells on the road, raising funds and representing the school, had limited appeal for most academics. And what about re-entry? The sudden 'drop' in status would involve a serious psychological readjustment. Nor was there any guarantee that one would be forgiven for decisions one had made while in charge. Given the absence of volunteers, the head of the search committee, Philippe Naert, did the only decent thing, and declared that he would be willing to make the sacrifice.

Naert had only arrived at the school 18 months earlier, in September 1984 from MIT, to take over from Edith Penrose as associate dean for research. As far as the board was concerned he was something of an unknown quantity, possibly even a loose cannon. The board was especially concerned about Naert's continued residence in Belgium. But Rameau's presence reassured board members sufficiently for them to take the chance. The overlapping mandates were certainly helpful in this respect, allowing the school to develop and change tack without excessive uncertainty or great upheaval. The relatively smooth transition from Thanheiser to Naert suggested a more robust and sustainable structure than had been anticipated – but also said a lot for Rameau's capacity to adapt.

Though fairly new to the school, Naert had considerable academic experience, especially in research, and had an uncluttered view of what needed to be done to hoist the school into the very top tier. In his presentation to the board in March 1986, Naert exposed what he saw as Insead's lingering weaknesses. He stressed the inadequacy of research per capita and the weak image in the 'academic community'. His proposed remedy was to "increase the size of the permanent faculty body by about 50 per cent" and to "create a doctoral programme".[33]

Naert's recruiting drive started immediately with an intensive tour of the top US campuses, in search of talent. What did he have to offer them? The doctoral programme was a hypothetical project, but Naert was adamant that it would see day. It was helpful that Europe was emerging as a region where exciting things were now happening. Naert also had an unexpected windfall. When the hefty increase in faculty salaries had been negotiated under the previous co-deanship, the dollar was worth about 10 francs and inflation was in double figures. By May 1987, the dollar had collapsed to under six francs

---

[33] Minutes of the Board Meeting, 10/3/86.

and inflation had dropped off by several points. All of a sudden, the school was proposing salaries which were competitive, even by US standards.[34]

THE GROWTH GAME

Naert implemented a number of measures to facilitate recruiting. A database of doctoral students in 25 leading US and Canadian business schools was established and professors were encouraged to attend conferences where they might approach or hear about potential candidates. Also, the term served by department heads, democratically known as 'area co-ordinators', was extended from one year to four years in order to facilitate continuity in the recruitment process.

Of course, there was no point in recruiting professors unless there was also teaching for them to do. Raw recruits could not immediately teach on executive programmes, so the only option was to expand the MBA programme. This view coincided with that of Antonio Borges, recently appointed MBA dean, who was also arguing for an increase in the size of the MBA programme.[35]

Partly, the co-deans were anxious to rebalance the school's activity mix back towards the MBA. With executive education growing apace, the school's flagship offering was in danger of turning into a sideshow, jeopardising the school's academic credibility. But equally, there was a sudden increase in market demand from all quarters. Applications for the 1986 intake were nearly three times those of the 1980 intake – and the school found it was turning away excellent candidates whose achievements were comparable to those admitted. Thus it would be possible to grow without lowering the quality of intake. In terms of placement, the number of interesting job offers far outstripped the number of graduating students – and there were plenty of companies waiting to recruit at the school. Expansion was therefore a low-risk option. In a sense, the risk actually lay with not expanding and seeing Insead's chief rivals mop up the high quality demand to develop their MBA programmes.

There was another market-driven argument too. New MBA programmes were springing up throughout Europe, often with dubious quality standards, but always proclaiming the same goals and methods as Insead's. The absence of a European accreditation system meant that anyone with a telephone and a fax could set up a programme. The scramble to board the MBA bandwagon was creating a lot of confusion, both among prospective students and employers. The *Economist* referred to "Friday-night MBAs" which were "in danger of lowering the tone of the MBA across Europe, where it has never

[34] Minutes of the Board Meeting, 20/3/87.
[35] Growth of the MBA programme, MBA Committee headed by Antonio Borges, 13/5/86.

had the same ring as in America".[36] Faced with an immature market, undermined by feeble programmes and bogus rankings,[37] Insead had to take forceful action. If the school did not want to see the prestige of the European MBA debased, then it needed to preserve a position of substantial impact. In business parlance, it had to maintain its market share.

Members of the board agreed that a small MBA programme did not seem compatible with becoming one of the world's top schools. Certainly, there were no known examples of this in North America. Growth would allow faculty numbers to reach critical mass in the majority of the school's areas. Also expanding the MBA "might be turned into a major opportunity for public relations."[38] Those associated with the school never lost sight of the opportunities to trumpet the school's name or achievements. It was second nature – part pride, part insecurity – the instinctive reflex of an institutional orphan.

In June 1987, the board voted to admit two extra sections of 70 participants each, one section in September 1988 and the other in January 1989. This would take the total student body from 320 to 420 – and would mean that the number of MBAs graduating in the 1980s would be equivalent to the total for the 1960s and 1970s put together.

Meanwhile, externally, Rameau continued to beat the drum, paying personal visits to company heads who might consider joining the school's national advisory boards (formerly national committees), and helping to create national advisory boards where they did not yet exist. The approach encouraged by Rameau was proactive. The school did not just send out brochures, but sent people to visit companies and talk to people directly. For everyone concerned it was time intensive and unmeasurable, in that the immediate result was often goodwill and referrals rather than funds or programme bookings. But progressively, the school was creating a vast web of contacts.

By December 1987, the school had created 13 national advisory boards – thanks largely to long-term supporters like Yves Dunant in Switzerland and André Bisson in Canada. The International Council had come to constitute a unique assembly of company heads on a worldwide basis. In this upbeat climate, the renewal of Rameau's mandate was virtually a formality.[39] Why upset a winning team?

[36] *The Economist*, 4/10/86.
[37] A particularly striking example was the league table featured in the September 1987 issue of *Business Administration*, a newsletter produced by William Cox, an independent adviser on European MBA programmes. Widely cited by the German press, including *Frankfurter Allgemeine Zeitung* (27/8/88), the table relegated Insead, IESE, LBS and IMEDE to fifth, sixth, seventh and tenth positions respectively in the European rankings. In the top four came two little known business schools which employed Cox as a marketing consultant.
[38] Minutes of Chairman's Meeting, 9/6/86.
[39] Minutes of the Board Meeting, 15/12/87.

REFLECTED GLORY

By the mid-1980s, Insead considered itself as "the leading institution of its kind in Europe."[40] As noted by Claude Janssen in a letter to board members in June 1986: "This position is now much more clearly established than a decade ago, and gives the school greater opportunities than ever, but also imposes a heavier responsibility on its leadership."[41]

In May 1988, *Fortune International* magazine provided dramatic confirmation of these perceptions. Featuring Antonio Borges, head of the MBA programme, on its cover, it hailed Insead as the top ranked business school in Europe. Moreover, it was not leader of a bunch of no-hopers. Far from being "pale imitations of Harvard,"[42] the five European schools surveyed were "winning high marks for their strikingly original programs and the fat, US-style salaries their graduates command".[43] Now they had the reader's attention! The message for the US was "Wake up to this threat!"

The story was significant for other reasons too. For example, the fact that *Fortune* should even take an interest in Europe's best business schools, much less make them its cover story, was a confirmation of the growing frenzy surrounding European integration. As the article put it: "As Europe sweeps away economic barriers on its historic march toward 1992, companies will turn increasingly to managers unfazed by linguistic and cultural boundaries."[44] The *Fortune* article was just one of several cover stories on Europe in the US press at the time.[45]

Previously, Insead had aroused little more than bemused curiosity in the US press. It had been a novel experiment in cross-cultural learning, something rather quaint and unthreatening. The *Fortune* story marked a new-found respect for Insead, "the school that virtually invented the concept of international business education ... the Rolls-Royce of European business schools."[46] The article even went as far as to defend the school's high-priced programme: "Tuition is no bargain. But Insead's ten-month program makes it cheaper than US business schools for their two year MBAs. And Insead students sacrifice regular paychecks for just one year instead of two."[47] The school itself could not have said it better.

For Insead, the article was a watershed event. The marketing department had the magazine's front cover blown-up into posters, and a number of

[40] Letter from Claude Janssen to board members, 26/5/86.
[41] Letter from Claude Janssen to board members, 26/5/86.
[42] *Fortune International*, 'Europe's Best Business Schools', 23/5/88.
[43] *Fortune International*, 'Europe's Best Business Schools', 23/5/88.
[44] *Fortune International*, 'Europe's Best Business Schools', 23/5/88.
[45] *Fortune* had already covered 'Europe's New Managers' (18/8/86) and in the last week of August 1987, *Newsweek* (US) and *BusinessWeek* (International) had both taken 'Europe Incorporated' as their lead story, one focusing on alliances and the other profiling the top company heads.
[46] *Fortune International*, 'Europe's Best Business Schools', 23/5/88.
[47] *Fortune International*, 'Europe's Best Business Schools', 23/5/88.

professors hung it up in their offices. It meant a lot to them. Borges was 38 years old. He was one of theirs, a member of faculty, not one of the school's two heads. And this was also telling. The decision to put the MBA dean on the cover of the magazine may seem bizarre, but as Borges recalls it was a compromise solution: "If you have two heads, who speaks for Insead? Who is Insead's voice? It is not by accident that neither of deans was on the cover of *Fortune* magazine. It was the associate dean for the MBA. Had there been only one dean, he would have been the obvious choice."

The article was heavily personalised: "Picked to head the MBA program in 1986, Borges is boldly expanding the faculty and putting a heavier accent on research." As head of the MBA, Borges actually had very little authority to do either of these things, but for the journalists he provided a striking symbol of the new Europe: dynamic, solid, multicultural. "By 1992, Borges plans to increase the number of full-time professors from 60 to 80. To recruit top talent, Borges is raiding the faculties of the best US schools. This year Borges helped lure Belgian Ludo Van der Heyden from a tenured post at Yale ... Under Borges, the pressure to turn out top-flight research is intense." Whatever his current position at Insead, for the journalists, this 'brisk extrovert', known to the students as 'gorgeous Borges', was clearly heading places.

Gareth Dyas, who had preceded Borges as head of the MBA programme, was once told by his son that it was a pity he had given up that responsibility. "If you'd stayed on as MBA dean, it would have been you on the cover of Fortune." "No," answered Dyas wryly, "they would have found someone else."

It may seem odd that a media event should have so much impact on the school. But Insead's image was still fuzzy and uneven, especially among academics. On the back of the article, recruiting faculty became easier. It also altered the profile of the American students which the school attracted. Mary Boss, who had just taken over admissions from Helen Henderson recalls: "When I arrived, the Americans who were here were not mainstream Americans. They were already living in Europe or very international. They had already made the decision to study outside the US. Quite quickly, we started to get more American candidates who were also getting offers from the top US schools – and some of them were starting to opt for Insead." In the year following the *Fortune* article the number of American candidates jumped from 322 to 554.

MINDING THE BUSINESS

Throughout the early and mid-1980s, executive education, under Philip Marchand then Jerome Foster, made up for the difficulties with fund-raising.[48] Both public and, to a lesser extent, tailor-made programmes fuelled Insead's development – and the less intensive use of Insead professors by

[48] Minutes of the Board Meeting, 15/12/87.

Cedep from 1980 onwards freed up faculty to teach on executives programmes.[49] The growth in corporate demand allowed the school both to increase its offer and to keep its prices ahead of inflation – which meant that the budget targets for executive education were systematically surpassed.

By the mid-1980s, Insead was becoming the price leader on many executive education programmes. This was both a sign of the school's self-confidence and a measure of the quality of its offering. Programmes were constantly updated to reflect emerging business concerns but were also designed to maximise exchanges and learning outside the classroom, through social events and gatherings. Indeed, the senior faculty and deans systematically invited groups of participants on some of the longer programmes, such as the MBA and AMP, to their own homes.[50]

Not to be underestimated, also, was the quality of the support received by participants. Programme coordinators were assigned to each programme. Though fairly junior in the organisational hierarchy, the success of individual programmes depended heavily on their ability to attend to the diverse needs of participants and to interact with them. It was emotionally wearing work and the front-line employees needed a lot of support from their supervisors, such as Siegi Schrinner and Mhairi Forbes.

This dual attention to learning and to customer service reflected the school's own balancing act between academia and business. Insead could not afford to neglect either dimension. Having fantastic performers on the faculty side was of little use, unless they were backed up by efficient and dedicated staff on the administrative side.

In the second half of the 1980s, demand for executive education intensified and the key success factor changed. The public programmes were filling themselves, but new programmes needed to be added. On the customer specific programmes, demand was such that the school could increase its supply and still cherry-pick. It was no longer a question of bringing business in, but of deciding which business to accept and then finding faculty willing to manage the programmes. These tasks were easier for an academic to perform than for a professional manager.

LEGITIMATE EARNINGS

When Dominique Héau took over from Jerome Foster, in 1987, customised programmes (MDU) were still regarded as slightly suspect by the academic community. Héau's self-appointed brief was to prove to faculty that these

---

[49] The aggregate number of sessions (Cedep plus executive education) taught on campus in 1977–78 totalled 2,688. By 1987–88, the total number of sessions had increased modestly, to 2,966, but the breakdown had changed significantly: Cedep had gone from 2,009 to 1,061 sessions, while executive education had climbed from 679 to 1,905 sessions.

[50] The active involvement of the spouses of various deans, director-generals, chairmen and senior faculty contributed significantly to the development of the school and to cultivating its 'family spirit'.

customised programmes could not only generate more funds, but generate real learning opportunities too. He combined close knowledge of faculty interests and a rare ability to define company needs. He was respected by colleagues yet sufficiently direct and pragmatic to be credible with business people. These skills, added to a persuasive manner, meant he could play his brokerage role to the full. His challenge was to try to identify those companies with the most intellectually stimulating problems, to determine what kind of programme they needed, and to persuade them to allow Insead to develop teaching material based on the information collected.

Finding professors to run or staff programmes was Héau's other preoccupation, but here again his background helped. To start with, it was not easy to turn down a request from a trusted fellow academic. Also, he led by example, teaching heavily and filling gaps in any programme that needed it. This allowed him to use moral blackmail and to twist arms to great effect. His own introduction to programme management had perhaps given him a taste for it. As he recalls: "Just before the 1981 summer break, Claude Rameau asked me if I would take over the Advanced Management Programme, without the Stanford 'safety net'. I was in my mid-30s at the time, so I was very flattered but I felt I wasn't experienced enough. I didn't dare refuse straight out, so I said let me think about it. When I returned from vacation my colleagues were all congratulating me on the promotion, and showed me the new AMP brochure which had me down as director. I shot straight to Claude's office to vent my anger and he told me, 'I know you'll do a good job. And anyhow, I knew it was the only way to get you to accept.'"

This rather cavalier approach highlights both the school's faith in 'youth' and the tremendous reserves of institutional loyalty on which the school could draw. As Héau himself later discovered: "People were willing to have their arms twisted because there was a great affection from most professors towards the institution." Yet there was a price to pay. In asking academics, like Héau, to run the institution, the school was also asking them to sacrifice their written output. Héau is one of several gifted scholars at the school of whom it can be said that 'Insead is their track record'.

By mid-1988, the contribution per week of in-company programmes was surpassing the contribution from public programmes.[51] The Advanced Management Programme announced a record participation, with six sections compared to the two, back in 1981 when the link with Stanford had been discontinued. At the same time, Héau had succeeded in rehabilitating an activity traditionally disdained as a 'cash cow'.

The school had become more selective in accepting new programmes. These should either have an institutional interest or should help professors in their particular research activities. Contracts with individual companies were

[51] Minutes of the Board Meeting, 20/6/88.

often agreed on the basis that the material could later be written up as a case. Thirty cases were produced in 1988 compared with only five the previous year.[52] Insead professors were evolving their own hands-on methods for studying the problems of large companies.

Company-specific programmes became the driver of a certain kind of research which focused on multinational companies and was heavily applied. It stimulated faculty thinking and interaction, and gave professors a wealth of contemporary examples for classroom discussions with MBAs and executives. It was long on practical lessons but short on academic substance. The school needed to push one step further.

TAKING THE PLUNGE

The idea of starting a doctoral programme had been floating in and out of the collective consciousness for a long time. It had briefly surfaced under Philippe Dennis who had been approached by the director of HEC about setting up a joint doctoral programme.[53] When Dean Berry arrived, the idea of setting up a doctoral programme was once again aired, but formally dismissed as an option.[54] Four years later, as Berry was preparing to leave, there were serious exploratory discussions about merging with the Brussels Institute of Advanced Studies in Management, the logic behind it being that: "Insead in terms of its own staff development needs more doctoral supervision work and more contact with the world of research and higher education."[55]

Steadily, the idea was making its way. Under Thanheiser and Rameau, there were informal discussions with the more academically inclined board members and, in September 1985, the issue was discussed extensively at the faculty retreat. In the autumn of 1985, a task force, chaired by Manfred Kets de Vries, was created. By the time Philippe Naert took over as co-dean, the real question was no longer whether Insead would start a doctoral programme but how and when. It was an initiative waiting for a champion.

The first question Naert had to confront was 'why now?' His official answer was couched in terms of securing a better balance between "the *transfer of knowledge* (teaching) and the *production of knowledge* (research)."[56] Naert talked of Insead's "responsibility to innovate" and to assert "leadership in the creation of new concepts and ideas".[57] He spoke of the school's need

[52] Minutes of the Board Meeting, 10/3/89.
[53] Philippe Dennis wrote two letters on the subject to Jean Marcou, 7/6/67 and 26/6/67. He had also written to Theodore Weinshall asking him to "to consider the question of doctoral studies at Insead and recommend a plan for this purpose" (June 1967). In October 1967, Weinshall had produced a 20 page report concluding that the school was "not yet ready for a fully fledged doctoral program".
[54] D. Berry, *A Proposal to the Ford Foundation on behalf of Insead*, 1/4/71.
[55] Letter from Dean Berry to Meinholf Dieckes, 19/6/75.
[56] *Financial Times*, 9/11/87.
[57] Minutes of the Board Meeting, 20/3/87.

"to contribute forcefully to thinking and knowledge in the particular European environment in which it operates".[58] But behind these lofty ideals lay more pressing issues, to do with faculty recruitment and development.

Insead's capacity to recruit and retain first-rate faculty increasingly hinged on the existence of a doctoral programme. From his intensive recruitment efforts, Naert was only too aware that the promise of such a programme was a decisive factor in many cases. On the development front, the faculty had a very concentrated age profile with 60 per cent of the professors in their forties.[59] In plain terms, the Dean Berry generation were entering middle age.[60] Like any other professionals, they were in need of permanent education. If the school was to avoid sclerosis, then something had to be done to regenerate the staff and provide an intellectual stimulus. It was expected that the presence of pushy doctoral students would provide "a significant buffer against the danger of early burnout".[61] In the business world they might have been called 'change agents'.

The future health of the school seemed to be at stake, but not everyone saw it that way. On the board, there were discussions about the high cost of the programme in relation to its expected output and the risk to Insead's reputation if it failed. Nor was it obvious how this development would actually benefit companies. Indeed, to some on the board, it seemed as though proposals such as the doctoral programme and the new library complex were more for the benefit of the faculty than to improve the excellence of the existing programmes.[62] Amongst the faculty, the objections were more subtle since no self-respecting academic could object to the idea of a doctoral programme 'on principle' – it would be like objecting to motherhood. So the debate revolved around the intensity of faculty involvement, the nature of the programme and the extensive damage to the school's reputation if it flopped. The school could not afford to launch a mediocre programme.

Naert's energetic recruitment drive between 1986 and 1988 had attracted an average of eight new recruits per year. This helped his cause enormously. They had come on the understanding that the school would shortly be offering a doctoral programme. They were enthusiastic and highly mobile. Now the school had to deliver or else risk losing these precious recruits. As expressed in one memo from those concerned: "For some years now promises have been handed out. It is time to fulfil them."[63] Through recruitment, Naert had built up internal pressure to follow through.

[58] Minutes of the Board Meeting, 18/3/88.
[59] Minutes of the Board Meeting, 20/3/87.
[60] As Manfred Kets de Vries had put it in an earlier memo to faculty (26/9/85): "Insead is entering a key phase where unless its faculty get serious about research, it might find itself obsolete."
[61] Minutes of the Board Meeting, 20/3/87.
[62] Minutes of the Board Meeting, 22/6/87.
[63] *Implementation Task Force on the Doctoral Programme*, R. Angelmar, K. Cool, S. Makridakis, D. Neven, T. Vermaelen, C. Wyplosz. 1/3/88.

He had also been busy generating external pressure on the school, through his contacts with the press. In late 1987, the *Financial Times* reported: "Although Insead has yet to decide whether or not to go ahead with its doctoral programme, Naert believes it would give a powerful impetus to the school's research."[64] Elsewhere, Claude Rameau had been broadcasting the school's determination "to be recognized as one of the world's top five business schools within the next few years."[65] Again, that implied having a doctoral programme.

By the autumn of 1987, a subtle shift had occurred. It was no longer a question of 'Can we afford to do it?' but rather 'Can we afford not to do it?' At the two-yearly faculty retreat of October 1987, the general principle of a doctoral programme was finally accepted. In March 1988, after thorough discussions, the Board also agreed 'in principle'.

REALISING THE INEVITABLE

The decision to launch a doctoral programme had two repercussions. First, it gave the final push needed for the board to accept the new library project. As described by Rameau, the current library was "a disgrace to the campus".[66] The facilities were described to the board as "totally inappropriate to the current needs of the school. The forty study places, in an area designed to accommodate half that number, fall way short of the needs of 300 MBA students, 60 permanent professors, 25 research assistants and numerous visiting professors."[67] Indeed, the imminent increase in the size of the MBA programme was set to "make the situation explosive".[68] To launch a doctoral programme with such facilities would be a guarantee of failure. The board finally gave the go-ahead for the construction project in June 1988.

The go-ahead for the doctoral programme also triggered a fresh debate among faculty concerning how to make it successful. There was consensus around certain elements. For example, the intake should be small to make sure that the students received sufficient personal attention through the programme and for job placement. An intake of six students per year, building up to a student body of 24 once the programme reached its steady state, was considered sufficient. The admission criteria should be stringent, and students should be both outstanding and international. These were straightforward issues.

On the other hand, the design of the programme generated heated discussions. This was perhaps natural, given the widely divergent profiles and

[64] *Financial Times*, 9/11/87.
[65] *International Management*, May 1987.
[66] Minutes of the Board Meeting, 12/12/88.
[67] Minutes of the Board Meeting, 20/6/88.
[68] Minutes of the Board Meeting, 20/6/88.

research traditions among the faculty. Finally, it became apparent that the answer lay in the debate itself. Part of the school's distinctiveness lay in "the variety of its faculty which, in addition to a high degree of specialisation, also have tolerance and respect for other fields, paradigms and methodologies".[69] The programme should therefore capitalise on the international and cross-disciplinary strengths of the faculty.

It was finally decided that the programme would be based on US lines, with a strong taught component on theory and research methodology, followed by two years of thesis work. But there would also be a strong concern to provide the students with the capacity to frame and define problems, not just apply methodologies and tools. The school wanted to turn out true researchers, not just people skilled at using sophisticated methods to deal with trivial issues. As Yves Doz put it: "We need to develop problem solvers, not puzzle solvers."[70]

Significantly, too, there was a firm belief that: "The programme should be discontinued if it ever appeared that the above objectives are not met."[71] With ten months to go before the launch, it looked to Charles Wyplosz, in charge of the programme, as if that might indeed be the case. Hundreds of PhD brochures and posters had been mailed out all over the world. This had resulted in hundreds of enquiries but few 'respectable CVs'. It was understandable. Insead's was not an established programme. It was unlikely to attract mainstream candidates. Wyplosz dispatched a rather panicky memo to all faculty, reminding them of their pledge: that the first graduating class should be outstanding to establish a track record; and that the faculty would use their networks to generate outstanding candidacies. Wyplosz complained that the second principle had fallen by the wayside: "It is now the time to do it. I urge every faculty member to do his or her best in this respect. This effort should not be delayed any further."[72]

In September 1989, six students of six different nationalities arrived to begin the doctoral programme. Fittingly, it was almost 30 years to the day since the first group of postgraduate students had arrived at the school. Once again, it involved a derisory number of students by the standards of the top schools, but they were bright and unusual. It was hugely symbolic for the school. As on the previous occasion, there was a huge collective sigh of relief.

FROM INSTITUTE TO INSTITUTION

The 1980s saw the school increase its physical plant, its faculty and staff, the size of its programmes, its operating budget and its research output. Such measures of progress do not lie, but nor do they tell the whole story.

[69] *PhD Committee Report on the First Year Course of Studies*, 25/1/89.
[70] Memo from Yves Doz to Charles Wyplosz, 3/1/89.
[71] *Implementation Task Force on the Doctoral Programme*, R. Angelmar, K. Cool, S. Makridakis, D. Neven, T. Vermaelen, C. Wyplosz. 1/3/88.
[72] Memo from Charles Wyplosz to all faculty, 2/11/88.

Underlying this quantitative expansion were three psychological advances for the school. First, it gained its independence, the dual deanship allowing the school to take charge of its own affairs, helped by a chairman who took care not to meddle in operational matters. Second, thanks largely to the *Fortune* article, the school finally became fully present on the US radar screen, the key barometer in matters of management education. Third, with the launch of a doctoral programme and the imminent addition of a purpose-built library constituting the final two pieces of the jigsaw, Insead was now an all-round business school.

There were also certain symbolic milestones which said a lot about the evolution of the school through the 1980s. For example, in 1984, the school literally moved into its second generation. Hugo Boreel enrolled on the MBA programme taken by his father, Geert, back in 1959. Representatives of the earlier generation were now on the board of the school, on the national committees, getting involved in fund-raising and were respected figures in the business community.

Or again, in January 1986, the French contingent dropped to 21 per cent of the intake and was overhauled by the British contingent, with 26 per cent. It was significant in that it confirmed that location had become secondary as a factor for choosing a school – and it laid to rest any lingering misconceptions of Insead as a 'French school'. The school also stopped referring to the number of nationalities as a meaningful indicator of its geographical spread and started instead to track the changing weight of various nationalities within the intake.

Finally, in 1988, the school took the inevitable but painful decision to abandon German as a language requirement. Already in 1972, it had been transformed from an entry requirement into an exit requirement, the idea being that students would learn German while at Insead. But the increasing geographical diversity of the student intake made this an untenable proposition. The idea, say, that a trilingual Latin American student, might not graduate, for lack of German proficiency, was simply unrealistic. The trilingual requirement was maintained but French and English became the only compulsory languages.[73]

All these changes pointed in the same direction. The school was increasingly international and increasingly established. At some point in the 1980s, the possibility of disappearing disappeared. The number of stakeholders, especially alumni[74] and assorted benefactors, was simply too great for the school to perish because of bad luck. Henceforth, it could only fail through incompetence. Resource constraints had given way to capacity constraints as the dominant issue in strategic discussions. Money could now

---

[73] See minutes of the Board Meeting, 12/12/88.
[74] Bearing in mind that the number of alumni produced in the 1980s was equivalent to the total for the 1960s and 1970s put together. Also many of Insead's older alumni were now in very senior positions.

be raised, so it was more a question of which orientations to pursue, which demands to accommodate.

These developments were made possible by a favourable context. Europe was heading towards a Single Market. The European economy was booming as was the demand for MBAs and executive education from European firms. Internal and external forces came together and the school's reputation suddenly gelled. By the close of the 1980s, Insead had ceased to be a private venture, much less an adventure, and had finally become an institution.

CHAPTER 8

Taking on the world

"Although nothing much can be seen through the mist, there is
somehow the blissful feeling that one is looking in the right direction."
Vladimir Nabokov, *Speak, Memory*.

A NEW PLAYING FIELD

As the 1980s drew to a close, Europe looked set to become a dominant
economic force again and Insead seemed to be sitting pretty. The euphoria
surrounding the impending Single European Market (1992) had indirectly
provided the school with several years of free publicity. It had also boosted
cross-border merger and takeover activity which in turn intensified demand
for Insead's professors who allied cultural consciousness to specialist
sophistication. Insead's message of internationalism had become a dominant
concern for most leading business schools. There was almost a sense of
'mission accomplished'. Then, unexpectedly, in November 1989, the Berlin
Wall came down.

All of a sudden, Insead was no longer comfortably dominating its 'home'
territory. The heart of Europe had shifted east, and Insead was sitting on the
wrong end of the Continent. The school had long cultivated good relations
with the Eastern European countries, initiated back in the 1960s by Roger
Godino, during the Cold War period. In the 1970s, there had been serious
talk of an East-West centre. Over the years, the school had even built up a
body of 33 Eastern European alumni, one third of them Poles, and had run
conferences on Eastern Europe. More recently, in November 1987, the
school had pulled off an academic coup in arranging a guest lecture by Abel
Aganbegyan, the architect of the economic reform drive implemented under
Mikhail Gorbachev. But these inroads were virtually irrelevant in the face of
a vast new demand for management education.

Very quickly, there were protracted discussions at board level concerning how the school planned to respond to this challenge. Already by March 1990, a number of new actions had been taken and were signalled to the board. But these were essentially individual initiatives by the professors, especially the economists who saw it as an opportunity to study the evolution of new markets. Some board members, notably Olivier Giscard d'Estaing and Roger Godino, considered that Insead had an institutional role to play and urged the school to take a pioneering lead.

In truth, the options for Insead were fairly limited. The Eastern European countries had no disposable funds, and Insead's own lack of discretionary resources impeded bold action. The school would need time to find sources of finance. The initial burst of enthusiasm from the West German companies, allowing Insead to organise an advanced management programme for East German managers, quickly petered out once the reunification costs became apparent. Meanwhile, other schools and several consulting companies were already on the spot prospecting, invading Insead's "back yard". It was a harsh reminder that the competitive arena was changing.

Within weeks of the Berlin Wall coming down, globalisation had already become the new buzzword, featuring prominently in Insead's annual report produced in early 1990.[1] Both Insead's clients and its competitors were becoming globally minded. The school had been preparing for the 1992 milestone. But from now on, the 'Single Market' referred not to a cosy club of rich European countries, nor even to an enlarged Europe, but to the whole world.

HITCHED AFRESH

In the midst of this geo-political upheaval, Ludo Van der Heyden, formerly head of R&D, took over from Philippe Naert as the new co-dean, alongside Claude Rameau. As in the previous case, no suitable external candidate had been found by a first committee[2] and Van der Heyden, as head of the second dean search committee, had been proposed to the board by the faculty. This was in danger of becoming a tradition.

Barely had Van der Heyden been offered the job than the Gulf crisis broke out, in August 1990. All in all, the external conditions did not auger particularly well for the start of his five-year mandate. To add to these

---

[1] There was a seven-page interview with Warren Cannon, Yotaro Kobayashi and Roger Godino entitled 'Three Perspectives on Globalization,' Annual Report, 1989.

[2] One candidate had been proposed to the board and turned down. Essentially the problem lay with a simultaneous, competitive selection process, whereby the proposed candidate had been a compromise solution, with only lukewarm support from the faculty. The selection process was changed as a result of this setback – and board members were integrated onto the dean search committee.

external difficulties, there were internal challenges. Naert would be remembered for two major accomplishments: getting the doctoral programme off the ground and bringing in 34 new professors over five years, to bring the total up to 79 in September 1990.[3] But Van der Heyden, who would take the lead on academic matters, had the unenviable task of making sure that the doctoral programme and the new professors actually became successful. Only a few months before Van der Heyden's appointment, Claude Rameau had pointed out to the board that the influx of new professors had "created two different groups within the faculty, a situation which is a bit difficult to manage".[4] There were differences in competence, expectations, and resource needs which would inevitably trigger tensions about fairness of treatment. Digesting such a heavy intake of fresh blood would not be easy.

Van der Heyden's first official function, in September 1990, was to inaugurate the MBA programme. His speech had all the hallmarks of creativity, intellectual style and commitment which he would bring to the position. He urged the incoming students to "engage in the classroom, discover the limits of the apparently obvious, and to dominate the apparently complex". He also told them that the MBA programme was "The central place ... [benefiting] both from the experience acquired in our executive education programmes, and from the leading edge research practised in our R&D laboratory. This is a bit idealistic, but this is what we aim for: a good mixture of relevance, rigour, and revelation." It was an early formulation of the 'virtuous cycle', refined later with Arnoud De Meyer: the idea that research, teaching and consultancy all fed on each other and that vital synergy could be generated by pushing simultaneously on all three fronts.

That same afternoon, Insead hosted the inauguration of the new library and information centre, financed in large part by bequests from the Ile de France Regional Council and from Digital Equipment Company.[5] Pier Carlo Falotti, the head of DEC International, represented the company at the inauguration. He reminded the audience that DEC's donation was a tribute to the strong relationship between the founder, Ken Olsen, and Georges Doriot. DEC had been launched thanks to seed money provided by American Research & Development.

Two years before the inauguration, when Claude Janssen had announced to Georges Doriot that Insead planned to name the library after him, Doriot had been flattered but asked that it should also carry the name of his late wife, Edna. Very soon after requesting this amendment Georges Doriot had died. Fittingly, the library featured both his statue and a plaque bearing a

---

[3] The faculty body had been 54 strong in September 1985 when Naert took over (see minutes of the Board Meeting, 10/12/90).
[4] Minutes of the Board Meeting, 9/3/90.
[5] See Chapter 1.

hallmark quote from him: "Without action, the world would still be an idea." For some members of the faculty, including Van der Heyden, the choice of such a motto for a library was inappropriate. They felt it should be the other way round, that ideas were central to action, and that the library should be a place of ideas. In many ways, the debate captured Insead's intermediary position between reflection and practice, between academia and business, between research and consulting – as well as the customary divergence of opinion among its faculty body.

The library was the crowning piece of the campus and also the last new building on the existing land. There was no more room for further construction. Yet this did not signal the end of Insead's development, as Claude Rameau observed: "Companies being more and more global, it seems obvious that if Insead wants to serve them properly, it needs to build critical mass: in terms of faculty size, in terms of research and in terms of the volume of the service proposed ... It is foreseeable that within two to three decades, Insead will double in size. So far we have focused essentially on Europe. In the last ten years, we have made a particular effort in Asia. That effort will continue and will develop exponentially."[6] However, as Rameau himself pointed out, this vision was not shared by all.

The completion of the new library also turned out to be Patrice Triaureau's swansong. With no new building projects on the horizon, the time had come to move on. The development of the physical infrastructure of the campus was largely his doing. At times he had shown more ambition and vision for the school than the deans themselves. But this had also brought him into conflict with the faculty who saw him as domineering and power hungry. The tensions had started to become public and, eventually, the liabilities of retaining him started to outweigh the advantages. As is often the case, his contribution became all the more apparent in retrospect. The next construction work, in 1997, would require the demolition of MBA residences erected two decades earlier, which had grown out of fashion with the students.

COMMUNICATION PROBLEMS

Through the 1980s, the scope and scale of the school's activities had grown tremendously. There was the new doctoral programme, the Euro-Asia Centre, numerous new executive programmes, as well as a mass of cases and working papers. There were multiple reunions of national councils, of alumni associations and of the International Council. There was the involvement of professors in world forums and the organisation of conferences on campus. The internal feeling was that, in contrast with the early years, the school was

[6] Video of inauguration of International Information Centre (IIC), 4/9/90.

under-communicating its achievements. This view, combined with the intensification of media interest in the school in the late 1980s, prompted Insead to reconsider its communication approach, starting with the basics. There was a growing awareness that the school could no longer pursue the *laisser faire* approach whereby instructional material, brochures, logos, stationery and business cards were refashioned at will by individual managers.

Part of the problem stemmed from the nature of the school itself. Diversity of culture and experience were givens. Entrepreneurialism was encouraged. The school was communicating in different languages, to different constituencies all over the world, and individuals were adapting the school's image as they saw fit. At the same time, the school's own professors were standing in classrooms stressing the importance of cost control, external communication, brand management and quality standards. Executives on courses, like alumni and board members, were swift to point out that it was perhaps time for Insead to practise what it preached. In early 1990, Claire Pike, who had been one of the most strident critics of the cacophony, was asked to streamline the school's external communications activities.

Although there was widespread agreement on the wastefulness of the current practices, this was not an easy mission. As an academic institute, substance was more important than form. The idea of calling upon the leading international design firm, Landor, for help looked dangerously commercial. For many insiders, image considerations came some way down the list of areas on which the school needed to concentrate. And the idea that it was worth spending serious money on such matters was even more debatable. Few of the school's professors deigned to get involved in an exercise which would be time consuming and which they sensed could be better spent on R&D. Yet these same professors would later hold the strongest opinions about the proposed designs.

There is a French saying that tastes and colours should never be discussed. It should have served as a warning. Deliberations over colour were overlaid with cultural preferences and associations. The school had traditionally shown a mild preference for shades of blue, since this was the colour of the European flag – but the school's catchment area was now much broader than Europe. Moreover, numerous competitors also used blue so it was important for Insead to distinguish itself. The discussions were emotionally charged in that the process itself surfaced different perceptions of the very mission and identity of the school. The existing logo, featuring a globe and an outline of Western Europe, was also considered outdated in terms of the international image the school wanted to project. Some felt it was reminiscent of a telecommunications company or, worse still, a football association. The school had a rather grander view of itself.

The internal diversity which had contributed to the problem in the first place also made it hard to reach consensus. The voting procedure on the final design options produced a very scattered response, both internally and among board members. Twice, the designers were forced to go back to drawing board. In some ways, this was actually reassuring. The debate reflected the extent to which people were attached to the school and believed strongly in its mission and originality. The fact that even board members, most of whom had never attended the school, should end up in heated arguments also said a lot for their attachment to the school. Finally, it took Ludo Van der Heyden's firm intervention to rally people round.

Inevitably, the final design was not as bold as some might have hoped but at least it was accepted by all.[7] Deep green, which reflected the school's forest setting, emerged as the colour of least resistance. Attempts to find a logo which would somehow express the essence of the school were abandoned, since it proved impossible to come up with a design which was neither too commercial nor too academic. Nevertheless, the original globe concept was preserved as a secondary, yet constant, 'decorative' device on brochure covers and letter paper. In the absence of a logo, a slogan was conceived which crisply captured the school's uniqueness: Enrichment through diversity.

A final recommendation from the design consultants, who had conducted lengthy interviews with external constituencies, was that the 'INSEAD' brand name was now sufficiently strong to stop spelling out the acronym in three languages. The existing policy was even misleading in that it harked back to an era when mastery of German was still an entry requirement. Like British Airways, Imperial Chemical Industries and British Petroleum before it, *L'Institut Européen d'Administration des Affaires* would now play down its geographical roots. It would be known by its initials so as to facilitate interaction with a global market.

Besides raising quality standards and harmonising communication efforts, the whole exercise firmly signalled the school's global intentions. It was the first time the school had paid concerted attention to its image, having recourse to a top consulting firm for help. These were signs of a growing professionalism – a desire to get advice, learn from and benchmark against the best.

WEATHERING THE STORM

Insead always prided itself on having no external wall to the campus, but with the outbreak of the Gulf war in January and February 1991 and the threat of retaliatory terrorism, this became a potential liability. People could simply stroll onto campus unchallenged. For Insead, the reinforcement of on-campus security measures was perhaps the most immediate consequence

---

[7] The minutes of the Board Meeting (9/12/91) noted laconically that the new visual identity "did not generate much enthusiasm among the members of the board".

of the conflict,[8] but there were plenty of others to follow.

The war triggered a worldwide recession which soon filtered via the companies through to the school itself. Within months, several high margin tailor-made programmes were cancelled or postponed, notably among IT firms which happened to be big consumers. Given that it took six to twelve months to find replacement activity, there was no way of filling the slots vacated. At the same time, several on-going pledges were cut back. And from October 1992, executive programmes started to suffer too. Even the MBA programme was not immune. There was a significant drop in applications and admissions for the 1991/92 MBA programme. Fortunately, enrolments remained steady owing to a much smaller number of 'no shows'.[9] These reduced revenues produced the first deficit in accounting results for over a decade.[10]

The situation did not improve the following year. In 1992–93, economic circumstances turned out to be even harder for many companies and, consequently, for Insead. More tailor-made programmes were cancelled than the previous year, and in public programmes real difficulties were noted from January 1993 onwards. For example, the Advanced Management Programme, in July 1993, ended up with 108 participants against a budgeted 150. These were heavy knocks for the school to withstand, especially as it fought to maintain the quality of an expensive doctoral programme. Like airlines and hotels, business schools have high fixed costs and as soon as enrolments start to drop off, programmes fall below the break-even point. Insead was particularly disadvantaged in this game by its independence and the fact that it had no endowment income to cover operational losses.

The drop in market demand was accentuated by heightened competition in the management education sector. There were more players trying to grab a piece of the cake. For example, among academic institutions, two existing trends had intensified. On one hand, there were more and more European universities developing MBA and executive courses. On the other hand, US schools were taking more meaningful steps to increase the international content of their programmes and, in some cases, reducing the length of their programmes. Insead's traditional sources of competitive advantage were therefore being eroded.

Competition between these rival establishments had been fuelled by more systematic ranking exercises, published by the likes of *Business Week*, *The Economist* and *Manager Magazin*. These compared not just MBA programmes, but also executive and even tailor-made programmes. As noted

[8] Several times the campus had to be emptied because of bomb threats called in anonymously over the telephone.
[9] Like airlines, the number of offers made by business schools exceeds capacity as there is always a significant proportion of "no shows".
[10] Minutes of the Board Meeting, 6/3/92.

in a Harvard Business School report, schools were paying closer attention to this feedback: "The highly publicized rankings in the mass media have triggered increased scrutiny of business schools and increased competitive activity among them."[11] The *Business Week* rankings, in particular, were credited with overhauls in the content and methods of several MBA programmes. Insead's own MBA programme was evolving faster than ever before: one third of the electives on offer had been created in the last three years.[12]

Besides the traditional sources of competition, there was more competition from adjacent sectors too. In particular, professional firms were increasingly combining their organisational consulting with educational support programmes, thereby encroaching on what had traditionally been academic turf. Similarly, there were more companies setting up their own training facilities and these centres could be leveraged for use by other corporations. There was also a more pernicious trend altogether. Companies were starting to put their own programmes together – treating Insead as a 'shop window' – and cherry-picking from the school's faculty. It was a sign of the growing transparency of the market and the growing sophistication of the 'consumers'.

The net result of these various influences was that the market was becoming tighter and outside expectations were rising. In executive education, companies were demanding shorter courses, expecting their managers to be 'immediately operational' on returning from a course, and were even asking the schools to bid for contracts – quite a reversal of the situation which Insead had enjoyed in the previous decade.

Bespoke programmes were increasingly sophisticated, demanding much more preparation, and often incorporating last-minute changes to cater for new competitive realities or preoccupations, typically the result of mergers or takeovers. In March 1993, David Scholey, head of the Warburg Group, confirmed to fellow Insead board members that companies wanted maximum yield from their investments in management education.[13] Again, this increased intellectual investment – though good for faculty development – tended to drive up the immediate costs for the school.

The levels of support and service expected were also higher. Those attending programmes were having notions of quality and customer service drummed into them at work and in class, and they expected similar standards outside class. As noted by Claude Rameau at the time: "Participants are becoming more and more demanding in their expectations and requirements across the board"[14] – notably in terms of sports facilities,

---

[11] "External Comparisons Summary Report: MBA: Leadership & Learning", External Comparisons Project Team, Harvard Business School, 6/4/93.
[12] See minutes of the Board Meeting, 3/12/93.
[13] See minutes of the Board Meeting, 5/3/93.
[14] Minutes of the Board Meeting, 15/6/92.

administrative support, and faculty contact. The point was unwittingly reinforced by an MBA student in the opening sequence of Insead's own promotion video, released in 1991: "[From attending Insead]... You don't expect anything. You just expect everything."[15] Expectations were perhaps getting out of hand.

Some faculty members also sensed a latent resentment from participating executives towards 'academics' with their 'sabbaticals' and 'tenured positions'. At the time Europe, in particular, was being hit by successive waves of restructuring, with lots of middle-aged executives losing their jobs. As Gareth Dyas recalls: "I remember walking into the first Advanced Management Programme I directed in 1992 and you had a bunch of shell-shocked executives out there. About 20 per cent of them didn't know if they would have a job to go back to." Professors who talked about growth, opportunity and innovation were not given an easy time. However close they might be to the hostile pressures of the business world, Insead professors always had the option of pulling back.

The cocktail of rising costs, inflated expectations and tougher competition did not make this an easy time to manage the school. Nor did it make it easy to recruit. Faculty salaries, which had once again fallen behind their US equivalents, could not be raised. Research budgets could not be increased nor heavy teaching loads reduced. Insead's research budget was around $4million compared to $40million for HBS and Wharton, institutions whose faculty size was roughly twice that of Insead.[16] It did not make the school a particularly attractive proposition for top-flight academics. Indeed, faculty recruitment between 1990 and 1993 barely covered turnover, with a positive balance of five for the period. None of this was commensurate with the school's stated ambition of becoming "one of the half dozen leading business schools in the world."[17] There had to be a better way.

A TESTING TIME

The recession provided a forceful reminder of the school's lingering financial vulnerability. Understaffed and overstretched, the existing fund-raising system developed from scratch by Jacqueline Tourlier-Pope could not easily make up for the shortfall in executive programme revenues. It was running out of steam. The on-going development of the school clearly required a fund-raising system of a completely different type and scale.

This was not really news. For several years, John Loudon had been urging the school to raise its sights, to think big and to consider a serious development campaign. The issue had already been formally raised with the

[15] Opening line of 'The MBA Experience', Insead video, 1991.
[16] Minutes of Board Meeting, 6/3/92.
[17] Philippe Naert in an interview with *Connexions*, Autumn 1988.

board in June and December 1988. In March 1992, the board tentatively agreed to launch a feasibility study. It may be worth considering why there was so much hesitation – both internally and at board level – over a course of action which, looking back, appeared to be the only way forward.

To start with, the school was coming out of a period of strong growth linked to the development of programmes. This had instilled a product logic and it was not easy to snap out of it. There was a certain comfort in self-sufficiency, even if it stunted the school's long-term ambitions.

There was also resistance, from the faculty, about getting drawn in to fund-raising activities, which a large-scale development campaign would surely demand. A prior attempt to involve faculty, Partners for the Future, had produced mixed results. It had met its financial objectives; but there had been shifts in faculty interest on certain research themes and general difficulties in mobilising faculty to work collaboratively in new ventures. This had led to embarrassing problems for the deans who had to repair relationships with companies and, in some cases, return funds. A repeat scenario, on a larger scale, would be catastrophic for the reputation of the school.

At board level, there was real scepticism about the school's ability to attract bigger funds. There were no similar campaigns in mainland Europe. The only obvious model was in Britain, where Oxford University had just launched its fund-raising drive. Yet drawing useful conclusions from the initial successes of Oxford's campaign seemed pretentious, to say the least. The University had an impressive history dating back seven centuries, not just three decades; it counted not just company heads, but several heads of state and Nobel prize winners among its living alumni; and it proposed a full range of classic academic specialities, not just a narrow focus on the *parvenu* discipline of management. Finally, Oxford offered public education and could not easily generate finance from its own activities. Conversely, Insead already charged high prices for its services, so how could it justify asking for additional money? Companies argued that a 'commercial' school should fund R&D out of sales (programme) revenues, just like they did.

There was also a cost barrier. Before a single donation rolled in, there would be significant up-front expenditure, starting with the feasibility study. A £2.5million gift from Shell, secured thanks to the influence of John Loudon, eased the decision considerably. It provided a confirmation of the feasibility of the campaign and helped initiate the school's fund-raising team to a new approach, not based on 'tit-for-tat' donations. It was an important 'test' case.

The reference for such campaigns was of course the US where Insead's campaign would have been unremarkable.[18] Yet, even in the US, campaigns

---

[18] To give an idea of the difference in scale and mentality, consider the major campaign launched by Harvard, in 1923, to obtain five million dollars for new buildings. The required sum was obtained from a single donor, George F. Baker, president of the First National Bank in New York, and the new school built at Soldiers Field became the George F. Baker Foundation.

tended to be launched by universities not stand-alone business schools. Given the US lead in this field, Insead was initially drawn towards American consultants for help. Very quickly, however, a difference of mindsets emerged. The consultants were accustomed to a set of conditions which did not prevail in Europe: a long tradition of alumni giving, helped by big tax breaks and encouraged by a culture which values the individual. As a consequence, the whole strategy was designed to reach out to as many alumni as possible, with little attention to corporate donations. The American consultants had difficulty conceiving that Insead's reality could be the reverse, with corporate donations making up the bulk of funding, while alumni donations barely covered the cost of soliciting them. Insead opted instead for the Ulanov Partnership which had steered the Oxford campaign in the US.

Their initial findings, presented in March 1993, proved surprisingly optimistic. Supporters of the school interviewed by the consultants confirmed that they would back a very ambitious campaign provided that Insead could present a clear and convincing development project. The exact figure would be determined by the school's ability to attract several large donations, before the official launch of the campaign, which should represent not less than a quarter of the total sum. The school could not afford to announce a campaign which would then fail to materialise.

In June 1993, the board members, whose time would be heavily solicited by the campaign, gave their blessing. This launched the preliminary phase of building the 'nucleus fund' under the guidance of a steering committee. The committee, led by the chairman of the board and the deans, comprised influential business figures such as Paul Desmarais Jr, Georges Muller, Gerard van Schaik and David Scholey. Their role was to examine potential sources of support and to use their contacts to persuade others to contribute. They were under no illusion, of course, that they would be expected to demonstrate their own financial commitment.[19] Their job was to help the school build up a chest for the 'R&D war'.

RETURN OF THE PRODIGAL SON

Shortly afterwards, in September 1993, Antonio Borges was lured back from a spell as deputy governor of the Bank of Portugal to be appointed co-dean. Before leaving Insead, Borges had been associate dean of the MBA programme, but since then he had spent three years away from academia. It was the closest the school had come to naming an 'outsider' since the appointment of Uwe Kitzinger as dean in 1976. Like the other two external

---

[19] Scholey, when given an Insead pen by Claire Pike, then director of the Campaign, noted wryly: "Thank you. Is this for signing a cheque?"

candidates shortlisted, Borges expressed a preference for a dual structure without ruling out the possibility of another option. Although very happy to work alongside Van der Heyden, the likely division of responsibilities did not look quite so clear cut as it had been with Rameau who had tended to specialise in non academic matters.

For Rameau, it was a blow that his mandate should run out when Insead's fortunes were not at their best. Yet his contribution was clear for all to see. He had overseen the explosive growth of the school and helped to fuel it by pressing hard on executive education and actively backing Insead's involvement in Asia.[21] But his steadying influence had also comforted the board and allowed the school to push on the academic dimension, notably with the introduction of a programme. His capacity to look beyond immediate operational concerns had provided a sense of strategic continuity. For example, when the school had run into trouble, in the wake of the Gulf war, he had insisted that this was a passing trend, that there was "no real reason to talk about a 'crisis' and that care must be taken not to hinder the development of the school, nor to alter its culture".[22] Indeed, in the very midst of that confusion, he had shown himself capable of strategic audacity by proposing the idea of a global multi-site institution to a restricted audience in September 1991.[23] Longstanding colleagues like Dominique Héau told him it was a terrible idea, but it planted a seed in the institutional consciousness.

For Borges, coming into the job in a climate of recession was a curse in disguise. The economic slowdown and successive financial deficits reminded the school of its vulnerability. It helped generate a sense of urgency which made it easier to make necessary changes.

In truth, the financial difficulties were not entirely attributable to the recession. The need for the school to market itself and its programmes more aggressively in a competitive market had also raised costs. Moreover, as a fast-growing organisation, in the 1980s, with plenty of opportunities and a very strong market, the portfolio of programmes had been allowed to grow unchecked. The school had developed bad habits, budgets had overrun.

Quickly there were freezes on staff salaries, a slowdown on investments, tightened cost control and a block on recruitment which, through job restructuring, meant that 18 positions were suppressed.[24] As Borges recalls: "The economic situation was not easy but it was helpful. It created the atmosphere that enabled us to get to grips with some basic tightening of

[21] Besides helping de Bettignies to look for potential corporate members, Rameau had also organised two faculty missions to Asia in the late 1980s. These missions helped to stimulate faculty interest in Asia and reasserted the school's commitment to the region at a time when the Euro-Asia Centre was being criticised internally.

[22] Minutes of the Board Meeting, 6/3/92.

[23] See 16-page document, "Insead 2005: Institution globale multipolaire?", Claude Rameau, 17/9/91.

[24] Minutes of the Board Meeting, 2/12/94.

systems and procedures and financial discipline, which helped us enormously afterwards." Borges did not shy away from dispensing painful medicine. But his resolute approach sometimes disturbed the more circumspect Van der Heyden.

While the school's financial situation was not at its best, some bright spots were nevertheless emerging. The first 'results' of the doctoral programme came at the top of that list. Back in June 1991, two years into the doctoral programme, Van der Heyden had been asked about the likely careers of the current doctoral students. Hedging his bets, he replied that most would probably become academics, but some of them might well end up in consulting firms, international organisations and investment banks.[25] In the event, the first graduating class, in June 1994, surpassed all expectations.

The first four students to graduate accepted places at IMD, Babson College, the University of Texas-Austin and, the icing on the cake, the University of Chicago's world-renowned finance department. Even inside the school, people were taken by surprise. Usually a doctoral programme takes years to establish a reputation. So how did this happen?

The critical starting point was that Insead attracted outstanding doctoral students, enticed by the school's unusual international and cross-disciplinary positioning. Significantly, half of the candidates had only applied to Insead, indicating that the school was projecting a distinctive image and that the faculty profile was internationally recognised as unique. Yet the fact that they selected an unknown doctoral programme, not attached to a university, also said something about them. They had to be risk takers, rather like the very first intake of postgraduate students had been; and they had to have tremendous faith in themselves because the school had never placed anybody and its qualification was not rubber-stamped by a higher authority.

These same factors also made a difference to the support they received. The faculty were fully aware that the school could not offer the same breadth of courses as a traditional university. In the top US programmes, doctoral students might take specialised courses in the faculty of mathematics, sociology, history or economics, as well as the business school. Insead's seminars would necessarily be narrower in focus, so the faculty compensated by giving students more teaching and advice, closer attention and guiding their research apprenticeship. Awareness of the school's limitations, by professors who had mostly been through the American system, stimulated an attitude of 'we try harder'. Placing bright mavericks through such a system had to produce interesting results. And so as not to spoil that chemistry, the doctoral programme would be kept fairly small.

[25] Minutes of the Board Meeting, 17/6/91.

Elsewhere, there were other encouraging signs. Even if the economic conditions were causing problems, executive education was holding up well against the competition. In September 1993, Insead's Advanced Management Programme was rated first by the *Wall Street Journal* in its survey of executive education worldwide. And in spite of the conditions, the school was still developing new initiatives. For example,[26] there was the AVIRA programme based on five days of intense reflection and aimed at company heads. Moreover, research centres for entrepreneurship, the management of environmental resources, advanced learning technology and healthcare were all being developed – and the output was quickly feeding into new MBA electives and executive programmes. Besides the advances in content, new multimedia cases and simulation exercises were being produced by the Centre for Advanced Learning Technology, headed by Albert Angehrn, upholding the school's long tradition for developing innovative learning tools.

There was progress on the eastern European front too. Lengthy negotiations, headed by Herwig Langohr, with the European Bank for Reconstruction and Development and the ABN-AMRO bank were about to culminate in early 1995 with the launch of a loan programme for students from central and eastern Europe. There was also an opportunistic link up with the *Handelshochschule Leipzig*, dubbed the oldest management school in Germany, whose aim was to train managers from the former East Germany. This was hoped to help Insead penetrate further into the German and eastern European markets. In fact, Leipzig never really resumed its pre-war position as the East/West gateway, so the partnership did not become the international platform hoped for, but it showed that the school was still taking initiatives in a period of adversity.

Another promising sign was the increasing presence of alumni on the school's multiple advisory committees – on the main board, international council, and on the national advisory boards.[27] This was a deliberate policy orchestrated by Claude Janssen to try to develop a cadre of suitable successors to take over from the still active 'founding' generation of Olivier Giscard d'Estaing, Roger Godino and himself. The effort had started in 1989, when Michael Butt (Class of '67) had succeeded John Loudon as head of the International Council, the aim being to "encourage the alumni to take a greater involvement in the various bodies of the school".[28]

This drive was further helped by the decision to merge the International Council, newly headed by Gerard van Schaik, with the 14 national councils. This had been widely perceived as a two-tier system, with membership of the

---

[26] AVIRA: Awareness, Vision, Imagination, Responsibility, Action.
[27] The national advisory boards were in parallel to the numerous alumni associations worldwide. Access to the national advisory boards was by invitation and alumni had not until the 1990s been heavily represented.
[28] Minutes of the Board Meeting, 12/12/88.

International Council conferring more prestige. Potentially, this might undermine the valuable commitment of those on the national councils and, with the forthcoming launch of the development campaign, Insead would need as much help as it could get. Moreover, the idea of 'compartmentalised' national councils, geographically limited in their field of action, no longer made sense. It quickly proved a shrewd move, providing a prestigious and very well attended forum. Of course, it also turned International Council gatherings into a logistical nightmare, but this was the price to pay for reinforcing the school's international web of support and its global aspirations. Insead was constituting its own mini-Davos.

Notwithstanding some promising indicators, all was not well between the two deans.

ONE HEAD IS BETTER THAN TWO

Since its introduction, in 1982, the dual deanship had always had its critics, not least because it was unique. If this was such a great idea, ran the argument, why were other schools not doing it?[29] The validity of the structure came under discussion with every change or renewal of co-deanship; and since there were two of those every five years, the issue never really went away. Moreover, successive dean search committees comprising both faculty and board members were spending large amounts of time identifying and interviewing potential candidates. It was a big effort that could be invested elsewhere.

The main virtue of the structure was held to be that two people had more time and energy to devote to a very demanding task involving extensive preparation, travel and contacts. It was two pairs of ears with different inner circles, four feet on the street, two sets of knowledge bases and capabilities. Some saw it as integral part of the school's delicate balance of interests and constituencies, cultures and generations, the embodiment of a collegial style of decision-making. Others saw it as inefficient, ineffective and a contributor to the current financial difficulties; a luxury the school had only been able to afford in more prosperous times. The financial troubles were perhaps a signal that the experiment had run its course. In truth, no one really knew to what extent the fortunes of the school were attributable to the structure, to the particular duo in charge, or to factors beyond their control. But the uniqueness of the structure meant that it was condemned to succeed in order to be preserved.

The impending departure of Claude Rameau had triggered more serious debate over the structure. In November 1991, Warren Cannon, a highly influential board member, considered that "the special circumstances which in the past favoured a dual deanship no longer exist. The school should

[29] As expressed in one confidential memo: "Few institutions save the family are led by two equal partners." Memo from the Management Structure Committee, headed by Erin Anderson, to faculty, 25/1/95.

express itself with one voice and envisage a single dean."[30] At around the same time, Rameau and Van der Heyden advanced their recommendation to the board that if a single dean were named, an associate dean for faculty should also be appointed.[31]

Once Borges was named alongside Van der Heyden, the debate was further fuelled by their difficulties in making it work. The two men liked and respected each other, they agreed on where the school should be heading, but their styles proved contradictory rather than complementary. Borges was forceful and determined, Van der Heyden more questioning and consensual. Borges had been expected to do the external work and Van der Heyden the internal work, but it mostly turned out to be the reverse. It was a frustrating time for both of them, and when the moment came to start looking for a replacement for Van der Heyden, Borges made it clear that he would carry on alone or not at all.[32]

In a strange way, it was a tribute to Claude Rameau. Working with three very different co-deans, he had adapted his approach and focus accordingly and had helped 'tutor' the incoming co-deans.[33] He had shown an ability to compromise and to keep conflicts 'behind closed doors' which had established the dual deanship as a workable structure. Most impressively, he had shown that joint responsibility could be reconciled with the efficient separation of tasks. With Rameau no longer in the picture, "the system experienced considerable tension ... now approximating a breakdown".[34]

A number of other factors were also pushing the school in favour of a single dean. In particular, there was a sense of declining faculty morale which needed to be addressed urgently. Here the logic was reversed, in that the recommendation of a single dean stemmed from the need to install a dean of faculty; someone who could devote full attention to issues of faculty management such as recruitment, retention and development which the co-deans currently neglected.[35] The single dean argument also made intuitive sense in the prevailing economic turbulence. The dual deanship had been associated with delays in decision-making, ambiguous responsibilities and lines of authority. The imminent development campaign, in particular, would require firm leadership and a strong message.

When put to a faculty vote in February 1995, the decision to change

[30] Report of interview with Warren Cannon from Ludo Van der Heyden to Claude Janssen, 25/11/91.
[31] Minutes of Board Meeting, 6/3/92.
[32] As Borges explained to the faculty at the time: "Given the changes [I] would like to envisage, a single Deanship is a requirement." Minutes of the Faculty Meeting, 12/10/94.
[33] Another key figure in the "tutoring" of incoming deans was Micheline Dehelly. Having taken responsibility for faculty services and organising board meetings, under Dean Berry, she quickly became an indispensable pivot in the running of the school. The fact that she assisted every dean from Berry through to Borges was a tribute to her conscientiousness, her organisational ability and her irreproachable discretion.
[34] Confidential memo from the Management Structure Committee to faculty, 25/1/95.
[35] Memo from Management Structure Committee to faculty, 5/10/94.

structure was widely supported. The second vote, two weeks later, was rather trickier. Did the faculty want to endorse Borges as its candidate for the single deanship? He had already ruffled some feathers and he was promising to ruffle plenty more. He made it very clear that, if selected, he would be making some sweeping changes.

There was rather more speculation regarding the likely outcome of the forthcoming vote. In the end, there were only 17 votes against, representing 24 per cent of the voting faculty. Based on intensive corridor discussions, Gareth Dyas, who had worked hard to build up consensus, had privately predicted 73 per cent in favour of Borges.[36] That Dyas was only three per cent out was a tribute to his unerring feel for the pulse of the school and his ability to oil its wheels. Yet Dyas was also quick to remind Borges that this did not mean that 76 per cent of faculty were enthusiastic about him being dean. The idea of looking for someone else and a possible succession crisis, had been strong inhibitors.

Meanwhile, Van der Heyden, an academic at heart, would return to the rank-and-file, rather like the passing head monk in a monastery returning to his cell. He had always positioned himself as a *primus inter pares*. In a period characterised by high teaching loads, eroding faculty salaries and external uncertainty, his natural empathy had been a great help. For young faculty needing to be integrated and seasoned faculty facing an tougher classroom environment, he provided a natural focal point and a source of comfort. He helped to consolidate the faculty and had a real impact on the culture.

Yet steering an organisation in a tempest does not always fit with a consensual style of leadership. The fact that he cared and was sensitive to human issues perhaps made it more difficult to move forcefully in a particular direction. He did much to encourage and protect the doctoral programme. But it is probably fair to say that Van der Heyden's legacy was more one of process and style than content. He provided the school with a common framework and vocabulary – the 'virtuous cycle' – for understanding the interactions between the various activities and the importance of balancing those activities as keys to Insead's uniqueness and success. He also helped the school to internalise the implications of a research orientation, and to prepare for the follow-up.

LAUNCH TIME

Assembling a 'nucleus fund' prior to officially launching the capital campaign took longer than expected. There were subtle ground rules and sequences to heed. First, do not ask for money from people you do not know.

---

[36] The faculty list showing the likelihood of support for Borges, on a scale of zero to ten, was pulled out of Dyas' desk drawer with a certain pride.

Second, listen to what donors are saying. Third, do not ask for money unless you know you are going to get it. Respecting these simple principles implied considerable planning and professionalism. It meant communicating to get people excited about the cause. It was a whole apprenticeship for Insead.

In some ways the delay proved helpful, preventing the school from making a big mistake. It had allowed Van der Heyden ample time to interview faculty members individually in order to establish a list of the research projects they had in mind. Had the campaign started without even token acknowledgement of faculty interests, it would only have reinforced faculty perceptions that this was not their concern, a matter for the dean and fund-raisers. As emphasised by the consultants, a development campaign needed to be taken up by the whole organisation. Consulting the faculty helped to bring them round to the idea and, if not to embrace the campaign, at least neutralised opposition towards it. As Jean-Claude Larréché, the faculty representative on the board, put it: "Awareness and support are two different matters."[37] It would take longer to make that transition.

The campaign was officially launched in late September 1995, coinciding with the mandate of Antonio Borges as single dean. By that stage, the school had collected substantial donations from a number of corporations thanks to the influence of senior alumni and long-term corporate supporters.[38] Less expectedly, it had also received large pledges from individual donors with strong ties to the school.[39] As Georges Muller (Class of '65) explained, his decision was driven as much by reason as by passion: "When you look at Insead's balance sheet and compare it with any institution of the same size in the service sector, you wonder how the Institute managed its superb development without equity, and how much stronger it could be with a certain equity base. It is the responsibility of all those like me, who benefited from the Insead experience, to build this equity and ensure the financial stability without which the Institute would not be able to reach its full potential."[40]

Strategically, John Loudon chose this moment to make a personal pledge for the creation of a chair, thus matching the earlier donation made by Claude Janssen to launch the nucleus fund. These were critical assertions of their personal belief in the need for a campaign and their faith in its outcome. Campaigns work very much on the basis of example; and this starts at the top. Big donations are confidence boosters. They allow the message to be delivered with more aplomb and the benchmark persuades others to go one better. At different stages in the process, and with considered timing, Janssen and Loudon set the tone.

[37] Minutes of the Board Meeting, 2/12/94.
[38] These included Sandoz, Boston Consulting Group, Timken, S.G. Warburg, CGIP, Arthur D. Little, Akzo Nobel and BP.
[39] In particular, from Georges Muller, Claude Rameau, Roger Godino, Youssef Bissada and Michael Ullmann.
[40] *The Insead Campaign*, document prepared to accompany the launch, September 1995.

For the same reason, new chairs were often inaugurated away from Fontainebleau; in London for S.G. Warburg, in Brussels for BP. Giving additional visibility to the inauguration was a way of publicly thanking the corporate benefactor, but it was also a way of encouraging others. Moreover, those donating chairs were asked to address the International Council and to explain why they were doing so. For the campaign to succeed, the school would have to work hard to build momentum and to stimulate a sense of healthy competition among its various constituencies.

The campaign launch itself was a grand affair which, with a salute to the past, took place in the courtyard of the palace before 350 guests. Several of the early benefactors, notably David Simon of BP, spoke to the audience to affirm their faith in the school. Later in the proceedings, Antonio Borges revealed the target figure of 700 million francs. He explained that the future of the school depended on its capacity to contribute to the production of new ideas in management, not just to disseminate existing knowledge. The message was not new, but Borges delivered it with characteristic assurance and intensity. He was the ideal front man for the campaign: no-nonsense, highly credible with the business community and capable of asking for large sums of money without flinching. He concluded with: "This campaign is not only about resources and about capital. In many ways, it is also the ultimate market test for Insead ... Nobody will support something they don't believe in. Nobody will continue funding Insead unless we are doing the right things."[41] The underlying message was simple: 'You will do this because you believe in us.'

However confident Borges appeared, the prevailing attitude in Europe towards donating money to business schools remained highly ambivalent. Even among Insead's own alumni there were divergent responses to the campaign launch. One alumnus wrote to the press, stating: "I give money to charities that I consider to be worthy and I cannot think of a list of needy institutions long enough to contain the name of any business school."[42] There was a response, shortly afterwards, from another alumnus who argued back that: "In giving money to Insead we are ensuring the school can continue to give others the advantages we now enjoy."[43] This was no foregone conclusion.

Whatever the final outcome of the campaign, the process engaged quickly had a rapid impact on the school. The dean's job became much more externally oriented. In particular, it tightened relations between the dean and chairman who jointly spearheaded the drive. It also encouraged closer and more regular interaction between the dean and the board, between the board and the faculty, and between the dean and the alumni. One of Insead's strengths had always been its closeness to the business community which

[41] *The Insead Campaign Launch*, Insead video, 30/9/95.
[42] *Financial Times*, 12/10/95.
[43] *Financial Times*, 17/10/95.

provided support and ideas, and served as a sounding board. The development campaign reinforced those exchanges and generated increased respect from both sides.

THE 'WRITE' STUFF

Having trumpeted top-grade research as the key to the school's global competitiveness, Borges then needed to set up conditions under which it could happen. He would be assisted in this challenge by a strong team of associate deans. Two new associate deanships, for faculty and external development, had been created to unburden the single dean of excessive responsibilities. Simultaneously, the associate deanships for R&D and MBA had come for renewal. Realising that he would need to delegate more than his predecessors, Borges picked a team capable of implementing the policies he had in mind.

In December 1995, he started out by advising the board of the current predicament: "If each professor were to teach only the contractual number of sessions, we would need up to 50 per cent more faculty members than today."[44] The current level of activity was clearly not sustainable and was undermining the school's "ability to invest in academic renewal".[45] Quantitatively, the early 1990s had not been good recruiting years. Although the school had attracted 35 new professors between 1990 and 1995, it had lost 28 in the same period.[46] 1995 was a particularly poor year, with seven departures and only four arrivals. In March 1996, Borges pressed home his point to the board: "Given the current teaching loads, the school would need around 120 professors, that is 40 more than currently."[47]

By June 1996, Borges was able to announce to the board that 12 new recruits would be joining the faculty in the following academic year. Of course, this was reflected in the budget for 1996/97 which included a "substantial investment in preparation for future growth".[48] There was also the first mention of the need to "begin to prepare for a moderate expansion in the MBA programme"[49] in order to build up to the introduction of a fourth section in September 1997. As mentioned elsewhere, MBA teaching, core and especially elective, is more suited to the competencies of younger more specialised and up-to-date faculty.

To help attract and retain a research-oriented faculty, a number of systems and incentives were introduced or changed. For incoming faculty, there was help with relocation costs, more efforts to help spouses find suitable work, reduced teaching loads, and two bonuses known as 'fifth day buyback' and

[44] Minutes of the Board Meeting, 8/12/95.
[45] Minutes of the Board Meeting, 8/12/95.
[46] See figures on new and departing faculty presented at the Board Meeting, 22/3/96.
[47] Minutes of the Board Meeting, 22/3/96.
[48] Minutes of the Board Meeting, 10/6/96.
[49] Minutes of the Board Meeting, 10/6/96.

'summer support', jointly representing a 40 per cent increase in base pay, for those willing to use their discretionary time to do research rather than outside consulting. For existing faculty, many of whom would have to shoulder the heavy teaching loads, there were different incentives: chairs, professorships, research support for programme directors and a strong programme of sabbaticals. In the four years that followed, new recruits would continue to be hired at a steady rate of 13 per year.

This was the good news. But Borges had to show he meant what he was saying about the school's commitment to research. As always, the evaluation process for promotions and contract renewals provided the most dramatic opportunity. The evaluation committee produced split votes on two of the young professors up for promotion. They were typical products of the Insead system: outstanding on teaching and institutional contribution, but relatively light on research output since joining the school. Borges had the casting vote and turned both down. It was a gamble. It sent an unmistakable message to incoming faculty about the quality of research output expected but might, at the same time, make it harder to appeal to institutional patriotism.

Changing the orientation of the school was by no means painless, but Borges took a textbook approach: renewing the people, aligning the systems and processes; using the full gamut of rewards and penalties at his disposal to support the strategy. He geared everything towards research in a coherent and single-minded manner. He was helped in this strategy by a number of factors. Of course, there was the boost in resources from the capital campaign and from an upsurge in executive education revenues, managed by Martine Van den Poel.[50] But there were also psychological considerations.

To start with, Borges had clearly announced the growth objective up front. A business school which is expanding fast, when competitors are growing more cautiously, projects a positive image. It attracts attention and more faculty candidates – and more of those candidates take the plunge because it looks like an exciting place to be. The growth objective can therefore turn into a self-fulfilling prophecy, which attracts talent and funds, even if the school could not originally afford to grow at that pace.

The other ingredient which helped Borges pull off this rapid change was his ambiguous insider-outsider status. As head of the MBA programme he had become familiar with the inner workings of the school. Returning to the school, he saw it with fresh eyes and understood more clearly what needed to be done. Capturing the dimensions of continuity and change, academia and business, he understood perfectly how the school worked and which levers to pull. Moreover, the likelihood that he would not be making his career at Insead, in the sense of returning to teaching after the deanship, made him

[50] In 1990, Insead was second to Harvard in terms of revenues from executive education programmes (see *Business Week*, 28/10/91). By December 1995, Insead had overhauled even Harvard and was easily number one.

more resistant to criticism. It was not rocket science, but it took resolve to push it through.

Setting such a strong academic course also required the full support of the board. This was easier to obtain than might have been expected from a group of business people. The board was increasingly coming round to the idea that the school could not survive only as a disseminator of knowledge.

FULL BOARD

The campaign also had a significant impact on the composition and running of the board. In 1994, six of the 24-strong board were alumni. By 1998, the number had climbed to ten and, even for Chris King as head of the Alumni Association, it was reaching its upper limit. The desire to bring in committed alumni[51] had to be set against Insead's long-standing principle of 'no dominant culture', or in this case 'mindset'. It was not just a matter of retaining a strong external perspective. The board also needed to consider the school's activities impartially and to maintain the balance between them. Excessive reliance on alumni might tend to favour the MBA programme, to the detriment of the research and executive programmes.

The board naturally tended to look to the International Council for new blood. Of the non-alumni on the board, many had headed one of the school's national councils or made large donations, often both. Key figures like John Clarkeson, Christophor Laidlaw, Gerard van Schaik, David Scholey, Ernest-Antoine Seillière or Horst Wiethüchter were all co-opted to the board while chairing their national councils. In this respect, the International Council served as a kind of nursery for potential new board members. On the other hand, so that making a large donation would not become a kind of entry ticket onto the International Council, the school created a 'Circle of Patrons' to reward people for services rendered.[52]

The progressive renewal of the board, driven in large part by the campaign, also changed the functioning of the board. The fact that most board members had made a financial or an educational investment in the school, often both, made them feel more like shareholders. They were not there for show. They expected to receive detailed information before board meetings and to participate fully in the decisions regarding the school's development. They were less docile than their predecessors who had tended to consider membership as more of an honorary position. For Janssen there was a striking manifestation of that change in motivation: "Today, a board

---

[51] Including Jean-Pierre Berghmans, Paul Desmarais Jr, Andrew Large, Cees Van Lede, Ronaldo Schmitz or Jürgen Zech.
[52] The first members included Georges Doriot, Raoul de Vitry, Jean Marcou (in memoriam) as well as Olivier Giscard d'Estaing, Roger Godino, John Loudon, Jean Martin, Warren Cannon and Washington Sycip.

member who cannot attend a meeting will telephone to ask about the issues and comment on them. Ten years ago, no one did that. Now they are much more involved."

When Janssen had first worked alongside Loudon, decisions had not been made by the board but by a small executive committee – and within that executive committee, if Loudon and Janssen agreed on something, the others tended to go along with it. Now, even by joining forces, the chairman and the dean of the school could no longer railroad the board, so they had to invest more time in explaining and persuading board members about the merits of particular initiatives. In many ways, it was a tribute to Janssen's capacity to adapt that he was able to accompany that change.

Like Loudon before him, Janssen refused to meddle with the internal running of the school, but was always on hand to advise and support the dean. Adapting to a succession of deans over the years, he had always exercised his influence discretely, never overshadowing the dean's authority. As he saw it, the role of the chairman, provided he agreed with the course of action proposed by the dean, was to secure the board's approval. In his 1993 leaving speech, Claude Rameau had observed: "Claude Janssen is never to be seen, he does nothing, but he holds everything." Of course, since then, the school had switched to a single dean and the capital campaign had been launched, both of which required Janssen's more active involvement in the external affairs of the school.[53] Having served the school in a variety of ways since before its creation, Janssen could justifiably be regarded as the 'guardian of the temple'.

BREAKING NEW GROUND

After experiencing some temporary difficulties in the late 1980s, the Euro-Asia Centre, chaired by Jeremy Brown, had regained momemtum in the early 1990s, under the direction of Gabriel Hawawini. The number of executive programmes conducted in Asia, rather than in Fontainebleau, increased significantly. Indeed, by 1994, Insead had become the biggest provider of executive education in South-East Asia. It could not continue working out of hotels. It needed to capitalise on this enviable position by establishing a local presence. Handing over to Arnoud De Meyer, as new head of the Euro-Asia Centre at the end of 1994, Hawawini made a strong plea in a faculty meeting for the school to do something 'really bold' in Asia.

At around the same time, Insead received an unexpected request from a number of Malaysian companies to set up a business school in Kuala Lumpur. While Malaysia boasted a dynamic economy and intriguing possibilities, there was some concern that it might not be sufficiently at the

---

[53] Having ceased his executive functions as Managing Partner of the Worms Group, in 1993, Janssen was able to devote extra time to Insead.

heart of the Asian business affairs. Hong Kong or Singapore might make more sense. So all three options were investigated concurrently. The emerging idea was that Insead should propose a full portfolio of activities in Asia, not just executive education.

Although it was an opportunistic response, the feeling quickly grew that this initiative actually made sense for Insead, and that the window of opportunity might not be open all that long. There were several strategic justifications for pursuing the idea. To start with, physical presence in Asia would give Insead access to an expanding market for business education. While Insead had benefited from a quasi-monopoly position in the 1980s, that market was of increasing interest to US schools, so Insead should capitalise on its 10-year head start. Intellectually, a local presence would help the school to attract Asian faculty and might serve as a useful base from which to observe new management concepts or innovative applications of existing concepts. There was also an image issue, in that it would enhance the credibility of Insead's position as the most international business school in the world; the natural partner for global businesses looking for international coverage of their needs.

The countervailing argument was that no one else had ever done it. The only comparable attempt was Harvard's eight-year foray into Switzerland, which had come to an end in 1983. But this argument was not taken very seriously. Proponents of the project considered that Insead's international expertise, together with its specific experience in Asia, gave it a unique ability to carry it off.

By the time the economic crisis hit Asia, in mid 1998, the idea of setting up a symmetrical campus in Singapore was sufficiently anchored not to be seriously menaced – and the project received a unanimous go-ahead from the board in December 1998. The resistance of the project to this threat perhaps signalled that the initiative actually corresponded to a much deeper need in the collective psyche. Insead had been built on a dream of a united Europe, and it had prospered on that dream. But the aim was not to build Europe anymore, so what was next? One could argue that a fundamental reason for going to Singapore was to find a new challenge, to refuel the vision-machine.

This does not make it an arbitrary move. Although a physical move to Asia could not have been anticipated at the outset, in 1959, the decision was perfectly in line with the pioneering spirit of the founders and the core values they instilled: international openness and opportunism, a desire to keep growing; the willingness to renew and take risks; daring to fail.

It was also the culmination of a longstanding institutional interest in Asia, traceable to the first encounter between Philippe Dennis and Henri-Claude de Bettignies and to a letter written by Philippe Dennis in March 1973: "I am very heartened that we have arranged a programme for 50 Japanese managers in September. But we need to think about going further. The idea of a 'Centre for Euro-Asian comparative management' is warmly welcomed by all the people to whom I have spoken about it. As soon as Henri-Claude de Bettignies returns, I would like to propose a meeting on this subject." The rest, as they say, is history.

An unfortunate casualty of the decision to set up in Asia was the need to drop French as an entry requirement. The omens had actually been apparent for a long time: the decline in the number of French students and faculty, and classes taught in French. Although the issue had moved the school many times before, there was no public debate. It was an unavoidable victim of the school's global ambitions. On the other hand, Insead maintained its trilingual entry requirement which had become a hallmark of its graduates. In this respect, the school managed to reconcile the past and the future.

HAVING IT BOTH WAYS

Ever since Dean Berry walked into Insead, in 1970, the school had lived with a permanent contradiction between a desire to be an academic institution and the need to earn its keep in the business world. In many ways, the co-deanship had been conceived to cope with that very duality. In the 1990s, this challenge reached new heights because of increasing competition and Insead's own global ambitions. To prosper, the school needed to push harder on the research dimension but without sacrificing its outstanding teaching reputation; it needed to deliver intellectual substance while remaining attentive to management trends; it needed to reconcile the personal outside interests of faculty and collective internal ones of the school.

This tightrope act was recognised by the corporate identity consultants in the early 1990s. Part of their challenge was to convey that idea visually. Like the principle of 'no dominant culture', the notion of balancing activities, of 'being in the middle', had proved impossible to render as a logo without appearing too wishy-washy, too trite or too abstract.

Internally, there was a growing consciousness of the need to manage these dualities. For example, among the special qualities required of the co-dean to work alongside Ludo Van der Heyden, two had been considered essential: "To recognise the unique character of the Institute which is not modelled on an American business school; and, to accept the duality which is at the very heart of the Institute and to adapt to this ambiguity for the success of the Institute."[54]

These qualities corresponded neatly to Antonio Borges who reflected the school's own dualities: a European with an American education; an academic having held a high powered business job; both a product of Insead and an outsider to it. In large part, the move to a single dean was possible because

[54] Minutes of the Board Meeting, 7/12/92.

Borges was both academically ambitious for the school yet business-like and credible with corporate audiences. But this did not signal that the battle had been won. Maintaining the fragile equilibrium between academic and commercial interests, recognising that the school needs to uphold its academic excellence while covering its costs with revenues and donations, is an on-going struggle. It happens to be more or less painful at different times.

Yet there were encouraging signs that Insead was at least on the right track. In particular, the 1990s saw the school's reputation endorsed by two supreme market tests. First, the success of the ambitious capital campaign substantiated the school's credibility with the business community. In particular, the board's enthusiastic response to the campaign, resulted in a more balanced and co-operative relationship with the faculty. The campaign generated not just funds and visibility, but commitment. Those who had given became even more forceful and vocal supporters of the school.

In parallel, the impressive placement record of Insead's doctoral students confirmed the school's status within the academic community. These two indicators of Insead's general performance suggested that it was possible to be market responsive while simultaneously engaging in leading-edge academic inquiry – and each new chair donated to the school reinforced this conciliation of academia and business.

Writing the history of the present is a risky enterprise, hence the tendency to skate over recent events. For example, the school has managed to resolve two longstanding issues relating to its physical development: renegotiating the lease on its original campus with the Paris Chamber of Commerce for another 40 years and securing new land adjacent to it. These arrangements will allow Insead to pursue its expansion in Fontainebleau, but if either of these negotiations had gone awry, Insead's 'future history' would have looked quite different.

It is only with hindsight that it becomes obvious where to throw the spotlight. Seemingly innocuous events can assume unexpected symbolic significance, rising stars can fizzle out, eccentric departures can become major strategic axes, and bit-players suddenly assume centre stage. Conversely, external influences can make a mockery of the best laid plans. Thus, speculating on the likely fate of the strategic initiatives of the past ten years would be foolhardy. On the other hand, it is clear that the school has developed a capacity to accompany change which is rare among establishments of higher learning. And this is another important duality: the aptitude to remain entrepreneurial while becoming increasingly established. It is impossible to say what Insead might look like in two or three decades, but it is safe to bet that it will look significantly different from the way it looks today – and that is not a prediction one would care to make about most educational institutions.

CHAPTER 9

Pillars of the establishment

"We should always be discerning, in choosing what to imitate." Yvan
Kaylov, *The Monkey and the Hunter*.

THE MEANING OF SUCCESS

Initially set up on the basis of little more than the vision and commitment
of a handful of individuals, Insead has come a long way in four decades. It
started out with no buildings or land. It had virtually no permanent faculty
and no prospect of soon affording one. It was unknown to prospective
students or prospective employers and it lacked the resources to establish a
distinctive image quickly with either group. The fact that it now ranks as a
world-class institution is a tribute to the imagination and energy of all those
associated with its development, from the founders onwards.

Tracking that evolution reveals an odd mix of grand vision and strategic
opportunism, of academic ambition and business instinct. Without being
planned that way, the school developed successive platforms which constantly
allowed it to reach upwards: it started by building up its teaching platform,
then it established an executive education platform, and finally it created a
research platform. In the process, it made the transition from obscurity to
visibility, from visibility to respectability, from respectability to prominence.

By any conventional indicator of performance, it is a tremendous success
story. Input measures show that the size, geographic diversity and intellectual
quality of the student body have never stopped progressing. Those students
are exposed to increasingly sophisticated learning as evidenced by the
growing number of articles in influential journals and prize-winning cases
written by the faculty. And in terms of output measures, the demand from
corporate recruiters, the starting salaries offered and the roll-call of glittering
alumni confirm Insead's top-tier reputation.

These are the kinds of yardsticks venerated by comparative guides and league tables. But there is also a revealing measure that never features in the rankings. Insead reunions attract unusually high numbers of alumni, typically over 50 per cent, even though they are scattered throughout the world. This says a great deal for their MBA experience which, though shorter than in other schools, is also culturally richer and socially more intense. It also says something about the type of people attracted to the school. Right from the outset, there was always a dual motivation for attending Insead. The first motivation was to learn about business and to get a qualification; the second motivation, initially embodied in the concept of building Europe, can be characterised as a commitment to the ideal of international exchange.

Taking a step back to consider what lies behind Insead's success, the inevitable starting point has to be this international dimension.

MIND-EXPANDING SUBSTANCE

The international credentials of a business school are easily boosted by initiating exchange programmes and alliances, or diversifying the international composition of students and faculty. Insead's difference is that it 'grew up that way'. Every group within the school, including the board, had to respect the principle of 'no dominant culture'. That ruling, applied 40 years ago, was way ahead of its time. Even today, how many so-called global firms, much less business schools, have anything like a multicultural board?

For the students, internationalism meant learning about other cultures. This learning was reflected in the content of the curriculum, but it really came to life in the *process* of working in groups and discussing cases. Long held certainties were suddenly shaken, as recalled by Claire Pike (Class of '69): "For my second group meeting, I was determined to show these men that I was just as capable as them, so I worked hard on the case. Then, summoning up my courage, I went to the blackboard and told them 'Gentlemen, this is how it is ...' I will always remember the British participant who followed me at the board, and in the same tone, just to show me, rubbed everything out and resolved the problem in totally the opposite way. You don't forget things like that. You realise that your approach is never *the* correct way, but one among others, and that you have every interest in soliciting, listening to, respecting and integrating other perspectives." It could even be argued that 'humbling experiences' of this kind opened up students' minds to learning, in a more general sense. In other words, internationalism is not just what is taught; it also affects the whole approach to learning. It stimulates curiosity and opens up minds to alternative viewpoints.

The same applied to the faculty. A natural consequence of internationalism was diversity of background and outlook. Although professors were mostly US trained, they came from different research traditions. The school ended up with an eclectic mix of faculty which made the school good at accommodating new influences, assimilationist. From an intellectual perspective this probably accounts for the success of the doctoral programme. Students were exposed to a multitude of approaches and paradigms which encouraged cross-fertilisation of ideas and allowed students to opt for the methodology which best suited them and the topic under investigation. Insead did not have a 'cookie-cutter' mould.

From a strategic perspective, diversity of faculty background and interests also had an impact on the school. It prevented the school from becoming set in its ways and made it more adaptable. The evolution of the school's management structure is a good example. Over time, there was a shift away from a structure headed by a director-general plus a dean, to a tandem of two deans, through to a single dean. Each arrangement corresponded to a different stage of the school's development. The internal diversity – embodied by the succession of deans from France, America, Britain, Austria, Belgium and Portugal – favoured experimentation and helped develop an impressive capacity to 'muddle through'.

Diversity enriched the strategic debate too. Different assumptions could be challenged which generated insights as well as reducing the number of blindspots. Interesting ideas would always be entertained, however far-fetched. Of course, faculty divergences sometimes made it difficult to find consensus, but the flip side was that there was no dominant coalition capable of quashing a proposal. If a project had merit and its champion was sufficiently determined, there was every chance of seeing it through. The birth of the Euro-Asia Centre and its Singapore offspring perhaps epitomise that possibility. Diversity made the school more sensitive to outside influences. It increased Insead's peripheral vision.

SURVIVAL AS A STRATEGY

There is the famous exchange between two expatriate American writers in Paris in the 1920s, on the subject of what it means to be rich: "The rich are different from us," asserted Scott Fitzgerald. "Yes," countered Ernest Hemingway, "they have more money." There is a tendency to assume that Hemingway won this exchange. But looking at Insead, one could argue that Fitzgerald had a point.

Compared to business schools with an endowment cushion, the support of a state university or huge corporation, Insead has had to earn its living the hard way. The early decision to establish the school as a private establishment has shaped not just the school's strategy but its whole culture.

Independence and lack of resources bred adventurousness. Footloose and free to make its own rules, Insead became a hotbed of educational enterprise. The partnership with Cedep, the early entry into company-specific programmes, the creation of the Euro-Asia Centre and the pioneering use of business simulations were all products of that independent spirit. But they were also manifestations of the need to generate revenues. Constraints and obligations were turned into opportunities. Things were tried which could not have been tried in other schools; and for a long time this drew people who were less attracted to mainstream business schools. The renegade spirit quickly rubbed off on new recruits.

Institutional isolation forged a strong collective spirit. Compared to other business schools, Insead developed what academics call 'generalised norms of reciprocity'. While people defended their own interests, there was a certain expectation that they would help each other and the institution without calculating precisely 'who owed whom'. Newcomers were thrown into a situation where the reputation and well-being of the school depended heavily on their willingness to pull together. Insead was an 'outsider' to the local education system and unlike other business schools in either its mode of financing or its mission. It therefore had to rely on its own efforts, to create its own markets and to shape its own environment: from conceiving the physical plant right through to defining the expected standards of academic professionalism. The threat to survival left a lasting impression on the school, fostering a culture of responsiveness, of proximity to business, of championship and of creativity. It made the school hungry.

It also gave the school a skewed view of risk. Because Insead had no protection, it needed to grow faster and to respond more quickly than rivals. When put to the board difficult proposals were often given a particular twist. The risk of not running a doctoral programme, of not launching a capital campaign, of not being present in Asia, were presented as bigger than the risk of making these moves.[1] Over several decades, arguments in favour of expanding the MBA programme were typically couched in the same terms. The implicit rule became: when in doubt, grow. The social construction of risk, allied to dark warnings about the dangers of complacency and competition, were part of developing an obsession with growth.

But independence also had its downside. Insead could not grow faster than it generated revenues. This meant that the school was not able to afford decent library facilities or to run a doctoral programme for a long time; it meant that the school was not able to take over Cedep when it was given the chance; and it meant that it has only recently been able to reduce teaching loads to levels which are compatible with sustained research output.

This financial precariousness affected the culture in that it made the school insecure, a characteristic which sometimes manifested itself in institutional boastfulness. After visiting the school in the mid-1960s, Anthony Sampson wrote: "If it fails, it will not be for lack of self-

---

[1] For example, see minutes of the Board Meeting, 2/12/94, p. 13.

promotion."[2] Though lessened, that trait was still evident in the mid-1980s when the school made premature claims that it would soon feature among the top five schools for research.[3] Financial vulnerability also tended to promote expediency, especially in dealings with the support staff who have often felt overstretched and underappreciated. The pace of development and the constant sense of urgency meant that Insead was never very strong on gratitude.

This may also explain the relative lack of organisational memory. Former deans have not been put on pedestals. Wall plaques make discrete references to those who built the school. Each incoming dean has felt the same pressure to finance the next phase of growth with limited means, has experienced the same struggle to keep the ship afloat and to stretch towards new objectives; the same sense of having to start again from scratch. The obsession with survival and growth has been such that there has rarely been time for tributes or looking back at past accomplishments. Yet, this lack of attachment to the past may also explain what allows the school to keep mutating.

EASY LISTENING

Staying 'close to business' was established as part of Insead's philosophy from the outset; and was backed up in practice by the school's private status. This was seen as a guarantee that the education dispensed would remain relevant to the evolving needs of business. Since the school had no money, it had to listen to what business wanted; and in order to listen it needed to establish links with business. Starting with its own board of directors, then through the alumni associations, the Advisory Committee for Management Education,[4] the boards of Cedep and the Euro-Asia Centre, the affiliation programme, the national councils and International Council, the Campaign support committees and the Circle of Patrons, the school progressively developed multiple links with the business community worldwide. A web of contacts was thus created which was unique in its quality and its geographical coverage.

That network was constantly enriched by fresh blood as new companies made use of the tailor-made or executive programmes, as new company heads or senior executives visited the campus, and as the national councils worked to identify and pull in local talent. Perhaps because the school was prepared to listen, busy outsiders were willing to devote enormous amounts of time to its development. They felt they had some say in what went on in the school; and Insead's modest size meant that they quickly saw the fruits of their efforts. Donations made were not 'a drop in the ocean' as they might be with the big US schools, but could have a real impact on Insead's strategic options.

[2] A. Sampson, *The New Europeans*, London: Hodder & Stoughton, 1968.
[3] See *Fortune* (23/5/88) and *Connexions* (Autumn 1988).
[4] Formerly called *Comité de Perfectionnement*.

Today, this dialogue between the school and the community it serves constitutes a built-in force for change and development. The school is not allowed to become complacent because it has given voice to outsiders. Insead is particularly unusual in giving a central role, as chairman of the board, to a business person.

Given these ties and this listening capacity, it is not particularly surprising that Insead has managed to stay in touch with business realities and to keep increasing its executive education activities. What is much more surprising is that it has done so while relentlessly improving its academic standards.

Gaining academic respectability required big changes in the composition of the faculty body: from part-time instructors to full-time teachers; from lay academics to professors with doctorates; from knowledge adapters to knowledge creators. That pendulum-swing from visiting practitioners to permanent academics with a strong research bias could easily have alienated the business community. But daily contact with managers through executive education, and particularly the early influence of Cedep, guaranteed that the incoming professors would keep their feet firmly on the ground.

Proximity to business has marked the culture of the school, sometimes giving a slightly schizophrenic feel. For example, Insead professors are unusually sensitive to their course evaluations. Such attentiveness to 'customer feedback' is closer to the norms of business than to the 'satisficing model' which tends to prevail in academia. In a more general sense, rubbing shoulders with business has instilled an emotional intensity, a capacity for renewal and an addiction to growth which are more typical of commercial concerns than of academic institutions. Opportunism and entrepreneurialism are words one rarely associates with educational establishments but which are recurrent features of Insead's development. In the case of Insead, the label 'business school' is not a contradiction in terms.

Of course, the simultaneous pursuit of academic and commercial opportunities creates a difficult balancing act, but it can also produce tremendous synergy. As Herbert Simon once put it: "The business school can be an exceedingly productive and challenging environment for fundamental researchers who understand and can exploit the advantages of having access to the 'real world' as a generator of basic research problems and a source of data."[5]

All this has made for a rather unusual strategic evolution. Where traditional universities and business schools have reluctantly moved towards business, Insead has fought hard to hoist its academic standards. Insead grew bigger and more respectable by listening to the market and, particularly, by quickly realising that the international market for management education was different from the MBA-dominated market which prevailed in the US.

---

[5] In a letter from Salvatore Teresi to Claude Janssen (8/4/75). The quote comes from Herbert Simon (1967) "The business school: A problem in organizational design", *Journal of Management Studies*, February, 1-16, 5.

Sensing the urgent need for management training among senior and middle managers, not just in Europe but also in Asia, the school shifted its strategy accordingly.

Insead used programme earnings and fund-raising to pursue its scholarly destiny, to better itself, to stretch outside the comfort zone, to invest in research and a doctoral programme. In this respect, the rise of Insead's academic excellence is the consequence as much as the cause of its institutional growth. It is very much a self-made school.

FAITHFUL SERVANTS

A school which comes to prominence from nowhere, without guaranteed finance, government endorsement or even a national identity must have something special going for it. The fourth ingredient – which catalysed internationalism, independence and proximity to business – was the human factor.

The crucible for this experiment was Harvard. Back in the 1950s, HBS was way ahead of the competition in terms of reputation, teaching methods and calibre of students. A group of French MBAs from Harvard called Olivier Giscard d'Estaing, Claude Janssen and Jean Raindre, later helped by Roger Godino, took up the challenge, set up by Georges Doriot, of launching the school. These were unusual people. They had shown openness and determination in heading out to the US and returned to France with precious competencies and breadth of vision. Notwithstanding the wealth of opportunities open to them, they chose to devote time and effort to an unknown school. The fact that Giscard d'Estaing, Janssen and Godino remain active members of Insead's board 40 years on, underlines the emotional and intellectual appeal of the initial idea.

The sheer originality of the school somehow touched people. It struck a chord with Jean Marcou and Jean Martin of the Paris Chamber of Commerce who lavished attention on the school, promoted it and helped it grow. It later seduced John Loudon, a hugely impressive figure, with high-powered contacts worldwide, whose stature was out of all proportion with the scale of the school. For over 20 years, he was heavily involved on the boards of the school and, like Doriot, infused Insead with a real sense of ambition. Loudon, Doriot, Marcou and Martin were still attending board meetings in the last year of their lives.

Amongst the faculty too, there are several who have found Insead irresistible. Lee Remmers, Claude Rameau, Heinz Thanheiser and Gareth Dyas were students at the school before it even had a campus, and returned to take up positions as faculty. Later Paul Evans and Jean-Claude Larréché followed their example. They were joined by mavericks like Henri-Claude de Bettignies or Dominique Héau who chose to invest in a fledgling institution rather than seek the security of an established one. Making institution-specific investments is not the done thing in academia. 'Real academics' do not have institutional loyalty. They have a loyalty to their profession and their discipline, not to the employing establishment. But, somehow, this was not the norm at Insead. A core of faculty members cared passionately about the school and its development – and passed that feeling on to others.

Then of course, there were the administrative troops represented by the likes of Micheline Dehelly, Odile Jacquin, Odette Jeanguenin, Gerrit Kohler, Raymonde Lefrançois, Nicole Orlhac, Claire Pike, Dusan Radivojevic, Uschi Renoux, Siegi Schrinner, Jacqueline Tourlier-Pope and Patrick Triaureau. With never enough resources and systematically working beyond the call of duty, they made it possible for Insead's modest engine to push its limits on a permanent basis.

Taken collectively, these people have provided sustained support to a school whose very survival was occasionally threatened. Continuity of people served as a surrogate for continuity of funding. Perhaps the embodiment of that continuity has been Claude Janssen himself. From participant in the pre-launch conception of Insead to chairman of the board, he has approved, accompanied or anticipated every stage in the development of the school. The trusted lieutenant of both Doriot and Loudon, their spirit flowed naturally through him. Finding a replacement with the same experience, legitimacy and understanding of the school will not be possible. This is just one of the challenges that lies ahead for the school.

A CASE IN ITSELF

Throughout the book readers have been alerted to the uncertainty and difficulty of choices which, in retrospect, seem obvious. It would therefore be inappropriate and intellectually dishonest to close on a euphoric note or to imply that Insead has now 'made it'.

There is no shortage of challenges for the coming generation. Rapid growth and the introduction of split locations will change the pattern of social and intellectual exchange. It will make it difficult to retain the same sense of team or level of goodwill. The push to climb the research ratings chart will force the school to apply quality standards imposed by others, namely the top US schools. Such dependence is troubling for a school which considers itself different and whose success probably relies on staying different.

To remain successful, the school will also need to maintain a due sense of humility. In terms of intellectual impact, for example, Insead has developed a kind of *laissez faire* research tradition. That was fine as long as the school's research ambitions were modest. They are no longer modest, yet the school is still not big enough to make contributions in every field. It will need to focus its efforts. The fact that it competes for the same MBA and doctoral students as Harvard does not make it Harvard!

Or again, Insead traditionally earned its money through activities not donations. This kept the school on its toes, obliged it to listen and made it responsive. An emerging challenge will be to make sure that the constitution of an endowment cushion does not create a certain remoteness or indifference to the concerns of the business community.

When an organisation achieves success, it is difficult to separate the critical factors from others which just happened to be there at the time. Looking forward, it is even tougher to anticipate which of the critical factors will help to sustain success and which can be regarded as having served their purpose. Perhaps this book can contribute to the discussion.

Appendices

CHAIRMEN, DIRECTORS AND DEANS OF INSEAD AND
ASSOCIATED ORGANISATIONS,
1959–1999

MEMBERS OF THE INSEAD BOARD, 1959–1999

CONTRIBUTORS TO THE INSEAD CAMPAIGN

MEMBERS OF THE CIRCLE OF PATRONS

Chairmen, Directors and Deans of Insead and Associated Organisations 1959–1999

INSEAD

Chairman of the Board

1959 – 69	Jean Marcou
1969 – 82	Jonkheer John H. Loudon
1982 –	Claude Janssen

Vice-Chairman of the Board

1959 – 74	Jean Martin
1968 – 69	Raoul de Vitry d'Avaucourt
1969 – 94	Olivier Giscard d'Estaing
1971 – 82	Claude Janssen (Executive Vice Chairman)
1993 –	Claude Rameau

President of the International Council

1982 – 89	Jonkheer John H. Loudon
1989 – 93	Michael A. Butt
1993 – 96	Gerard van Schaik
1996 –	Sir David Scholey, CBE

Director General

1960 – 63	W. Chr Posthumus Meyjes
1963 – 66	Olivier Giscard d'Estaing
1966 – 74	Philippe Dennis
1974 – 82	Pierre Cailliau

Deans

1959 – 63	Olivier Giscard d'Estaing (Director)
1964 – 70	Roger Godino (part-time Dean of Faculty)
1971 – 76	Dean Berry
1976 – 80	Uwe Kitzinger
1979 – 82	Claude Rameau (Deputy Director General)
1980 – 82	Heinz Thanheiser
1982 – 86	Claude Rameau and Heinz Thanheiser

1986 – 90	Philippe Naert and Claude Rameau
1990 – 93	Claude Rameau and Ludo Van der Heyden
1993 – 95	Antonio Borges and Ludo Van der Heyden
1995 –	Antonio Borges

Academic Directors and Associate Deans,

MBA PROGRAMME

1971–73	Peter C Smith (then one-year programme)
1973–77	Lee Remmers (then Post Graduate Programme)
1977–80	Claude Rameau
1980–87	Gareth Dyas
1987–90	Antonio Borges
1990–92	Arnoud De Meyer
1992–96	Herwig Langohr
1996–98	Daniel Muzyka
1998–	Landis Gabel

EXECUTIVE EDUCATION

1971–73	Gilbert Sauvage
1973–85	Claude Rameau
1985–87	Jerome Foster
1987–92	Dominique Héau
1992–99	Arnoud De Meyer

R&D

1971–74	Claude Faucheux
1974–78	Richard Meyer
1978–82	Jean-Claude Thoenig
1982–84	Edith Penrose
1984–85	Philippe Naert
1985–89	Charles Wyploz
1989–90	Ludo Van der Heyden
1990–95	Yves Doz
1995–98	Landis Gabel
1998–	Luk Van Wassenhove

PHD

1990–93	Wilfried Vanhonacker
1993–98	Lars T. Nielsen
1998–99	Gabriel Hawawini

FACULTY

1995–	Hubert Gatignon

INSEAD EURO-ASIA CENTRE

Chairman of the Board

1981 – 88	Washington Sycip
1988 –	Jeremy Brown

Director

1981 – 88	Henri-Claude de Bettignies
1988 – 95	Gabriel Hawawini
1995 – 99	Arnoud De Meyer

CEDEP

Chairman of the Board

1971 – 73	Renaud Gillet
1973 – 97	Guy Landon
1997 –	Igor Landau

Director General

1971 – 91	Salvatore Teresi
1991 –	Claude Michaud

INSEAD ALUMNI ASSOCIATION

President

1960 – 65	Jean-Marie d'Arjuzon
1965 – 68	Jeremy Leigh-Pemberton
1968 – 74	Piet van Waeyenberge
1974 – 79	Jorgen Friisberg
1979 – 82	Willem Prinselaar
1982 – 86	Jürgen Zech
1986 – 89	Michael Butt
1989 – 92	Roger Wippermann
1992 – 95	Eddie Moerk
1995 –	Christopher King

INSEAD ALUMNI FUND

Chairman

1976 – 88	Michel Gauthier
1988 – 96	John Cutts
1996 –	Jack Boyer

Members of the Insead Board, 1959–1999

Dr Giovanni Agnelli, Président, FIAT
1967–1970

The Rt. Hon. Lord Aldington, Chairman, National & Grindlays Bank Ltd
1971–1980

Maurice Amiel, Chairman of the Advisory Council, The Timken Company
1982–1998

Malcolm Anson, Chairman, Imperial Group
1980–1982

The Rt Hon. Lord Armstrong of Sanderstead, President, Midland Bank
1977–1980.

Louis d'Arras d'Haudrecy, Directeur des Services d'Information, INSEAD
1992–1995

E. Arrighi de Casanova, Directeur Général, CCIP
1971–1977

Murielle Aubert, Responsable de la Taxe d'Apprentissage, INSEAD
1995–1998

Dr Ahmet Aykaç, Professeur Associé d'Economie, INSEAD
1982–1984

Jean Bailly, Vice-Président Trésorier, CCIP
1971–1974

René Baken, Président de la Fédération des Chambres de Commerce Belges
1959–1969

George Baker,, Dean, Harvard Graduate School of Business
1963–1971

Dr S.C. Bakkenist, Deputy Chairman, AKZO NV
1973–1977

S.E. Monsieur Joseph Bech, Ancien Ministre des Affaires Etrangères du Luxembourg, Président de la Chambre des Députés
1960–1972

Lord Beeching, Vice-Président, Imperial Chemical Industries Ltd
1967–1971

André Bénard, Directeur Général, Groupe Royal Dutch-Shell
1983–1998

M. Benvenuti, Président du Conseil de l'Europe
1960–1965

* **Jean-Pierre Berghmans**, Président du Comité Exécutif, Groupe Lhoist
1996–

Dr Dean F. Berry, Doyen du Corps Professoral & Directeur Général Adjoint, INSEAD
1975–1976

Dr Paul Beyer, Vorstandsmitglied der Deutschen Industrie – und Handelstages
1960–1961

André Bisson, Directeur Général, Banque de la Nouvelle Ecosse
1975–1998

André Blondeau, Directeur de l'Enseignement, Chambre de Commerce et d'Industrie de Paris
1977–1984

* **Dr Antonio Borges**, Professeur Associé d'Economie, Doyen, INSEAD
1993–

* **Ana Patricia Botín**, Consejera Delegada, Santander Investment
1999–

Dr Walter Boveri, Président, S.A. Brown, Boveri & Cie
1960–1965

Sigismund Freiherr von Braun, Botschafter a.D.
1976–1982

Jonkheer M.L. de Braun, Ancien Ministre des Pays-Bas
1977–1982.

* **Jeremy J.G. Brown**, Director, Matheson & Co Ltd
1988–

Michael A. Butt, Chairman, Sedgwick international Ltd
1982–1998

Pierre Cailliau, Directeur Général, INSEAD
1975–1882

Philip Caldwell, Vice-Chairman, Ford Motor Company
1977–1982

Louis Camu, Président, Banque de Bruxelles
1960–1976

Warren Cannon, Directeur, McKinsey & Co
1969–1990

Frédéric Chabaud, Technicien audiovisuel, INSEAD
1989–1992

* **John S. Clarkeson**, President & Chief Executive Officer, Boston Consulting Group
1998–

Paul Coirre, Trésorier, CCIP
1967–1968

Graham Corbett, Senior Partner Continental Europe, Peat, Marwick, Mitchell & Co
1984–1987.

J. Corpet, Vice-Président, CCIP
1971–1974

Roger Couratier, Trésorier, CCIP
1968–1971

Henri Courbot, Trésorier, CCIP
1962–1967

Pierre-Bernard Cousté, Président Directeur Général, Lumière S.A.
1975–1989

François Dalle, Président Directeur Général, l'Oréal
1969–1973

Armand Daussin, Directeur Général, Administration & Finances, Conseil de l'Europe
1969–1978

Paul Delouvrier, Président, Electricité de France
1972–1981

Arnoud De Meyer, Directeur Général, Centre Euro-Asie and Doyen Associé, Education Continue, INSEAD
1996–1998

Philippe-Jean Dennis, Directeur Général, INSEAD
1974–1978

*__Paul Desmarais Jr.__, Chairman & Co-Chief Executive Officer, Power Corporation of Canada
1998–

*__Vincent Dessain__, Directeur de Développement, INSEAD
1999–

Professeur Giacomo Devoto, Ancien Président, Chambre de Commerce de Florence
1960–1965

René Dewael, Président, Chambre de Commerce de Bruxelles
1960–1972

Général Georges F. Doriot, Professeur, Harvard Graduate School of Business
1960–1974

Pierre Dumont, Membre, Conseil Economique et Social. Former Président, CCIP. Président de l'Association pour l'Encouragement de l'Enseignement de l'Administration des Affaires
1960–1972

Yves Dunant, Président, Sandoz
1968–1988

Dr Gareth P. Dyas, Professeur Associé de Politique de Gestion, INSEAD
1976–1980
1992–1995

Jacques Ehrsam, Président Directeur Général, Singer S.A. and Vice-Président, CNPF
1974–1982

François Essig, Directeur Général, CCIP
1984–1991

Jean Eudes, Président, Comite de Liaison CCIP-INSEAD
1966–1972

Dr von Falkenhausen, Président, Fédération des Banques Privées de la RFA. Président, l'Union des Banques du Marché Commun. Co-Président, Chambre de Commerce franco-allemande
1965–1968

Pier Carlo Falotti, President & CEO, Digital Equipment Corporation International (Europe)
1991–1992
1994–1999

Professor Lawrence E. Fouraker, Dean, Harvard Graduate School of Business
1970–1977

Louis Franck, CBE
1975–1981

Maurice Frère, Président, SOFINA
1960–1969

Jørgen Friisberg, Senior Partner, Egon Zehnder International
1974–1982

Jean-Louis Gilliéron, Président, Chambre de Commerce Suisse in France
1965–1981

Olivier Giscard d'Estaing, Directeur Général, INSEAD
1966–1996

* Roger Godino, Président Directeur Général, Sté les Montagnes de l'Arc, CEGIF
1979–

Pieter Goedkoop, Président-Directeur Général, Nederlandse Dok
1960–1973

René Granier de Lilliac, Président de la Française des Pétroles
1967

Maurice Guigoz, Président, Fédération des Jeunes Chefs d'Entreprises d'Europe
1960–1967

Dr Carl H. Hahn, Vorsitzender des Vorstandes, Continental Gummi-Werke AG
1976–1999

S.E. le Dr. Walter Hallstein, Président, Communauté Economique Européenne
1960–1969

The Right Hon. Lord Robert Hankey, Head of the UK Delegation to OECD
1962–1982

* **Dr. Gabriel Hawawini**, Professeur de Finance, Directeur du Centre Euro-Asie, Doyen Associé, INSEAD
1989–1992
1999–

Dr. Dominique Héau, Professor of Business Policy, Associate Dean for Executive Education, INSEAD
1986–1992

Etienne Hirsch, Président, Euratom
1960–1967

H.E. the Hon. Amory Houghton, Former Ambassador of the United States in France
1961–1965

James Houghton, Area Manager Europe, Corning Glass Works
18 juin 1965 1970

* **Frederik Wouters Huibregtsen**, Managing Director, McKinsey & Co, Inc
1990–

Norman C. Hunt, Professor of Organization of Industry and Commerce, Edinburgh University
1960–1966

Hideo Ishihara, Chairman, Goldman Sachs (Japan) Ltd
1998

* **Claude Janssen**, Associé Gérant, Groupe Worms & Cie
1971–

Odette Jeanguenin, Chef des Services Comptables, INSEAD
1976–1980
1982–1985

Professeur P.W. Kamphuisen, Président du Conseil d'Administration, AKU
1960–1961

Dr. Alexander King, Chairman, International Federation of Institutes for Advanced Studies
1975–1980

* **Christopher King**, CBE, Chairman, Avon Rubber plc.
1996–

Uwe Kitzinger, Doyen, INSEAD
1976–1983

Bo J. Kjellen, Chef de Cabinet de M. E. van Lennep, Secrétaire Général de l'OCDE
1970–1973

Walther Kniep, Président, CPC Europe, Ltd
1975–1982

Jonkheer Gualtherus Kraijenhoff, Former President of AKZO NV
1978–1982.

Thorkil Kristensen, Secrétaire Général, OECD
1961–1970

Sir Christophor Laidlaw, Deputy Chairman, British Petroleum Co
1980–1994

René Lamy, Vice-Gouverneur, Société Générale de Belgique
1980–1982

* **Igor Landau**, Directeur Général, Rhône-Poulenc
1997 –

Guy Landon, Vice-Président, L'Oréal
1973–1997

Dr Kurt Lanz, membre du Conseil de Surveillance, Groupe Hoechst
1981–1987.

* **Dr. Jean-Claude Larréché**, Professeur de Marketing, INSEAD
1982–1986
1992–

* **Sir Andrew Large**, Deputy Executive Chairman, Barclays plc
1998 –

Dr. André Laurent, Professeur de Psychosociologie des Organisations, INSEAD
1976–1980
1979–1982

Robert Layton, Vice-Président, Ford Werke
1964–1969

Raymond-François Le Bris, Former Préfet, Directeur Général, CCIP
1991–1995

* **BG Lee Hsien Yang**, President & CEO, Singapore Telecommunications Ltd
1999–

Dr. Franz J. Leibenfrost, Vorstand der Steyr-Daimler-Puch AG
1978–1982

Jonkheer Aarnout A. Loudon, Président, AKZO
1988–1991

Jonkheer John H. Loudon, Président d'Honneur, Royal Dutch Shell
1967–1996

Jacques Maisonrouge, Président, IBM Europe
1975–1980

Jean Marcou, Former Président, CCIP
1960–1990

Jean Martin, Vice-Président, CCIP
1960–1996

Emmanuel Mayolle, Vice-Président, CNPF
1960–1977

Johan Melander, Managing Director, Den Norske Creditbank
1981

* **Edward S. Moerk**, Corporate Executive Vice-President, Royal Ahold NV
1992–

The Hon. David Montagu, Président, Orion Termbank Ltd
1975–1982

Dr. Marc Moret, President et Administrateur Délégué, Sandoz AG
1988–1998

Etienne Moulin, Président Directeur Général, Galeries Lafayette
1973–1982.

* **Georges Muller**, Senior Partner, Bearbull S.A.
1993–

Dr Philippe Naert, Professeur de Marketing and Doyen, INSEAD
1986–1990

Hans-Olle Olsson, Chef de cabinet du Secrétaire Général, OCDE
1973–1974

René Perrin, Président, Compagnie Française de Raffinage
1960–1968.

Pierre Piketty, Membre-Trésorier, CCIP
1960–1962

* **Didier Pineau-Valencienne**, Président d'Honneur, Schneider
1982–1988
1999–

Claude Postel, Directeur du Développement, Air France
1974–1982

S.E. M. W. Chr. Posthumus Meyjes, Former Ambassador of the Netherlands. Directeur Général, INSEAD
1963–1967

Willem J. Prinselaar, Director, EVC International SA
1978–1989

* **Claude Rameau**, Professeur de Sciences de la Décision, Directeur Général Adjoint, Doyen, INSEAD
1980 1993
1994–

Sir Patrick Reilly, Chairman, British & French Bank Ltd
1969–1976

Professeur Franco Restivo, Président, ISIDA
1960–1973

Jean Rey, Président, Commission du Marché Commun
1967–1980

Dr. G. Riedberg, Représentant à Paris du Bundesverband der Deutschen Industrie
1963–1971

P.L. Roederer, Area manager Europe, Corning Glass Works
1970–1972

Baron Edmond de Rothschild, Fondateur and Président, Compagnie Financière Benjamin et Edmond de Rothschild SA and Président, Banque Privée Edmond de Rothschild SA
1967–1982.

Dr Guido Sandler, Generalbevollmächtigter des Oetker-Konzerns
1974–1982

Gerard van Schaik, Chairman of the Executive Board, Heineken NV
1991–1996

* **Ronaldo Schmitz**, Member of the Board, Deutsche Bank AG
1996–

* **Sir David Scholey**, CBE, Chairman, S.G. Warburg Group plc
1991–

* **Ernest-Antoine Seillière**, Président du Directoire, CGIP and Vice-Président, Medef
1988–

René Sergent, Secrétaire Général, OECD
1960–1961

Lord Simon of Highbury, CBE, Chairman, The British Petroleum Company plc
1996–1997

M. Smithers, Secrétaire Général, Conseil de l'Europe
1968–1970

Christopher Stratos, Membre du Comité National grec
1963–1969

Washington Sycip, Chairman, SGV Group
1982–1988

Stanley F. Teele, Dean, Harvard Business School
1960–1962

Dr Heinz Thanheiser, Professeur de Politique de Gestion, Doyen, INSEAD
1976–1977
1979–1980

Lars-Erik Thunholm, Directeur Général, Skandinaviska Banken
1962–1982

Chevalier A. Thys, Président, ELECTROBEL
1972–1977

Dr José de la Torre, Professor of International Business, INSEAD
1980–1982
1984–1985

Jacqueline Tourlier-Pope, Directeur du Développement, INSEAD
1979–1982
1986–1989

V. Valetta, Président, FIAT
1960–1967

Dr Ludo Van der Heyden, Professeur de Recherche Opérationnelle et Gestion des Opérations, Doyen, INSEAD
1991–1995

* Cees Van Lede, Chairman & Chief Executive Officer, Akzo Nobel NV
1997–

Dr A.D. Vas Nunes, Royal Dutch
1960–1963

* Daniel L. Vasella, Président, Novartis AG
1998–

Professeur G.M. Verrijn Stuart, Président du Conseil Economique et Social
des Pays-Bas
1960–1968

Victor P. Victor-Michel
1975–1977

Raoul de Vitry d'Avaucourt, Président, Péchiney
1960–1969

Arnaud de Voguë, Président, Saint-Gobain
1960–1973

* Christian Vulliez, Directeur Général Adjoint, Chargé de la Formation,
CCIP
1996–

Piet van Waeyenberge, President, De Eik NV
1970–1973

Eric M. Warburg, Senior Partner, Bankhaus MM. Warburg, Brinckman,
Wirtz & Co
1970–1981

Arthur K. Watson, Président, IBM World Trade Inc
1961–1970

Dr Horst Wiethüchter, Chairman, Bentley Pipe Corporation Ltd
1987–1996

Roger Wippermann, Vice-President and Managing Director, Allied-Signal
Europe SA.
1988–1996

* Philip Yeo, Chairman, Economic Development Board
1999–

* Dr Jürgen Zech, Vorstandsvorsitzender, Koelnische Rueckversicherung AG
1981–1989
1996–

* Current member of the INSEAD Board, 30 June 1999

Contributors to the Insead campaign

SUPPORTERS

Georges and Edna Doriot Library
Beaucourt Foundation
Bell & Howell Company
Digital Equipment Corporation
Private Individuals & Foundations
Région Ile-de-France

FACULTY POSITIONS

Chairs
The Alfred H Heineken Chair in Marketing
Professor Jean-Claude Larréché

The Boston Consulting Group Bruce D Henderson Chair in International
Management Professor W Chan Kim

The BP Chair in European Competitiveness
Professor Karel Cool

The Paul Desmarais Chair in Partnership and Private Enterprise
Professor Philippe Haspeslagh

The Henry Ford Chair in Manufacturing
Professor Luk Van Wassenhove

The Henry Grunfeld Chair in Investment Banking, endowed by the S.G.
Warburg Group plc
Professor Gabriel Hawawini

The INSEAD Chair in International Banking and Finance
The Claude Janssen Chair in Business Administration
Professor Hubert Gatignon

The John H Loudon Chair in International Management
Professor Erin Anderson

The L'Oréal Chair in Marketing – Innovation and Creativity
Professor Amitava Chattopadhyay

The Novartis Chair in Healthcare Management

The Raoul de Vitry d'Avaucourt Chair in Human Resource Management
Professor Manfred Kets de Vries

The Rothschild Chair in Banking

The Sandoz Chair in Management and the Environment
Professor Robert Ayres

The Schroders Chair in International Finance and Asset Management, endowed in recognition of Georg W von Mallinckrodt, KBE
Professor Theo Vermaelen

The Shell Chair in Human Resources and Organisational Development
Professor Ronald Burt

The Solvay Chair for Technological Innovation
Professor Ludo Van der Heyden

The Timken Chair in Global Technology and Innovation
Professor Yves Doz

The Wendel/CGIP Chair for the Large Family Firm
Professor Ludo Van der Heyden

The Unilever Chair in Marketing
Professor Marcel Corstjens

Professorships & Fellowships
ABN-AMRO Professorship in Global Universal Banking
Professor Dominique Héau

The Akzo Nobel Fellowship in Strategic Management
Professor Arnoud De Meyer

The Berghmans, Lhoist Professorship in Management

The Bielenberg REL CIFM Fellowship

The IAF Professorship in Entrepreneurship
Professor Daniel Muzyka

The INSEAD Fellowship and Research Fund for Strategy and International Management
Affiliate Professor Renée Mauborgne

The Price Waterhouse Professorship in Management Accounting Information & Control
Visiting Professors William Kinney and Eric Noreen

The Salmon and Rameau Fellowship in Healthcare Management
Professor John R Kimberly

The Shell Fellowship in Business and the Environment

The Shell Fellowship in Economic Transformation

The Van Leer Professorship of Industrial Marketing Professor David Weinstein

RESEARCH FUNDS

3i Venturelab

The Arthur D Little Fund for the Enrichment of the Learning Experience

The Booz Allen & Hamilton Research Fund for CIMSO

The Tele Danmark Research Fund for Corporate Renewal and Entrepreneurship

SUPPORTERS OF R&D

Chartered Institute of Bankers (CIB) for Commercial Banking
Eli Lilly for HMI
Heineken for R&D
Johnson & Johnson for HMI
Lucent Technologies for CIMSO
The Reuter Foundation for CALT
Swedish Trade Council for CALT
Xerox Foundation for Knowledge Management

INDIVIDUAL DONATIONS

Les Amis de Raoul de Vitry   John H Loudon
Robert Bauman   Charles Mackay
Heinrich Baumann   Georges Muller
Michael Butt   James Phelan
John Cutts   Claude Rameau

Jan Frøshaug
Roger Godino
Mickey Huibregsten
Claude Janssen
Samuel Laidlaw
Sir Andrew Large

Sir David Scholey, CBE
Rinji Shino
Michael Ullmann
Graham Williams
Anonymous Donors

OTHER MAJOR CONTRIBUTORS

Aon
Canadian Foundation for International Management
Chambre de Commerce et d'Industrie de Paris
The Economist Group
Fondation de l'Entreprise
Fondation de France
Fondation Mondiale INSEAD
Fondation INSEAD
GEA
INSEAD Gesellschaft Deutschland
INSEAD Management Education Foundation
INSEAD Trust for European Management Education
J.P. Morgan

ASIAN CAMPUS

Air France
Bank Brussels Lambert
China Consortium
Economic Development Board, Singapore
Eddie Moerk
Eli Lilly
Michael and Ute Roskothen
Reuters
Starr Foundation

MBA SCHOLARSHIPS

Antoine Rachid Irani/Bissada
Arnoud De Meyer
Belgian Alumni and Council
Børsen/INSEAD Danish Council
Broadview
Canadian Foundation

Giovanni Agnelli
Henry Grunfeld Foundation
INSEAD Alumni Fund (IAF)
INSEAD Gesellschaft Deutschland
Dr Paul-Robert Wagner
Judith Connelly-Delouvrier INSEAD

Chr Thams (Orkla ASA)
Danone
Danuta
Dredging International
Edmond Israel Foundation
Eli Lilly
Elmar Schulte
Elof Hansson Foundation
Freshfields
Gemini Consulting

Landis Gabel
Lister Vickery Memorial Award
Lord Kitchener
L'Oréal
Louis Franck
Misys
Minute Maid Company
Olivetti
Sasakawa/Sapec
Sisley-Marc D'Ornano

MBA PRIZE

Ford Motor Company, The Henry Ford II Prize

EXECUTIVE EDUCATION SCHOLARSHIP

CZ Ltd Scholarship for the Young Managers Programme

PHD SCHOLARSHIPS

Andersen Consulting
Euroforum
Gabriel Hawawini
GE Capital Foundation
JNICT
Luzenac Group
NatWest Group
The Sasakawa Young Leaders Fellowship Fund

EQUIPMENT AND FACILITY GIFTS

Ever
Reuter Foundation
Hewlett-Packard France

ANNUAL SUPPORT

Corporate Affiliation Programme
INSEAD Alumni Fund (IAF)
Taxe d'Apprentissage

as of 31st August 1999

Members of the Circle of Patrons

The INSEAD Circle of Patrons was created on 29th September 1995 to recognise a select group of friends who made an outstanding contribution to the development of the Institute. The thirty eight Members have been listed in alphabetical order, as of 1st October 1999.

MEMBERS

Maurice Amiel	Chairman of the Advisory Council, The Timken Corporation
Win Bischoff	Chairman, Schroders plc
Warren M. Cannon	Former Board Member, INSEAD
John S. Clarkeson	President & CEO, The Boston Consulting Group Inc
Paul Desmarais Jr.	Chairman & Co-CEO, Power Corporation of Canada
General Georges Doriot	Founder of INSEAD, in memoriam
Michel Franck	Président, Chambre de Commerce et d'Industrie de Paris
Olivier Giscard d'Estaing	Président, Fondation INSEAD
Roger Godino	Président, Holding International de Développement
Frederik W Huibregtsen	Managing Director, McKinsey & Company, Inc
Claude & Tuulikki Janssen	Chairman of the Board, INSEAD
Baron Daniel Janssen	Chairman of the Board of Directors, Solvay SA
Brian Larcombe	Chief Executive Officer, 3i Group plc
Jonkheer John H. Loudon	Honorary Chairman of the Board, INSEAD (deceased)

Jean Marcou	Founder and first Chairman of INSEAD, in memoriam
Jean Martin	Président d'Honneur, INSEAD Recherche (deceased)
Georges & Caroline Muller	Senior Partner, Bearbull Group
Jacques A. Nasser	President, Ford Automotive Operations, Ford Motor Company
Lindsay Owen-Jones	Président Directeur Général, L'Oréal
Claude & Annie Rameau	Professor Emeritus, Former Dean of INSEAD
Michael & Ute Roskothen	Former President Global Oral Care, Colgate Palmolive
Sir David Scholey, CBE	Senior Advisor, Warburg Dillon Read
Ernest-Antoine Seillière	Président Directeur Général, CGIP and President, Medef
William F. Stasior	Chairman & CEO, Booz•Allen & Hamilton Inc
Peter D. Sutherland	Chairman, The British Petroleum Company plc
Washington SyCip	Chairman, SGV Group
Lo C. Van Wachem	Chairman of the Supervisory Board, Royal Dutch/Shell NV
Dr. Daniel Vasella	Président, Novartis International Inc
Raoul de Vitry d'Avaucourt	in memoriam
Karel Vuursteen	Chairman of the Executive Board, Heineken NV
To be named	Roland Berger & Partner GmbH
To be named	Rothschild Bank AG
To be named	Unilever NV

EMERITUS MEMBER

Henry Grunfeld	Former President, S.G. Warburg Group plc (deceased)

INDEX